ADVANCES IN THE NEUROLINGUISTIC STUDY OF MULTILINGUAL AND MONOLINGUAL ADULTS

This edited volume examines current themes in the neurolinguistic study of multilingual and monolingual adults and highlights several new directions the field is moving toward.

Divided into three sections, Part I of the book focuses on language processing in multilingual and monolingual adults, Part II explores language processing in multilingual and monolingual adults with dementia, and Part III centers on language processing in multilingual and monolingual adults with stroke-induced aphasia. Chapters feature empirical data and/or literature reviews, discussing the key issues in the field that are currently engaging scholars and practitioners, with topics including language attrition, cognitive flexibility, aging and the brain, eye-tracking studies of aphasia, translanguaging, and multilingualism in dementia. The book includes cutting-edge research from researchers and practitioners who are all alumni and colleagues of Professor Loraine K. Obler, to whom this book is dedicated.

Presenting crucial topics in the field, the book is highly relevant for students, researchers, and practitioners in the fields of neurolinguistics, psycholinguistics, sociolinguistics, applied linguistics, and language disorders.

Mira Goral, PhD, CCC-SLP, is a professor of Speech-Language-Hearing Sciences at Lehman College and The Graduate Center of The City University of New York (CUNY), New York. She is also an adjunct professor at the Center for Multilingualism in Society across the Lifespan, the University of Oslo, and an adjunct research professor at NYU School of Medicine, New York.

Aviva Lerman, PhD, SLP, is an adjunct lecturer at Hadassah Academic College, Jerusalem. She also works as a speech-language pathologist in the Rehabilitation Department of Hadassah Hospital, Mt. Scopus, Jerusalem, where she directs the Communication Disorders research program and runs the out-patient clinic.

ADVANCES IN THE NEUROLINGUISTIC STUDY OF MULTILINGUAL AND MONOLINGUAL ADULTS

In honor of
Professor Loraine K. Obler

Edited by Mira Goral and Aviva Lerman

Routledge
Taylor & Francis Group
NEW YORK AND LONDON

Designed cover image: © Getty Images

First published 2024
by Routledge
605 Third Avenue, New York, NY 10158

and by Routledge
4 Park Square, Milton Park, Abingdon, Oxon, OX14 4RN

Routledge is an imprint of the Taylor & Francis Group, an informa business

ISBN: 978-1-032-36113-0 (hbk)
ISBN: 978-1-032-36096-6 (pbk)
ISBN: 978-1-003-33031-8 (ebk)

DOI: 10.4324/9781003330318

Typeset in Sabon
by MPS Limited, Dehradun

This book is dedicated to Loraine K. Obler, with gratitude, appreciation, and admiration.

CONTENTS

CONTRIBUTORS

Suvarna Alladi, DM, is a Professor of Neurology at the National Institute of Mental Health and Neurosciences, Bangalore, India. She coordinates a multidisciplinary service that has provided support for more than 4,000 people living with dementia and has coordinated multicentric studies to adapt cognitive tests for different Indian languages. Her research focuses on cross-cultural neuropsychology for diverse linguistic and educational contexts and investigates the complex influence of life-course experiences especially bilingualism, education, and social engagement to understand the development of risk and resilience against dementia.

Carmit Altman, PhD, is the Head of the Child Development Program in the Faculty of Education and is affiliated with the Gonda Multidisciplinary Brain Research Center, Bar Ilan University, Ramat Gan. Her academic career has followed a psycholinguistics-sociolinguistics interdisciplinary trajectory and her research has focused on bilingual language development and narrative intervention, funded by BSF, ISF, and Ministry of Education grants. She is co-director of Bilingualism Matters, Israel.

Sameer Ashaie, PhD, is a Research Scientist at the Shirley Ryan AbilityLab and a Research Assistant Professor in the Department of Physical Medicine and Rehabilitation at the Feinberg School of Medicine, Northwestern University, Chicago. His research focuses on aphasia rehabilitation, particularly post-stroke depression and related psychosocial disorders. He employs a variety of techniques in his research including eye-tracking and heart-rate variability.

Mellissa Bortz, PhD, CCC-SLP, is an Assistant Professor in the Department of Communication Disorders at St John's University, Queens, New York.

Jose G. Centeno, PhD, is a Professor in the Master of Science Program in Speech-Language Pathology in the Department of Rehabilitation and Movement Sciences in the School of Health Professions at Rutgers University, New Jersey.

Peggy Conner, PhD, CCC-SLP, is an Associate Professor and Chair of the Department of Speech-Language-Hearing Sciences at Lehman College of The City University of New York (CUNY), New York where she teaches, publishes, and presents on the topics of aphasia, multilingualism, and fluency disorders.

Hia Datta, PhD, is an Associate Professor at the Department of Communication Sciences and Disorders (CSD) at Molloy University, New York. She teaches courses in Neural Bases of Communication, Acquired Neurogenic Disorders, Cultural Linguistic Diversity, and Research. She obtained her doctorate from The Graduate Center of The City University of New York (CUNY), and her research involves understanding cultural linguistic diversity in CSD and equity as well as neural processing of language in children and adults.

Susan De Santi, PhD, is the Executive Director for External Stakeholder Engagement in Global Medical Affairs, Alzheimer's Disease, and Brain Health at Eisai Inc., located in Nutley, New Jersey.

E. Susan Duncan, PhD, is a Speech-Language Pathologist and Cognitive Neuroscientist. She is an Associate Professor in Speech-Language-Hearing Sciences at The Graduate Center of The City University of New York (CUNY), New York.

Zohar Eviatar, PhD, is a Professor at the School of Psychological Sciences, and a member of the Institute for Information Processing and Decision Making (IIPDM), both at the University of Haifa. Her main areas of research are multilingualism, reading in different languages and writing systems, and hemispheric division of labor during simple and complex cognitive processes.

Elizabeth Galletta, PhD, CCC-SLP, CBIST, is a Clinical Associate Professor at NYU Grossman School of Medicine, New York.

Mali Gil was the Director of the Department of Communication Disorders at Beit Lowenstein Rehabilitation Hospital, Raanana, for 30 years until her retirement. She initiated, conducted, and headed numerous research projects focused on the assessment and diagnosis of people with aphasia. She has mentored hundreds of Speech-Language-Pathologists and treated thousands of monolingual and bilingual patients.

Martin R. Gitterman, PhD, is a Professor Emeritus at Lehman College and The Graduate Center, The City University of New York (CUNY), New York and Ombuds Officer at The Graduate Center. His areas of specialization include neurolinguistics, bilingualism, and second language acquisition.

Pernille Bonnevie Hansen holds a PhD from MultiLing – Center for Multilingualism in Society Across the Lifespan, at the University of Oslo, Oslo. She works as an Associate Professor at Inland Norway University of Applied Sciences.

Eve Higby, PhD, is an Assistant Professor in Speech, Language, and Hearing Sciences at California State University, East Bay, California. She received her B.A. in Spanish with certificates in Linguistics and Latin American and Caribbean Studies from Florida International University and her PhD in Speech-Language-Hearing Sciences with a concentration in Cognitive Science from The Graduate Center of The City University of New York (CUNY). Her research focuses on cross-linguistic influence in bi-/multilingualism across the life span.

JungMoon Hyun, PhD, is an Assistant Professor in the Department of Speech-Language Pathology at Hunter College, The City University of New York (CUNY), New York. Her research interests include language and cognitive function changes in typical and atypical aging populations.

Elizabeth Ijalba, PhD, CCC-SLP, is an Associate Professor of Linguistics and Communication Disorders, Queens College, The City University of New York (CUNY), New York.

Reem Khamis, PhD, CCC-SLP, is a Professor of Speech-Language Pathology and director of the Neurophysiology in Speech-Language Pathology Lab (NSLPLab) at Adelphi University, New York.

Swathi Kiran, PhD, CCC-SLP, is the James and Cecilia Tse Ying Professor in Neurorehabilitation at Boston University College of Health and

Rehabilitation Sciences, Sargent College, Boston, Massachusetts. She is also the Director of the Aphasia Research Laboratory and the Research Director of the Aphasia Resource Center, Boston. She is the co-founder of Constant Therapy Health.

Marion C. Leaman, PhD, CCC-SLP, is an Assistant Professor at the University of Kansas Medical Center, Kansas, where she is the Director of the ALL-CAN-Converse Aphasia Lab.

Taryn R. Malcolm, PhD, CCC-SLP, is an Assistant Professor in the Department of Communication Disorders at Mercy College, New York, and a practicing Speech-Language Pathologist in New York. Her current research investigates the effects of cross-linguistic influence in speakers of Jamaican Creole and English. Other treatment research investigates the influence of dual-language societies on acquired language disorders and treatment outcomes, including research on bilingual individuals with primary progressive aphasia and the cross-cultural impact of self-disclosure for individuals with aphasia.

Merav Raveh-Malka, MA, is a Speech-Language Pathologist who is an Adjunct Lecturer in Ariel University, Ariel, as well as in the Department of Adult Rehabilitation and in the NICU in Hadassah Hospital, Mt. Scopus, Jerusalem. She also is a part of the Omer team, Ezer Metzion, who are a team of experienced Speech-Language Pathologists and Occupational Therapists specializing in Augmentative-Alternative Communication in adults and children.

Klara Marton, PhD, is a Neuropsychologist and Professor at Brooklyn College and The Graduate Center, City University of New York (CUNY), New York, and Barczi College of Special Education, ELTE, Budapest.

Sara Meilijson, PhD, was the Chairperson of the Department of Communication Disorders, Hadassah Academic College, Jerusalem, until her retirement in 2017.

Yael Neumann, PhD, CCC-SLP, is an Associate Professor and Director of the Undergraduate Program in Communication Sciences and Disorders in the Department of Linguistics and Communication Disorders at Queens College, The City University of New York (CUNY), New York.

Marjorie Nicholas, PhD, CCC-SLP, is the Chair of the Communication Sciences and Disorders Department at MGH Institute of Health Professions in Boston, Massachusetts.

Alexandre Nikolaev, PhD, is a Senior Lecturer at the University of Eastern Finland and an Adjunct Professor at the University of Helsinki (General Linguistics), Helsinki. His work includes computational studies on Finnish language morphology and experimental studies with healthy Finnish speakers and people with Alzheimer's disease.

Monica I. Norvik, PhD, is an SLT/researcher at MultiLing – Center for Multilingualism in Society across the Lifespan, Department of Linguistics and Scandinavian studies, University of Oslo, Oslo, and the Department of Acquired Brain Injury, Statped, Oslo.

Dafna Olenik, MA, is the Director of the Adler Aphasia Center, Department of Communication Disorders, Hadassah Academic College, Jerusalem.

Avanthi Paplikar holds a PhD from The Graduate Center of The City University of New York (CUNY), New York, and subsequently did her post-doctoral fellowship at NIMHANS, Bengaluru, India. Currently, she is working as Associate Professor at Dr. S. R. Chandrasekhar Institute of Speech and Hearing, Bengaluru, India.

Ingeborg Sophie Ribu, PhD, is an Associate Professor in special education at the Oslo Metropolitan University, Oslo.

Valerie L. Shafer, PhD, is a Professor of Speech-Language-Hearing Sciences at The Graduate Center of The City University of New York (CUNY), New York. Her research focuses on first and second-language acquisition in typical and atypical populations with a particular interest in neural measures and phonological systems.

Hanne Gram Simonsen, PhD, is a Professor Emeritus in Linguistics at MultiLing – Center for Multilingualism in Society across the Lifespan, Department of Linguistics and Scandinavian Studies, University of Oslo, Oslo.

Lisa Tabor Connor, PhD, MSOT, OTR/L, is the Elias Michael Professor and Associate Dean for Occupational Therapy at Washington University in St. Louis School of Medicine, Missouri. Her laboratory focuses on the biopsychosocial determinants of recovery from stroke and the ability of people to reintegrate into their communities, particularly people with aphasia.

Joel Walters, PhD, is a Professor Emeritus of the Department of English/Linguistics in Bar Ilan University, Ramat Gan. He is the former head of the Department of Communication Disorders at Hadassah Academic College, Jerusalem.

Amy Vogel-Eyny, PhD, SLP, is an Assistant Professor at Hunter College, The City University of New York (CUNY), New York.

Zhilong Xie, PhD, is a Professor and Vice Dean at Foreign Languages College, Jiangxi Normal University, Nanchang, China.

PREFACE: ABOUT LORAINE K. OBLER

Loraine K. Obler is recognized internationally as a leading scholar in the study of neurolinguistics. She is currently a Distinguished Professor in the Program in Speech-Language-Hearing Sciences at The Graduate Center of The City University of New York (CUNY), with appointments as well in both Linguistics and Cognitive Neuroscience. She served recently as Acting Ombuds Officer for the entire Graduate Center, adding to a period of service as Ombuds Officer about 25 years ago. Within the very broad and multifaceted terrain subsumed under the heading *neurolinguistics,* Loraine has developed a research agenda encompassing many relevant sub-disciplines including, but not limited to, the neurolinguistics of bilingualism, language in aging, and the cross-language study of aphasia, to name a few.

Loraine's scholarly achievements are evident in a range of activities typically engaged in by productive scholars. The voluminous listing of her published articles and books, for example, reveals that she has long been at the cutting-edge of research. One of her earliest works, *The Bilingual Brain: Neuropsychological and Neurolinguistic Aspects of Bilingualism* (1978, with M. Albert, Academic Press) is truly a seminal work in the field. It suggests findings about the organization of language in the brain with a focus on comparing a first language with a second language. The book, widely cited, served as the basis for much additional research that helped refine theories and advance our knowledge within this specialization. Other books co-authored or co-edited by Loraine over the years have also addressed key research interests of the day, thus leading, undoubtedly, to additional relevant research deemed to be needed. The range of topics addressed in her books is made clear by perusing some of the titles in addition to the aforementioned volume: *The Exceptional Brain: Neuropsychology of Talent and Special Abilities*, 1988, with D. Fein, The Guilford Press; *Bilingualism Across the Lifespan: Acquisition, Maturity, and Loss*, 1989, with K. Hyltenstam, Cambridge University Press; *Non-Fluent Aphasia in a Multilingual World*, 1995, with L. Menn, M. O'Connor and A. Holland, John Benjamins; *Communication Disorders in Spanish Speakers: Theoretical, Research and Clinical Aspects*, 2007, with J. Centeno and R. Anderson, Multilingual Matters; *Aspects of Multilingual Aphasia*, 2012, with M. Gitterman and M. Goral, Multilingual Matters. Articles authored or co-authored by Loraine have appeared regularly in professional journals for some 4 decades. These publications provide a critical source of knowledge to the academic community and, when considered in their entirety, are illustrative of the reason Loraine is indisputably among those scholars considered prolific researchers and writers.

Any truly fruitful effort to capture the essence of Loraine's scholarly achievements necessitates the mention of factors extending beyond publications. Loraine has been a consistent presenter for many years at professional conferences, including numerous invited and keynote addresses. She has engaged in research funded by the National Institute of Health (NIH; M. Albert co-PI) at the Harold Goodglass Aphasia Research Center (Language in the Aging Brain Lab), Boston University School of Medicine. She was awarded a Doctorate Honoris Causa from Stockholm University (1993) and from Turku University (2011), among numerous other honors.

To limit a discussion aimed at providing an overview of Loraine K. Obler to solely academic achievements would not be doing justice to the topic. Her praiseworthy personal characteristics call out for inclusion. Loraine's outstanding interpersonal communication skills are based on her ever-present objectivity and sensitivity as well as a recognition of the importance of tact and logic in building and maintaining effective communication. She is an outstanding listener. Some of her students and former students over the years have commented to me how much they admire that trait. A typical comment of this type relates that Loraine has a very busy schedule, but when you are meeting with her you always have her undivided attention conveying the feeling that you are the only thing on her mind at that time. She has great respect for her students and has maintained a long-term association with many of them, often resulting in co-authorships. She is a model of dedication to students, concerned not only with their academic advances, but with their overall professional development as well.

While the material above only touches the surface in presenting an overview of Loraine K. Obler, it is hoped that it provides sufficient information for the reader to understand that Loraine is indeed a great scholar and a remarkable person. She has enriched the lives of so many people.

Thank you, Loraine!

Martin R. Gitterman

ACKNOWLEDGEMENT

The editors wish to thank all the contributors for their hard work on this book, and Erika Levy for her proofreading help.

1

INTRODUCTION

Mira Goral and Aviva Lerman

This book, *Advances in the Neurolinguistic Study of Multilingual and Monolingual Adults: In Honor of Professor Loraine K. Obler*, has been written by colleagues and former students of Loraine in honor of her contribution to the field of adult neurolinguistics. Loraine has been a pioneering researcher of neurolinguistics and during an academic career spanning over 50 years she has always been at the forefront of this changing and developing field. This book is a culmination of work by scholars who have been inspired and encouraged by Loraine throughout their careers so far, and each chapter is a testament to Loraine's academic influence and ties to the future of the field of neurolinguistics in multilingual and monolingual adults.

This edited volume highlights a number of new directions that the field of adult neurolinguistics is moving toward. One is the importance of assessing and treating communication skills, in addition to linguistic skills, in acquired language disorders (aphasia and dementia), for example by examining discourse and conversation, rather than single words and sentences. This approach harmonizes with a shift toward embracing functional, life participation approaches to aphasia rehabilitation. Increasingly, clinicians and researchers emphasize the importance of not only impairment-based but also, and maybe first and foremost, participation-based intervention and management. Similarly, researchers increasingly acknowledge different cultures and cross-cultural aspects within multilingual populations and multilingual individuals, including those embracing translanguaging as an inclusive framework in healthy and clinical multilingual populations. Other new directions include the employment of integrative approaches to

DOI: 10.4324/9781003330318-1

understanding bilingual language processing, taking into consideration a multitude of variables, as well as the focus on neuroanatomical changes, neuropathology and biomarkers to inform behavioral changes in healthy and clinical populations. Finally, the development and increased use of cutting-edge technologies for assessment and intervention in clinical populations, such as eye tracking and transcranial Direct-Current Stimulation (tDCS), represent promising avenues for future research.

Part I of the book focuses on language processing in multilingual and monolingual adults. In Chapter 2, Klara Marton and Valerie L. Shafer describe bilingual processing in adults and argue that the two different approaches – top down and bottom up – can be combined into a single model. The authors discuss attention-dependent and attention-independent systems, and explain how factors such as age of acquisition, language proficiency and use, and manner of acquisition affect these different networks. In Chapter 3, Elizabeth Ijalba and Zohar Eviatar discuss bilingualism, diglossia, and standard-with-dialect linguistic contexts, focusing on two countries: the U.S. and Israel. The authors describe standard-with-dialect situations in the U.S. setting, and diglossia in the Palestinian-Israeli setting, and how research suggests that the degree of difference between two dialects or varieties of a language is dynamic and changes within individuals with age and proficiency. Consequences for literacy acquisition are discussed. In Chapter 4, Reem Khamis and Mellissa Bortz discuss translanguaging as a framework for providing effective education as well as assessing and planning intervention for clinical populations. The authors consider translanguaging in terms of its relationship to the prevalent monolingual-centric viewpoint in the field of Speech Language Hearing Sciences and suggest ways of changing that viewpoint to encourage positive development in the field that better captures real-life communication. In Chapter 5, Hia Datta and Zhilong Xie define and describe processes of language attrition in aging in monolingual people, as well as attrition of a first language and of a later-acquired language in bilingual individuals. Furthermore, the authors provide a fascinating insight into attrition within societies, focusing on the negative effect that attrition of indigenous languages can have on biodiversity. In Chapter 6, JungMoon Hyun and Alexandre Nikolaev provide an overview of healthy aging from the perspective of structural and functional neural changes and how they underlie linguistic and non-linguistic cognitive changes that are observed with aging. They highlight the contribution of advances in neuroimaging technology to our understanding of behavioral changes associated with healthy aging.

Part II of the book focuses on language processing in multilingual and monolingual adults with dementia. In Chapter 7, Taryn R. Malcolm and Susan De Santi provide an overview of the clinical profiles of dementia due to Alzheimer's disease and of Primary Progressive Aphasia (PPA) and their underlying neuropathologies. The authors also describe current research on and clinical uses of imaging and fluid biomarkers, and how the field is moving forward toward finding effective treatments for these dementias. In Chapter 8, Monica I. Norvik, Ingeborg Sophie Ribu, Pernille Bonnevie Hansen, and Hanne Gram Simonsen provide an overview of first and second language production in dementia, focusing on connected speech (discourse, narratives, and conversation). The authors also present their own research and suggest that detailed analyses of connected language in people with dementia or suspected dementia are useful in defining language impairment and in dissociating the contribution of dementia and of linguistic background (e.g., bilingualism) to the observed changes. In Chapter 9, Avanthi Paplikar and Suvarna Alladi provide an overview of research into bilingualism in dementia from cognitive, linguistic, and social viewpoints, with a particular focus on the cultural context in India. The authors explain that knowledge from research on bilingual people with aphasia can inform the field of research on bilingual people with dementia, and they highlight services that have improved for bilingual people with dementia in India, as well as those that need further attention. In Chapter 10, Amy Vogel-Eyny and Elizabeth Galletta review the history of the use of tDCS paired with behavioral treatments in PPA and summarize relevant studies. Their review emphasizes that the majority of earlier studies focused on targeting naming, while recent studies have extended this novel intervention to discourse. The authors describe this promising field of research, which is still in its infancy, and give suggestions as to the direction of future research.

Part III of the book focuses on language processing in multilingual and monolingual adults with stroke-induced aphasia. In Chapter 11, Jose G. Centeno and Eve Higby present an intersectional neurocognitive approach to management of post-stroke aphasia in multilingual geriatric populations. The authors provide background information on ethnoracially and linguistically diverse populations in the U.S., and consider relevant factors in the management of post-stroke aphasia, including cognitive, linguistic, socioeconomic, political, medical, and neurological factors. They also discuss the complexity of assessing and treating these populations, offering valuable information regarding resources that are currently available, and those that need to be developed in the future. In Chapter 12, Lisa Tabor Connor, Sameer Ashaie and Marjorie Nicholas discuss the Life Participation Approach to Aphasia (LPAA) and how it has become one of the leading frameworks in clinical aphasiology. The authors review two components of the A-FROM (Living with Aphasia–a Framework for

Outcome Measurement) model: (1) personal factors affecting life participation of people with aphasia, including depression, fatigue, anxiety, and apathy, and (2) the role of the environment. They present results from several studies they have conducted and discuss the challenges involved in measuring life participation and also offer some solutions. In Chapter 13, Dafna Olenik and Sara Meilijson offer a vivid depiction of the implementation of the LPAA in an Aphasia Center that was established within an academic program in the Department of Communication Disorders, Hadassah Academic College, Jerusalem. The authors describe the vision behind the center and the mutual advantages for the academic program and the Aphasia Center, and provide a number of case studies to illustrate the remarkable potential for centers such as these. In Chapter 14, Yael Neumann and Marion C. Leaman describe the history of conversation therapy in aphasia, from the beginning of this subfield to its current state. The authors describe four main treatment protocols for conversation therapy, including a protocol that one of the authors developed herself and is currently testing. The chapter provides details of the effectiveness of these therapies, and suggest future directions for researchers and clinicians, including conversation therapy in multilingual people with aphasia. In Chapter 15, Aviva Lerman, Joel Walters, Merav Raveh-Malka, Mali Gil, and Carmit Altman describe narrative analysis in monolingual and bilingual adults with and without aphasia and aim to dissociate the contribution of linguistic background (i.e., bilingualism) and the contribution of aphasia to the observed patterns of language production. The authors present data that highlight the importance of analyzing multiple aspects of language production of bilingual people with aphasia both across groups and within individuals. In Chapter 16, E. Susan Duncan and Peggy S. Conner provide a comprehensive literature review of eye tracking and its use in understanding language processing in bilingualism and in aphasia, as a complementary methodology to behavioral studies and brain imaging studies. The authors demonstrate that eye tracking has been instrumental in providing evidence for the co-activation of the languages of bilingual people, and review three studies on eye tracking in bilingual people with aphasia. The chapter addresses the potential for eye tracking to improve our understanding of language processing.

In the concluding chapter, Chapter 17, Swathi Kiran together with the co-editors, Aviva Lerman and Mira Goral, situate the chapters in the context of the contribution of Loraine K. Obler to the field in her pioneering work, her ongoing collaborations, and her influence on current research.

PART I

Language Processing in Multilingual and Monolingual Adults

2

BILINGUAL LANGUAGE PROCESSING AND INTERFERENCE CONTROL FROM AN INTEGRATED PERSPECTIVE

Klara Marton and Valerie L. Shafer

Introduction

Considerable research has established that knowledge and use of more than one language fundamentally changes how a speaker/listener processes language. In particular, bi-/multi-lingual speakers need to control processes (top-down control) that allow them to facilitate the selected language and suppress the non-target (interfering) language(s) in a given situation/context (Marian & Spivey, 2003; van Hell & Tanner, 2012). Many studies, particularly those focusing on lexical access, semantics, and syntax, examine interference and facilitation in bilingual language processing under the lens of cognitive-control models. Fewer studies, however, consider bilingual processing in terms of the more attention-independent processes (bottom-up) engaged during language processing (Hamrick et al., 2018; Shafer, in press; Strange, 2011). An understanding of bilingual language processing requires integrating findings from these two approaches into a single model that explains how these various mechanisms operate in bilingual individuals. The goal of this chapter is to provide a brief overview of this research, and to take the first steps toward developing a general integrative framework that can predict behavior and neural processes across all levels of language.

We begin this chapter by providing some theoretical background and important terminology used in the study of bilingual (and multilingual) language interaction. We then explain models of cognitive control, focusing specifically on facilitation, interference, and monitoring. We briefly review key findings from studies using this framework. Following this, we

DOI: 10.4324/9781003330318-3

present research that has focused on the role of attention-independent mechanisms in bilingual processing. Finally, we provide a general framework for a more comprehensive model.

Language Interaction, Facilitation, and Interference

Current models of cross-language interaction suggest a constant bidirectional influence between the two languages of a speaker/listener in the context of other cognitive processes (Kroll et al., 2015). Even when an individual is using only one language to perform a task, elements of the other language – that is, the one currently not in use – may hinder access to the target language through interference (Assche et al., 2012). Interference between the languages has been found at every level: in speech production and comprehension, in sentences, and most commonly in single words (Kroll et al., 2014; Libben & Titone, 2009). Items that share linguistic features may interfere with each other at any stage of encoding or storage, but particularly during retrieval. If the retrieval cues are not sufficient to distinguish between target and distracting items, then interference will occur (Van Dyke & McElree, 2006). Thus, interference is clearly a source of performance deficits.

Bilingual development and the use of two or more languages affect both specific language functions and general cognitive mechanisms (Kroll et al., 2015). However, the extent to which interference operates independently at different language levels or is a function of higher-level cognitive processes (e.g., memory) is not clear. Some findings suggest that cross-linguistic effects do not occur in isolation; when one language influences the other, the effect is not limited to that specific language level (e.g., lexical-semantics) but it may be apparent in broader cognitive-linguistic changes such as the reorganization of the memory system. For example, cross-linguistic differences in narrative construction may affect bilingual individuals' memory retrieval because speakers of different languages focus their attention on different linguistic categories (Pavlenko, 2003). In contrast, other outcomes indicate independence of interference control even within the different language levels, specifically in the semantic and the syntactic domains. For example, in Arabic-Hebrew bilingual individuals, interference control at the lexical-semantic level did not correlate with interference management at the grammatical level (Prior et al., 2017). Moreover, various aspects of the bilingual experience, such as language proficiency and the language context interact with these control processes. For example, it is well known that phonetic and phonological similarities between the target and distractor languages influence bilingual listeners' processing of sentences in the auditory modality, but the extent of interference between the two languages is modulated by the speaker's level of proficiency (Kim et al., 2019).

Cognitive Control in Bilingual Language Processing

Cognitive control is a theoretical concept that encompasses processes that are needed to adapt the cognitive system in response to changing conditions to achieve goal-directed behavior even if there are other compelling or habitual acts (Botvinick et al., 2001; Cohen, 2017). These processes require attention (top-down processes) and are supported by a distributed frontoparietal network, including the anterior cingulate gyrus (ACC) (Botvinick et al., 2004; Shenhav et al., 2013). Cognitive control supports the retrieval of relevant content from memory, as well as the selection and suppression of irrelevant information. Two distinct features that determine these processes are flexibility and adaptation (Botvinick et al., 2001). Cognitive flexibility is a marker of cognitive control and it supports the system's adaptation processes through frequent updating when task goals, contexts, or other demands are changing (Dreisbach & Fröber, 2019). It refers to the system's readiness to selectively switch between mental processes in order to execute goal-directed behavior by disengaging from a previous task, reconfiguring new responses, and carrying out the current task (Dajani & Uddin, 2015). For example, the Dimensional Change Card Sort task, described below, requires updating of task goals and corresponding responses. Despite the differences in previous findings regarding the nature of linguistic interference, most point to the critical role of cognitive control in preventing and/or reducing cross-language interference, even though there is no agreement about the specific mechanisms that underlie language control (e.g., Abutalebi & Green, 2007; Bialystok, 2009; Prior et al., 2017).

One widely studied question in our field that has not yet been resolved is whether language control is part of a more general cognitive-control system. A common method to examine this question uses a task- or language-switching paradigm. While task switching is often studied using variations of the Dimensional Change Card Sort (Doebel & Zelazo, 2015; Eichorn et al., 2018), language switching is typically examined with naming tasks (Calabria et al., 2012). In both cases, participants have to keep two sets of rules active in working memory and select the appropriate one according to the task cues (e.g., sort cards according to color or shape; name pictures in one or the other language). There is some evidence supporting the idea of overlapping control mechanisms that are responsible for both linguistic and non-linguistic task switching (De Baene et al., 2015; Linck et al., 2012; Liu et al., 2014); however, other findings suggest distinct processes underlying these two switching domains (e.g., Branzi et al., 2016; Prior & Gollan, 2013). The mixed outcomes in the literature are primarily related to differences in populations, tasks, and data analysis procedures across studies. Participants in various studies differed in age (from children to older adults), in language proficiency and dominance of the target language, and in social status, among other relevant factors. The linguistic and non-linguistic tasks were markedly different in a number of studies and the results were often based on simple correlations. These shortcomings further undermine confidence in claims about the independence of cognitive-control processes operating in linguistic versus non-linguistic domains.

Studies that designed tasks that were similarly structured for linguistic and non-linguistic stimuli have shown at least some overlapping mechanisms underlying switching regardless of domain, even though they also identified some task-specific effects that influenced the outcomes (Declerck et al., 2017). In the language-switching task used by Declerck and colleagues, participants had to name digits either in German or in English; in contrast, in the non-linguistic task they had to perform magnitude judgments by indicating whether the given digit was smaller or larger than five. The two tasks were matched with regard to cues, response modality, and response alternatives. The authors suggest that these similarities in structure contributed to the similarities between the language-switch costs and task-switch costs (Declerck et al., 2017).

Neurophysiological findings further revealed the need for matching task requirements across linguistic and non-linguistic task-switching paradigms. When the task requirements were matched, highly proficient bilingual individuals activated very similar brain circuits within the distributed frontoparietal network during language control and cognitive control (De Baene et al., 2015). With an increasing number of well-designed studies, we are closer to identifying the critical factors of language control and cognitive control; at the same time, we are also acquiring more information about the complexity of these systems.

Training studies may provide a different approach to examining these questions by focusing on transfer effects within and across domains. Wadhera (2020) compared cognitive and linguistic improvement in English-language learners with an adaptive, working memory updating and binding training design. This design used an n-back task and included interference conditions. This training was carried out over four weeks in 12 sessions. Transfer effects were found in a number of different tasks; performance improved from pre-training to post-training on both non-verbal measures of cue-based retrieval with interference conditions, on linguistic tasks that included English word categorization using a conflict paradigm, as well as on a task that required lexically-ambiguous sentence processing. Nevertheless, there was no transfer to other language tasks that did not include interference conditions, such as a simple reading comprehension task. Hence, this study provided strong evidence for the relationship between interference control and second-language (L2) processing in English-language learners.

In a much shorter but intense training study that employed well-matched linguistic and non-linguistic switching tasks (i.e., color/shape and digit naming sequences) with different groups of bilingual (early Spanish-English; early Mandarin-English; late Hebrew-English) and English monolingual young adults, Prior and Gollan (2013) found some unexpected results of transfer across the two tasks. The authors measured both mixing and switching costs. The mixing cost is calculated by comparing participants' responses to stay trials – in which no switching is involved – between a single block and a mixed block. While a single block includes stay trials only, a mixed block includes both stay and switch trials. Thus, the mixing cost indicates how the different contexts affect participants' responses to stay trials. If participants practiced language switching prior to color-shape task-switching, then they exhibited larger mixing costs for the color-shape task than those who practiced color-shape task-switching prior to language switching. However, cross-task transfer only occurred in the non-dominant language, and it was the mixing cost and not the switching cost that revealed significant transfer and practice effects, as well as associations between linguistic and non-linguistic switching. Prior and Gollan's findings are interesting because the mixing cost reflects global mechanisms related to monitoring in both linguistic and non-linguistic tasks.

Monitoring is another critical component of control to prevent and/or reduce interference between the two language systems in bilingual individuals. In their seminal work, Green and Abutalebi (2013) explored the cognitive-linguistic demands of three social contexts: single-language use, dual-language use, and dense code-switching context. Communication in all three contexts requires different cognitive-control skills to prevent cross-language interference. However, all three contexts involve a high level of monitoring in order to maintain the current goal and prevent interference from irrelevant and/or distracting items. Evidence from neurophysiological literature has shown that the ACC is essential in detecting the conflict and engaging the attentional control mechanisms in the dorsolateral prefrontal cortex to achieve goal-directed behavior (Shenhav et al., 2013). The dorsal ACC is highly activated in general conflict monitoring and in the maintenance of control during task performance (Botvinick et al., 2004; Luna et al., 2015).

Similar to the behavioral studies, a central question in neurophysiological research of bilingualism has been whether conflict monitoring through language control in bilingual individuals relies on the same neural system as monitoring in general cognitive control. Abutalebi and colleagues (2012) used a neuroimaging technique to reveal that the ACC plays a critical role in monitoring for both general cognitive control and language control. In agreement with Botvinick and colleagues' (2001) conflict monitoring and cognitive-control theory, the ACC detects and signals when irrelevant items interfere with the current task goal in both linguistic and non-linguistic tasks.

In summary, considerable research has established that bilingual individuals have honed cognitive-control skills to manage their two languages. Open questions remain on the extent to which these skills are specific to language or extend more generally to non-linguistic domains.

Attention-Independent Processes in Bilingual Language

One aspect of bilingual language processing that requires more research is the role of attention-independent processes. Attention-independent processing relies on different brain systems than the attention-dependent systems. As described above, the attention-dependent systems, which are involved in cognitive control, include the ACC and a frontoparietal network. The brain networks supporting attention-independent processes include the basal-ganglia-frontal network for procedural memory and learning (implicit learning) (Hamrick et al., 2018; Jorge et al., 2022), and sensory cortex for establishing memory representations that can be accessed without attention (Crick & Koch, 1990; Koch, 2004). In learning a first language (L1), listeners become automatic at selecting the phonetic cues that allow for fast and efficient recovery of linguistic categories (Shafer, in press; Strange, 2011; Strange & Shafer, 2008). Some aspects of morphosyntactic processing also appear to rely on procedural mechanisms, and thus, are attention-independent (Hamrick et al., 2018). In contrast, research has revealed that L2 learning and processing often relies on attention-dependent systems, at least in the early stages of L2 learning (Strange, 2011). These types of learning and memory have been referred to as declarative or explicit learning and memory in the literature (Hamrick et al., 2018). These "explicit" systems include the cognitive-control mechanisms discussed above.

There has been some debate over whether learning an L2 later in life (after about 13 years of age) differs from early learning, with a greater reliance on attention-dependent systems in later learning (Hamrick et al., 2018). The extent to which early L2 learning versus late L2 learning engage these different systems remains an open question. Furthermore, the type of learning (e.g., classroom versus immersion) is likely to modulate how attention-dependent and independent systems operate in bilingual language processing (Saito et al., 2022).

Below, we describe in greater detail how the automatic processes of L1 speech perception might interfere with L2 speech perception for late bilingual individuals, as proposed by Strange's Automatic Selective Perception (ASP) model and further discuss how factors, such as age of acquisition (AoA), length of exposure, and type of learning/training can modulate how attention-dependent and attention-independent systems are engaged in bilingual language processing.

The ASP model was designed specifically to address the role of attention in L1 versus L2 speech perception (Strange, 2011). The ASP model posits that L1 speech perception is automatic, and thus does not need focused attention to recover the relevant cues for accurate speech perception. These automatic processes are termed selective perceptual routines (SPRs). Considerable research support the claims that L1 SPRs are robust (accurate) even under conditions of high cognitive load (e.g., divided attention, background noise) (e.g., Hisagi et al., 2010). In contrast, evidence shows that L2 speech perception, specifically in late learners of an L2, often requires focused attention (Hisagi et al., 2010). Thus, under difficult task conditions that draw attention to some other language level or that tax working memory, speech perception in the L2 suffers. Furthermore, studies reveal that under conditions where attention is drawn away from the L2, listeners fall back on their L1 SPRs (e.g., Hisagi et al., 2010; Shafer et al., 2021). Reverting to the L1 SPRs can be viewed as a type of interference. Whether to view this reversion as a failure of cognitive control (failure to suppress the L1 SPRs) or as simply the default mode of processing for late learners is unclear. It will be important to determine whether native-like speech perception in late learners is more strongly correlated with better cognitive-control skills or with measures of attention-independence of L2 speech processing, such as the mismatch negativity (MMN) neural discrimination measure. To date, studies of late L2 learners, who are immersed in the L2 environment at the time of testing, have shown no more than weak correlations between the attention-independent MMN measure and L2 speech perception accuracy (e.g., Shafer et al., 2021). Thus, for these late learners, high performance on L2 speech perception behavioral tasks is a function of attention-dependent mechanisms (possibly interference control mechanisms), rather than changes in dependence on attention of speech perception. Intensive training of L2 categories might increase attention-independence, but to date, training studies have shown somewhat mixed results, with some studies observing improvements in attention-independent processes (the MMN) and others suggesting that improvements are supported only by attention-dependent skills (Tamminen et al., 2021).

The nature of speech perception in early bilingual learners (learning the L2 before 6 years of age) presents an interesting case. For late L2 learners, the L1 phonological system is firmly established early in life (Kuhl's neural commitment to the L2 speech patterns; Kuhl, et al., 2008). The question for early bilingual learners, however, is whether they can develop "automaticity" (that is, attention-independence) for both language systems, or whether one system (the dominant one) is more independent of attention than the other system. In addition, it is possible that early bilingual speakers engage in processing both languages in a different manner than monolingual or late bilingual individuals.

Research findings support both of these proposals. Specifically, for some bilingual speakers, one system is dominant (attention-independent). For example, the early Spanish-English bilingual individuals in Hisagi et al. (2015) showed behavioral performance in attention-dependent identification and discrimination tasks on an English vowel contrast, /ɛ/ versus /ɪ/, equivalent to monolingual English listeners, but showed attenuated neural discrimination (i.e., smaller MMN) when attention was focused away from the stimuli. This finding suggests that these listeners favored the Spanish vowel system, consistent with the claim that they have neurally-committed to Spanish before beginning to learn English (in the U.S., Spanish-English bilingual children often first encounter English in the public school system). However, in another study from the same lab, testing a different cohort of early bilingual speakers, no difference in MMN was observed to the same vowel contrast between the monolingual English and bilingual Spanish-English groups, for adults or for 8- to 10-year-old children (Datta et al., 2020). An interesting additional finding in this study was an increase in an attentional measure (called the Processing Negativity or PN, also called Nd) for the bilingual group compared to the monolingual group, suggesting that the bilingual speakers were monitoring the speech signal at some level, even when instructed to ignore the speech sounds. Taking these findings together, and considering findings from other studies (e.g., Peltola et al., 2012), we suggest that multiple factors, including age of acquisition and amount of use will modulate the degree to which speech perception is attention-independent in either the L1 or L2. We also suggest that the PN attentional effect reflects monitoring of the speech signal to determine which system is relevant for further processing.

The literature indicates that bilingual speakers engage attention-dependent mechanisms to support speech perception to a greater extent than monolingual listeners. Few studies have examined attention dependence of grammatical processing, but findings of reduced accuracy in grammatical judgments with increasing age of L2 acquisition are consistent with the hypothesis that late learning of morphosyntax will result in greater reliance on attention-dependent processes. Below, we discuss how these various accounts of bilingual language processing can be integrated into a coherent model of bilingual language processing.

Unifying the Models

Cognitive-control models of bilingual language processing have focused on explaining how high-level (attention-dependent and conscious) brain systems support bilingual processing. In contrast, the ASP model and Ullman's declarative-procedure model emphasize how some language processes are attention-independent (Hamrick et al., 2018). Specifically, procedural learning and memory processes are largely automatic, whereas declarative learning and memory processes are attention-dependent. Attention-independence of L1 phonetic cue processing, but not of L2 cue processing, for late L2 learners correctly predicts accuracy and speed in perception tasks, as well as robustness of neural discrimination. However, studies also suggest that attention-dependent abilities correlate with L2 performance on grammar for both bilingual speakers with lower and higher L2 experience, but, in addition, the higher-experienced groups showed significant correlations between attention-independent procedural memory and grammar abilities (Hamrick et al., 2018).

Thus, a more comprehensive model of bilingual language processing must include both attention-dependent and attention-independent mechanisms to fully explain performance. The attention-dependent system is supported by the prefrontal cortex, attentional networks (ACC and frontoparietal system), and memory systems (prefrontal and hippocampus) (Luna et al., 2015). Attention-independent processes are supported in the sensory cortex and by a basal-ganglia-frontal network (for implicit/procedural learning and memory) (Hamrick et al., 2018; Koch, 2004). These systems work in tandem to support language learning and language processing.

Cognitive control and procedural and sensory functions all play a role in bilingual language learning and processing. In early stages of L2 learning, L2 information (phonology, morphosyntax) is perceptually difficult because accurate representations and procedures have not been established. With focused attention to one aspect of information processing (e.g., repeating speech sounds or repeating verb conjugation paradigms), the learner can perform well because the task is simplified. However, language use is typically more complex (e.g., producing or comprehending discourse) and requires processing on multiple levels. Thus, in the early stages of L2 acquisition, the L1 is expected to interfere with processing of the L2. For the novice L2 learner, selective attention and cognitive-control systems will be strongly engaged in the attempt to suppress the L1. These cognitive-control mechanisms, however, will often be insufficient because for success, the novice learner needs to focus resources on multiple language levels (phonology, morphosyntax, semantics, discourse). In these early stages of L2 learning, listeners with better cognitive-control skills are expected to show better performance than those with weaker skills. With increasing L2 experience and proficiency, certain language skills may become automatized and allow for overall improved performance because cognitive resources are freed up for other tasks. For example, if L2 grammatical processing becomes more independent of attention, resources are freed up for processing speech. As Hamrick et al. (2018) observed, procedural memory performance correlated positively with L2 grammar abilities only for participants with higher L2 experience. The interpretation of this finding is that the procedural performance advantage was only apparent when sufficient experience allowed certain linguistic patterns to be supported by the procedural system. As a result, focused attention does not need to be engaged in processing information that is supported by the procedural system and is free to be allocated to processing other aspects of language. Thus, an apparent increase in cognitive control in experienced bilingual speakers could be directly due to improvements in cognitive control, or could be a side-effect of the shift of certain processes to the procedural system.

An additional observation is that bilingual experience changes how the speaker/listener interacts with the environment because an additional decision must be made, that is, which language is the target language. This possibility may fundamentally change how attention is engaged for bilingual speakers, specifically leading to heightened monitoring of the linguistic environment (Datta et al., 2020).

In sum, the bilingual listener who is proficient in both languages may show superior abilities to resist inference than a less proficient bilingual individual for two reasons: 1) certain L2 skills, such as speech perception and morphosyntactic processing, have become less dependent on attention, which frees up cognitive resources for suppressing interfering information, and/or 2) proficient bilingual speakers have honed cognitive control skills to allow efficient monitoring of the auditory landscape and suppression of the non-target language. Future studies will be needed to test these hypotheses.

Conclusion and Future Directions

The various theoretical frameworks approach the understanding of bilingual language processing from different directions. Studies of higher-level language processes (e.g., semantics and discourse) have focused on attention-dependent processing, and therefore have favored models of cognitive control modulating non-target language interference. In contrast, studies of bilingual speech perception and morphosyntactic processing have focused on attention-independent processes, and therefore have examined attention-independences in cue selection (as in the ASP model) and procedural memory (Ullman's model). Recognizing that bilingual language processing engages cognitive-control, sensorimotor, and procedural-brain mechanisms will allow us to reach a deeper understanding of bilingual language performance.

An important future direction will be to test the implementation of these various brain mechanisms in processing the same stimuli in the same participants, while considering how factors such as AoA and experience modulate engagement of these processes. For example, a switch task, requiring Spanish-English bilingual speakers (with varying levels of experience, proficiency, and AoA) to identify a target category (e.g., Voice-Onset Time of /ba/ among /pa/) could be used to investigate suppression of interfering phonology from a target to a non-target language in a case where the phonetic realization of the categories differ (prevoice versus short-lag for Spanish, and short-lag versus long-lag for English). This type of design would shed light on how attention-dependent cognitive control processes interact with more attention-independent processes during bilingual language processing.

References

Abutalebi, J., Della Rosa, P. A., Green, D. W., Hernandez, M., Scifo, P., Keim, R., … & Costa, A. (2012). Bilingualism tunes the anterior cingulate cortex for conflict monitoring. *Cerebral Cortex*, *22* (9), 2076–2086.

Abutalebi, J. & Green, D. (2007). Bilingual language production: The neurocognition of language representation and control. *Journal of Neurolinguistics*, *20* (3), 242–275.

Assche, E. V., Duyck, W., & Hartsuiker, R. J. (2012). Bilingual word recognition in a sentence context. *Frontiers in Psychology*, *3*, 174.

Bialystok, E. (2009). Bilingualism: The good, the bad, and the indifferent. *Bilingualism: Language and Cognition*, *12* (1), 3–11.

Botvinick, M. M., Braver, T. S., Barch, D. M., Carter, C. S., & Cohen, J. D. (2001). Conflict monitoring and cognitive control. *Psychological Review*, *108* (3), 624–652.

Botvinick, M. M., Cohen, J. D., & Carter, C. S. (2004). Conflict monitoring and anterior cingulate cortex: An update. *Trends in Cognitive Science*, *8*, 539–546.
Branzi, F. M., Calabria, M., Boscarino, M. L., & Costa, A. (2016). On the overlap between bilingual language control and domain-general executive control. *Acta Psychologica*, *166*, 21–30.
Calabria, M., Hernandez, M., Branzi, F. M., & Costa, A. (2012). Qualitative differences between bilingual language control and executive control: Evidence from task-switching. *Frontiers in Psychology*, 2. 10.3389/fpsyg.2011.00399
Cohen, J. D. (2017). Cognitive control: Core constructs and current considerations. In. T. Egner (Ed.). *The Wiley Handbook of Cognitive Control* (pp. 3–28). John Wiley & Sons.
Crick, F. & Koch, C. (1990). Towards a neurobiological theory of consciousness. *Seminars in the Neurosciences*, 2, 263–275.
Dajani, D. R. & Uddin, L. Q. (2015). Demystifying cognitive flexibility: Implications for clinical and developmental neuroscience. *Trends in Neurosciences*, *38*(9), 571–578.
Datta, H., Hestvik, A., Vidal, N., Tessel, C., Hisagi, M., Wróbleski, M., & Shafer, V. (2020). Automaticity of speech processing in early bilingual adults and children. *Bilingualism: Language and Cognition*, *23*(2), 429–445. 10.1017/s1366728919000099
De Baene, W., Duyck, W., Brass, M., & Carreiras, M. (2015). Brain circuit for cognitive control is shared by task and language switching. *Journal of Cognitive Neuroscience*, *27*(9), 1752–1765.
Declerck, M., Grainger, J., Koch, I., & Philipp, A. M. (2017). Is language control just a form of executive control? Evidence for overlapping processes in language switching and task switching. *Journal of Memory and Language*, *95*, 138–145.
Doebel, S. & Zelazo, P. D. (2015). A meta-analysis of the dimensional change card sort: Implications for developmental theories and the measurement of executive function in children. *Developmental Review*, *38*, 241–268. 10.1016/j.dr.2015.09.001
Dreisbach, G. & Fröber, K. (2019). On how to be flexible (or not): Modulation of the stability-flexibility balance. *Current Directions in Psychological Science*, *28* (1), 3–9.
Eichorn, N., Marton, K., & Pirutinsky, S. (2018). Cognitive flexibility in preschool children with and without stuttering disorders. *Journal of Fluency Disorders*, *57*, 37–50. 10.1016/j.jfludis.2017.11.001
Green, D. W. & Abutalebi, J. (2013). Language control in bilinguals: The adaptive control hypothesis. *Journal of Cognitive Psychology*, *25* (5), 515–530.
Hamrick, P., Lum, J. A. G., & Ullman, M. T. (2018). Child first language and adult second language are both tied to general-purpose learning systems. *Proceedings of the National Academy of Sciences of the United States of America*, *115*(7), 1487–1492. 10.1073/pnas.1713975115
Hisagi, M., Garrido-Nag, K., Datta, H., & Shafer, V. L. (2015). ERP indices of vowel processing in Spanish–English bilinguals. *Bilingualism: Language and Cognition*, *18*(02), 271–289.
Hisagi, M., Shafer, V. L., Strange, W., & Sussman, E. S. (2010). Perception of a Japanese vowel length contrast by Japanese and American English listeners: Behavioral and electrophysiological measures. *Brain Research*, *1360*, 89–105.

Jorge, A., Lipski, W. J., Wang, D., Crammond, D. J., Turner, R. S., & Richardson, R. M. (2022). Hyperdirect connectivity of opercular speech network to the subthalamic nucleus. *Cell Reports*, *38*(10), 110477. 10.1016/j.celrep.2022.110477

Kim, J., Marton, K., & Obler, L. K. (2019). Interference control in bilingual auditory sentence processing in noise. In. I. A. Sekerina, L. Spradlin, & V. Valian, (Eds.). *Bilingualism, Executive Function, and Beyond. Questions and insights* (pp. 103–116). John Benjamins Publishing Company.

Koch, C. (2004). *The Quest for Consciousness: A Neurobiological Approach.* Roberts and Co.

Kroll, J. F., Bobb, S. C., & Hoshino, N. (2014). Two languages in mind: Bilingualism as a tool to investigate language, cognition, and the brain. *Current Directions in Psychological Science*, *23* (3), 159–163.

Kroll, J. F., Dussias, P. E., Bice, K., & Perrotti, L. (2015). Bilingualism, mind, and brain. *Annual Review of Linguistics*, *1*, 377–394.

Kuhl, P. K., Conboy, B. T., Coffey-Corina, S., Padden, D., Rivera-Gaxiola, M., & Nelson, T. (2008). Phonetic learning as a pathway to language: New data and native language magnet theory expanded (NLM-e). *Philosophical Transactions of the Royal Society of London. Series B, Biological Sciences*, *363*(1493), 979–1000. 10.1098/rstb.2007.2154

Libben, M. R. & Titone, D. A. (2009). Bilingual lexical access in context: Evidence from eye movements during reading. *Journal of Experimental Psychology: Learning, Memory, and Cognition*, *35* (2), 381–390.

Linck, J. A., Schwieter, J. W., & Sunderman, G. (2012). Inhibitory control predicts language switching performance in trilingual speech production. *Bilingualism: Language and Cognition*, *15* (3), 651–662.

Liu, H., Rossi, S., Zhou, H., & Chen, B. (2014). Electrophysiological evidence for domain-general inhibitory control during bilingual language switching. *PLoS One*, *9*(10), e110887.

Luna, B., Marek, S., Larsen, B., Tervo-Clemmens, B., & Chahal, R. (2015). An integrative model of the maturation of cognitive control. *Annual Review of Neuroscience*, *38*, 151–170.

Marian, V. & Spivey, M. (2003). Competing activation in bilingual language processing: Within-and between-language competition. *Bilingualism: Language and Cognition*, *6*(2), 97–115.

Pavlenko, A. (2003). "I feel clumsy speaking Russian": L2 influence on L1 in narratives of Russian L2 users of English. In V. Cook (Ed.). Effects of the Second Language on the First. *Multilingual Matters* (pp. 32–61). Bristol: Blue Ridge Summit.

Peltola, M. S., Tamminen, H., Toivonen, H., Kujala, T., & Näätänen, R. (2012). Different kinds of bilinguals: Different kinds of brains: the neural organisation of two languages in one brain. *Brain and Language*, *121*(3), 261–266. 10.1016/j.bandl.2012.03.007

Prior, A., Degani, T., Awawdy, S., Yassin, R., & Korem, N. (2017). Is susceptibility to cross-language interference domain specific? *Cognition*, *165*, 10–25.

Prior, A. & Gollan, T. H. (2013). The elusive link between language control and executive control: A case of limited transfer. *Journal of Cognitive Psychology*, *25*(5), 622–645.

Saito, K., Kachlicka, M., Suzukida, Y., Petrova, K., Lee, B. J., & Tierney, A. (2022). Auditory precision hypothesis-L2: Dimension-specific relationships between auditory processing and second language segmental learning. *Cognition*, *229*, 105236. 10.1016/j.cognition.2022.105236

Shafer V. L. (in press). Automatic Selective Perception Model. In M. Amengual (Ed.). *The Cambridge Handbook of Bilingual Phonetics and Phonology*. Cambridge University Press.

Shafer, V. L., Kresh, S., Ito, K., Hisagi, M., Vidal, N., Higby, E., Castillo, D., & Strange, W. (2021). The neural timecourse of American English vowel discrimination by Japanese, Russian and Spanish second-language learners of English. *Bilingualism: Language and Cognition*, 1–14. 10.1017/S1366728921000201

Shenhav, A., Botvinick, M. M., & Cohen, J. D. (2013). The expected value of control: An integrative theory of anterior cingulate cortex function. *Neuron*, *79* (2), 217–240.

Strange, W. (2011). Automatic selective perception (ASP) of first and second language speech: A working model. *Journal of Phonetics*, *39*(4), 456–466. 10.1016/j.wocn.2010.09.001

Strange, W. & Shafer, V. L. (2008). Speech perception in second language learners: The re-education of selective perception. *Phonology and Second Language Acquisition*, 153–191.

Tamminen, H., Kujala, T., Näätänen, R., & Peltola, M. S. (2021). Aging and non-native speech perception: A phonetic training study. *Neuroscience Letters*, *740*, 135430. 10.1016/j.neulet.2020.135430

Van Dyke, J. A. & McElree, B. (2006). Retrieval interference in sentence comprehension. *Journal of Memory and Language*, *55* (2), 157–166.

van Hell, J. G. & Tanner, D. (2012). Second language proficiency and cross-language lexical activation. *Language Learning*, *62*, 148–171.

Wadhera, D. (2020). *Working Memory Training: Cognitive and Linguistic Implications in Adult English Language Learners* (Doctoral dissertation, City University of New York).

3

DYNAMIC RELATIONSHIPS AMONG MULTIPLE LANGUAGES

Elizabeth Ijalba and Zohar Eviatar

Introduction

The relationships between multiple languages within an individual and linguistic diversity within a population are complex. Here we examine three types of relationships between languages: bilingualism, diglossia, and standard-with-dialects. Our focus is on the manner in which individuals deal with multiple languages, referring also to sociolinguistic data about linguistic environments.

Bilingualism is defined as the case in which an individual or population uses two or more languages on a regular basis, sometimes with language separation by topic, and sometimes with much mixing. *Diglossia* is defined as the case in which there are two levels of a language, a high (H) level used for formal occasions and a low (L) level that is used in everyday speech. *Standard-with-dialects* is defined as the situation where one form of a language is considered the standard, with different forms used by different communities considered as dialects (e.g., standard American English vs. African American English, Cajun English, etc.). Sociolinguists (e.g., Mejdell, 2017) differentiate diglossia from bilingualism and from standard-with-dialects because speakers in the diglossic context do not access all versions/registers, whereas speakers in the standard-with-dialects and bilingualism contexts access all versions/registers. When the H and L versions of a diglossic language have little overlap, speakers in formal registers almost always utilize the H form and speakers in informal registers almost always use the L form.

DOI: 10.4324/9781003330318-4

We focus on bilingual and standard-with-dialects situations in the U.S. and on the diglossic situation in the Palestinian-Israeli environment. In both countries, the diversity of linguistic experience impacts the education, socialization, and integration of minoritized populations into society at large.

The Context of Linguistic and Cultural Variation in the United States

The U.S. has been a polyglot multicultural nation since its inception. By the 1800s there were over one million enslaved Africans, who spoke Niger-Congo languages, pidgins, and creoles. These linguistic forms gave rise to what is today known as African American English or Black American English (BAE). The 1800s marked the suppression and genocide of Indigenous Native Americans. Their languages and cultures were suppressed to the point of extinction; however, 170 Indigenous languages survive to this day. Additionally, the 1800s marked the annexation of Florida and large parts of Mexico and Puerto Rico, bringing in large numbers of Spanish speakers, while the Louisiana purchase brought in French speakers. At that time, approximately one quarter of the nation's European immigrants were non-English speakers, predominantly German speakers, who settled in Pennsylvania. Large numbers of Chinese immigrants arrived in the mid-1800s for the California Gold Rush and the building of the first Transcontinental Railroad. Migration from China was banned with the Chinese Exclusion Act of 1882 and restarted with the passage of the Immigration and Nationality Act of 1965. This law removed discrimination based on ethnicity, primarily directed against Asians, Southern and Eastern Europeans, and non-western groups. See Rumbaut and Massey (2013) for a concise analysis of immigration and language diversity in the U.S.

The multilingual and multicultural fabric of the U.S. expanded after 1965, placing language rights and education at the core of the Civil Rights movement. The Bilingual Education Act (BEA) of 1967 and its amendments in 1974 recognized the special language and education needs of immigrant children and children of immigrants, giving rise to bilingual education programs. These changes influenced a flourishing of research in bilingualism in education, psycholinguistics, and neurolinguistics – including our understanding of bilingualism/multilingualism across the lifespan.

Linguistic Diversity, Ethnicity, Education, and Literacy

Multilingualism in the U.S. is rooted in history and migration from many parts of the world. According to the 2020 U.S. Census, the five predominant languages in the U.S. today, other than English, are Spanish, Chinese, Tagalog, Vietnamese, and Arabic. However, Spanish is predominant and spoken by 76.44% of all English learners (Office of English Language Acquisition, 2016-17).

Despite its multilingual and multicultural history, the U.S. has been described as a "zone of language extinction" (Rumbaut & Massey, 2013), where immigrant languages are replaced with English. This occurs largely through a social system that places value on standard American English (SAE) and by a public school system that enforces SAE. Accordingly, most bilingual programs are transitional and aimed at mainstreaming students to English within 1 to 3 years. Additionally, content-based instruction for reading, writing, and academic language is primarily provided in English (see Ijalba & Velasco, 2019).

The scarcity of reading materials and literature in other languages compared to SAE, further reinforces its superior status. For example, bilingual teachers have the additional burden of "invisible work" by often having to translate curriculum materials from English (Amanti, 2019). Spanish-speaking parents often lack books in Spanish for early literacy and are ambivalent about reading to their children in a language other than English (Ijalba, 2014). The lack of literacy materials for all grade levels is intensified in the case of BAE, which is often associated with race and "slang" in the U.S. (Washington & Seidenberg, 2021). BAE has been described as a transplant dialect arising from African American speakers moving from southern states into northern cities. This migration gave rise to ethnolinguistic divergence that sets BAE apart from other English vernaculars (see Wolfram, 2000).

Questions associated with bilingual instruction are particularly important when considering reading acquisition, and the challenges that students with limited English proficiency face when learning to read English. However, for speakers of BAE, the challenge is not lack of English proficiency, but limited awareness about the differences between BAE and SAE. Bilingual instruction does not address the educational challenges of BAE speakers. Moreover, students and teachers lack literacy materials in BAE. This state of affairs has consequences for educational outcomes among minoritized groups. For example, the National Assessment of Educational Progress (NAEP, 2019) reading report indicates report (NAEP, 2019) indicates that only 35%–37% of 4th–12th graders read at grade level, with scores essentially unchanged in the last 10 years. The lowest performance scores are linked to Hispanic, Black, and Native American students. This points to a failure within the U.S. educational system to address linguistic diversity in reading and academic instruction.

Orthographic Transparency, Linguistic Diversity, and Reading

Spanish has orthographic transparency in its grapheme-to-phoneme correspondences (GPC), which facilitates reading (e.g., Ellis et al., 2004). This is relevant, considering that over 76% of English learners come from Spanish-speaking homes and are among the groups with lowest national reading scores. Developmental dyslexia in Spanish is primarily associated with challenges in fluent reading; whereas in English it includes inaccuracy in word/nonword recognition and problems in reading comprehension (e.g., Wimmer & Schurz, 2010). Additionally, language proficiency is crucial in developing phonological awareness, lexical retrieval, and morphosyntax – core components of reading in English and Spanish.

A focus of bilingual research in reading has been to determine predictors of reading success across languages. Ijalba et al. (2021) administered a battery of reading and language tasks to 3rd, 4th, and 5th graders in a dual-language program in Uruguay. Findings revealed strong correlations between accuracy in word reading and decoding nonwords in each language. However, phonological awareness in English was the only measure strongly correlated with reading comprehension across languages, suggesting that it could predict reading success. In contrast, phonological awareness in Spanish did not yield correlations with reading comprehension in either language. It may be that the consistent GPC of the Spanish writing system facilitates self-teaching (Share, 1999), including phonological awareness and reading fluency for all readers, despite their reading challenges.

In a direct test of the influence of orthographic transparency on word reading, Ijalba and Obler (2015) compared adults learning to read invented words and symbols with corresponding phonemes in a 1:1 and in a 1:2 GPC. Twenty adult Spanish-speakers and 20 English-speakers followed a structured teaching routine to learn both GPCs. Results showed increased accuracy among participants for the reading of invented words in the 1:1 GPC. Importantly, the English-speakers outperformed the Spanish-speakers in the 1:2 GPC, suggesting the influence of their first-learned language in learning to read an additional script with multiple GPC. Thus, orthographic transparency and consistency may play a facilitative role in learning to read a new language.

Clinical case studies shed light on the assessment of language and reading in bilingual speakers. Ijalba et al. (2020a) showed the relevance of measuring accuracy and timing for the reading of words and nonwords, and accuracy, fluency, and reading comprehension in English for three bilingual participants (English/Spanish) with prior monolingual reading instruction. The researchers noted that reading is learned through systematic and structured reading instruction; therefore, bilingual students should only be assessed in their language of instruction. A detailed reading assessment of the three participants (ages 10, 10, and 18 years old) revealed problems in phonological processing. In the case of one 5th grader, her challenges in phonological processing impaired her word reading ability, resulting in slow reading and poor reading comprehension. Interestingly, this reader was subsequently placed in a dual-language bilingual program, and she readily learned to read in Spanish. Moreover, within 1 year she also showed improvement and enjoyment for reading in English (mother's report).

Does learning to read in Spanish, with its 1:1 GPC, facilitate learning to read in English, with its 1: many GPC, and does simultaneous dual-language reading instruction facilitate transfer at the phonological, morphosyntactic, and lexical levels? A substantial body of research suggests the latter may indeed be the case, given the positive reciprocal interactions between phonemic awareness and reading development (Castles & Coltheart, 2004; Geva & Siegel, 2000; Hanley et al., 2004; Lallier & Carreiras, 2018). The view of multicompetence posits that transfer between languages is bidirectional because bilingual/multilingual speakers shift among languages in their mind – forming a linguistic superstructure, rather than establishing separate language systems. Based on this perspective, Talebi (2013) argues that improvements in reading in any language will result in improvements in reading across languages.

Questions regarding linguistic and cultural identity often impact whether bilingual speakers retain or lose any of their languages. Ijalba et al. (2020b) explored how shifts in linguistic/cultural identity influenced language choices among Hispanic and Asian college students. Questionnaires and individual interviews revealed that participants who strongly identified within their own culture also reported proficiency in their heritage language. Participants who lost their heritage language reported difficulty integrating within their families and communities. In contrast, bilingual participants described the benefits of speaking more than one language, such as promoting an inclusive world view, improving their understanding/insightfulness of other cultures, and increasing job opportunities.

Integrating Linguistic Diversity in the Classroom

Translanguaging is an approach to academic instruction that views the linguistic resources of bilingual/multilingual speakers from a unitary perspective and encourages speakers to access all languages in their repertoire. This conceptualization positions all language forms on a par with SAE. Moreover, translanguaging integrates social justice, cultural/linguistic identities, collaboration, and learning across linguistic modalities. Its dynamic and inclusive framework makes it a promising educational approach in bilingual/multilingual and standard-with-dialects context (see also Chapter 4, this volume).

Whereas translanguaging has been primarily used with bilingual students representing standard languages, such as English and Spanish (García & Kleyn, 2016), it may hold promise for speakers of BAE who may be unaware of the differences between BAE and SAE (Seltzer & García, 2020; Smith, 2020). There are two distinct approaches: spontaneous translanguaging and pedagogical or structured translanguaging. The former relies on a unitary perspective and encourages speakers to spontaneously shift among their languages (García, 2009). The latter relies on systematic instruction, comparison, and transfer among languages (Cenoz & Gorter, 2022; Cummins, 2021; Fuster, 2022).

The overlap between BAE and SAE may present particular challenges for bidialectal students throughout their academic careers. Key features of BAE are found in verb morphology, syntax, and phonology, with concomitant effects on reading, writing, and academic expression. Washington and Seidenberg (2021) suggest that for early readers, subtle linguistic and cultural transformations within a language may be more difficult to detect and resolve than those between different languages. However, for bidialectal college students, the challenges include academic conversations and self-expression, reading and writing across academic genres and disciplines, and the emotional toll associated by using SAE at the cost of BAE.

Work in progress by Ijalba focuses on developing inclusive pedagogical practices with college students who identify as linguistically diverse (i.e., bilingual, bidialectal, or multilingual). Queens College of the City University of New York is a 4-year institution with high student diversity (29% Hispanic, 29% White, 27% Asian, 9% African American, and a growing number of international students). Such diversity raises the challenges of language, culture, and education at the academic level. Moreover, distance learning has added to the complexities of teaching and assessment. This research study will compare how participants perform on oral and written persuasive discourse samples after brief interventions using spontaneous translanguaging or structured translanguaging.

Diglossia in Palestinian-Israeli Society

In Israel, diglossia is an inherent characteristic of Palestinian-Israeli society, similar to other Arabic-speaking countries. The spoken form of Arabic (SA) is different from its written form (Modern Standard Arabic, MSA). SA is the native language of all Arabic speakers; it varies geographically, is not traditionally written, and is considered the low (L) form of the language. MSA is acquired through schooling; it is standard across the Arab world, it is written, it is used in formal occasions, and it is considered the high (H) form of the language. Although the two forms of Arabic share substantial vocabulary, their linguistic distance is found within the phonological, morphosyntactic, and lexical-semantic domains (Saiegh-Haddad, 2005). For example, in some Palestinian dialects in Israel there are vowels that exist in SA and not in MSA. SA and MSA utilize different plural markings/insertion rules for function words and have different constraints on word order in sentence structure (see Saiegh-Haddad & Henkin-Roitfarb, 2014, for a review of differences in the Palestinian-Israeli context). Saiegh-Haddad and Spolsky (2014) highlighted the lexical differences between SA and MSA by mapping the vocabularies of Palestinian-Israeli kindergarteners. Only 21.2% of the words were identical between SA and MSA, 40.6% were phonologically related but not identical, and 38.2% of words in children's vocabulary were unique to MSA. Importantly, the two forms of Arabic are intertwined in everyday life, for example, preliterate children are exposed to MSA via picture books and cartoons, adults and literate children study in MSA, and the news is written and reported in MSA.

Many studies have shown that reading acquisition is slower in Arabic than in Hebrew, which is similar in structure and writing system, but uses a different script. These studies have generally suggested that this slowness is due to diglossia, where children learn to read a language that they do not speak (e.g., Saiegh-Haddad, 2003). Saiegh-Haddad and Schiff (2016) and Eviatar et al. (2016) showed that adult skilled readers of Arabic read complex texts in Arabic more slowly than adult-skilled readers of Hebrew read complex texts in Hebrew. Both reports suggest that this slowness results from diglossia. This hypothesis is supported by the findings of a recent eye-movement study of ecological reading by adult skilled readers (Lahoud et al., 2023), who showed longer fixation durations and dwell times on words unique to MSA than on words that are cognates or identical to SA. Thus, the effects of diglossia on reading persist at all levels of skill.

Whereas the status of SA as the native language of all Arabic speakers is clear, the status of MSA has been debated (e.g., Eid, 1990; Eviatar & Ibrahim, 2000; Hellmuth, 2022; Khamis-Dakwar & Froud, 2006). In this chapter, we suggest that the status of MSA within an individual is dynamic and changes with age. Thus, there is a continuum between the representation of dialects of a single language, diglossia, and bilingualism, rather than a qualitative categorical difference. More than 50 years of neurocognitive research suggests that the differences between language representations in the brains of mono- and multi-lingual speakers are quantitative rather than qualitative. We suggest that as Arabic speakers become more proficient in the H form of the language, it becomes easier for them to code-switch between the L and the H forms, such that they become integrated. This has been termed "Educated Spoken Arabic" (ESA) and may indicate that the H form becomes more similar to a high register of the L form, than another language.

Eviatar and Ibrahim (2000) proposed that when children are first exposed to MSA, they treat it as an additional language. The authors showed that SA-speaking kindergarteners and 1st graders who were exposed to MSA in order to prepare them to learn to read, performed very similarly to a bilingual Russian-Hebrew control group, and differently from a monolingual Hebrew-speaking group on a series of language tests. The authors used three measures: phonological awareness, language arbitrariness (Piaget's sun and moon task), and vocabulary size. The Russian-Hebrew bilingual group showed the canonical bilingual pattern: higher awareness of phonology and arbitrariness, and smaller vocabulary, than the monolingual group. The Arabic-speaking children closely patterned with the Russian-Hebrew bilingual children (see Figure 3.1). We concluded that SA and MSA are sufficiently different such that the cognitive system of young children treats them as different languages.

The distance between SA and MSA may shrink as proficiency in MSA rises. This has been facilitated in the last several decades by computer-mediated communication. The social taboo on writing SA was broken with the advent of smartphones and social media, where the informal context of digital chats invited Arabic-speaking teenagers and young adults to write in SA (e.g., Hoigilt, 2018; Warschauer et al., 2002). Until keyboard software was updated to accommodate Arabic, youngsters wrote SA using a combination of Latin letters and numbers (the orthography known as "Arabizi", Yaghan, 2008). Abu-Leil et al. (2019) examined literacy in the H and L versions of Arabic by asking computer-savvy 8th graders to read single words and texts in SA in Arabizi, and in MSA. Results showed that the youths read texts in MSA faster than texts in Arabizi. The authors interpreted this finding in two ways: First, this reflects higher proficiency in reading normal Arabic orthography vs. the relatively new Arabizi. Second, Arabic orthography and Arabizi belong to different writing systems. Arabic orthography is an abjad[1] and Arabizi utilizes an alphabetic system. In the Arabic abjad, there are two forms: the voweled form includes diacritics that are inserted above or below letters and is used in children's books, poetry, and religious texts. It represents the phonological forms of words completely; the unvoweled form omits the diacritics and includes only long vowels. This results in more frequent use of the faster lexical versus the slower phonological route in reading. Voweled texts are read more slowly by skilled readers than unvoweled texts, reflecting the relative slowness of full phonological processing (this was also found for Hebrew readers who use a different abjad script with voweled and unvoweled versions; e.g., Frost

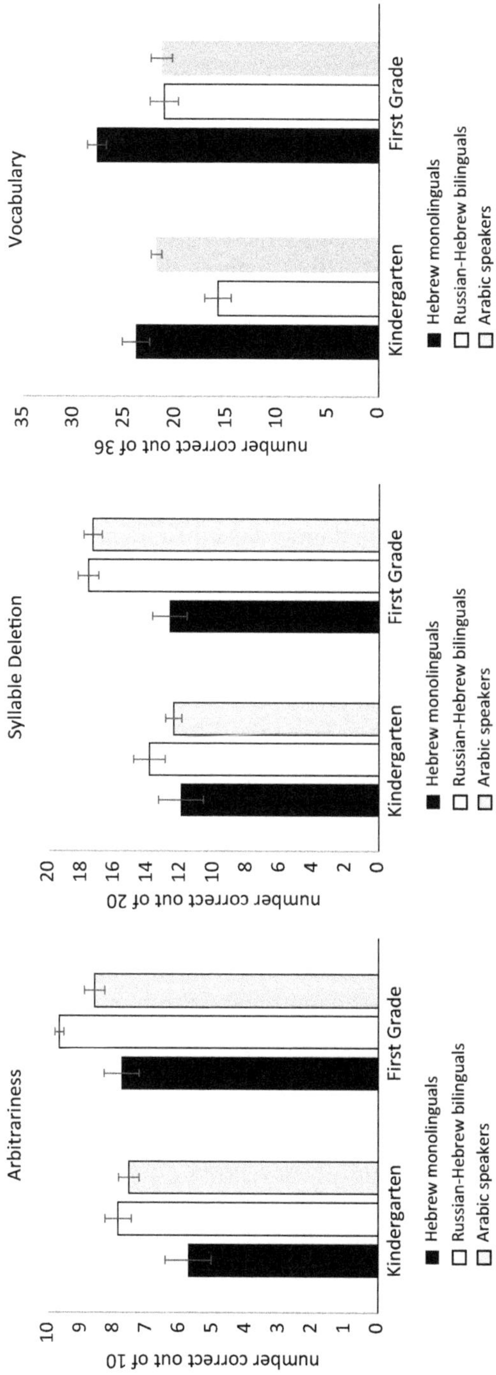

FIGURE 3.1 Response patterns of Arabic speakers compared to bilingual and monolingual control groups.

& Bentin, 1992). Arabizi includes all vowels, similar to abjad voweled texts, and thus may slow reading down. Interestingly, in comprehension measures, we found an interaction between text genre and script type. Narrative texts were better comprehended in Arabizi, and expository texts were better comprehended in MSA. This probably reflects the frequency with which narratives are encountered on social media, while MSA is used in textbooks in an expository context.

The same 8th graders also took part in a survey of their attitudes toward SA and MSA (Abu-Leil et al., 2020), where they acknowledged the usefulness of SA in the computer-mediated-context and their feeling of ease and comfort in writing it because it is their native language. However, they did not want SA to replace MSA in the formal sphere. These teenagers reported feeling obligated to MSA and a responsibility to preserve it (the majority agreed with the position: "*We live in a country that does not recognize the official status of the Arabic language, so it is my responsibility to keep it and use it*"). Both Christian and Muslim youths reported a sense of pride in MSA as a symbol that represents their identity and culture. Thus, living in a country with a different majority language (Hebrew), these native Arabic speakers consider MSA an important source of ethnic identity and culture. Interestingly, similar attitudes are reported for Egyptian and Moroccan young people (Hoigilt, 2018), where the status of Arabic as the national language is not endangered.

Previous authors (e.g., Boussofara-Omar, 2003; Helmuth, 2022; Hoigilt, 2018; Mejdell, 2006, 2017) have suggested that educated Arabic speakers move quite freely between the H and the L versions of Arabic, a register called *wusta*, middle Arabic, or ESA. In this version of Arabic, features of both SA and MA are interwoven in fluent speech. This has led sociolinguists to suggest that the L and H versions of Arabic are not different categories, but rather lie at ends of a continuum of formality and style. This mixing of MSA and SA is supported by new research (Dallasheh-Khatib et al., in preparation) which examines emotional speech in multilingual Arabic speakers. In Israel, literate Arabic speakers navigate between SA, MSA, Hebrew, and English. The authors examined the way that female university students, native speakers of SA, talk about emotions. Given that these participants are highly proficient multilingual speakers (all matriculated from high school in MSA and passed proficiency exams in Hebrew and English to enter the university), we focused on their code-switches. We showed these women 20 emotion-arousing pictures from the International Affective Picture System collection (Lang et al., 1997). This is a collection of over 1000 photographs of people in different situations, which have been categorized emotionally by a large population. The participants were asked to talk for at least 1 minute about the emotions aroused by each picture.

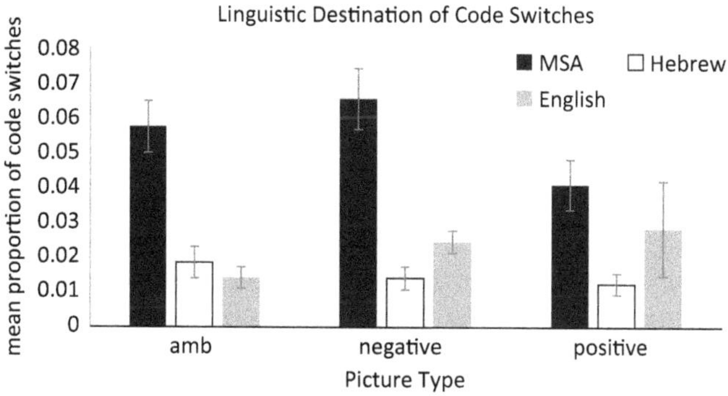

FIGURE 3.2 Proportions of code-switches made by Arabic speakers into MSA, Hebrew, and English. Amb=ambiguous pictures.

The experiment took place in SA, with instructions to talk freely about the pictures. The authors transcribed these recordings and counted the number of emotional words and the number of code-switches. It was found that code-switches were made on 11% of the words, with a quarter of these made on emotional words. See Figure 3.2 for the pattern in linguistic destination of code-switches.

More switches were made into MSA than into Hebrew or English. These data suggest that MSA is more accessible to our participants when they are speaking SA than their other languages, supporting the view that for these educated adults, SA and MSA are on a continuum, rather than different languages.

To summarize, research on the manner in which Arabic speakers in Israel function in the diglossic environment suggests that the status of MSA changes with age. When children are first introduced to MSA, their cognitive system seems to treat it as an additional language. As proficiency in MSA rises, it becomes closer to SA and represents a higher register rather than a different language. Further research is needed to shed light on the dynamic relationship between the H and L versions of Arabic at varying levels of skill. Detailed study of language breakdown in aphasia and old age has just begun in this context (e.g., Khamis-Dakwar, 2020), and is of interest for speech-language-pathologists and for psycholinguists.

Conclusion and Future Directions

We have considered linguistic diversity and its effects on reading, cognition, and identity, while focusing on the U.S. and Israel. In the U.S., we considered the suppression of a rich multilingual and multicultural collective in favor of SAE, with concomitant reading and educational challenges for linguistically diverse groups (i.e., Hispanic, Black, and Native American students). We looked at orthographic transparency and its relevance for Spanish speakers, who often experience reading difficulties in English and constitute a majority of English learners. We looked at the assessment of reading in bilingual students and the role of phonological processing among readers with dyslexia. Research points to phonological awareness in English as a predictor of reading success across English and Spanish. We considered multicompetence and the positive interactions of transfer across languages and the challenges faced by bidialectal speakers due to the overlapping nature of BAE and SAE. Moreover, we explored how cultural-linguistic identity influences language choices and language proficiency among bilingual speakers during the school years.

When considering diglossia in Israel, the research points to languages and literacies functioning along a continuum and changing across the lifespan, rather than forming separate language systems. A central premise of our view is that the status of MSA within an individual is dynamic and changes with age. Whereas children initially treat MSA as an additional language, MSA becomes closer to SA and functions as a higher register, rather than a different language. We also considered the sociolinguistic complexity in Israel, where literate Arabic speakers navigate between three to four languages (SA, MSA, Hebrew, and English) and three different writing systems, and how Arabic-speaking youth take pride in MSA as a symbol of identity and culture.

To conclude, despite the sociolinguistic differences and complexities found in Israel and in the U.S., a common thread is the unified construct of language(s) among diglossic, bilingual, and bidialectal speakers. Theoretically, our research points to a continuum between these constructs, rather than to qualitative categorical differences. We suggest that inclusive sociolinguistic conditions, equity, and an education rooted in recognizing linguistic diversity will benefit our societies.

Note

1 An abjad writing system includes mostly consonants, where short vowel information is not included in the unvoweled version and is included as diacritics in the voweled version. In Hebrew and Arabic, most written materials except children's books, liturgical materials, and poetry are unvoweled.

References

Abu-Liel, A. K., Eviatar, Z., & Nir, B. (2019). Writing between languages: The case of Arabizi. *Writing Systems Research*, *11*(2), 226–238.

Abu Leil, A. K., Eviatar, Z., & Nir, B. (2020). Arab adolescents' attitudes towards standard and nonstandard writing systems: The case of Arabizi and Modern Standard Arabic. *Journal of Cultural Cognitive Science, 5*, 125–142.
Abu-Liel, A. K., Ibrahim, R., & Eviatar, Z. (2021). Reading in multiple Arabics: Effects of diglossia and orthography. *Reading and Writing, 34*, 2291–2316.
Amanti, C. (2019). The (invisible) work of dual language bilingual education teachers. *Bilingual Research Journal, 42*(4), 455–470. 10.1080/15235882.2019.1687111
Boussofara-Omar, N. (2003). Revisiting Arabic diglossic switching in light of the MLF model and its sub-models: The 4-M model and the Abstract Level model. *Bilingualism: Language and Cognition, 6*(1), 33–46. doi:10.1017/S136
Castles, A. & Coltheart, M. (2004). Is there a causal link from phonological awareness to success in learning to read? *Cognition, 91*, 77–111.
Cenoz, J. & Gorter, D. (2022). *Pedagogical translanguaging. Elements in language teaching, Cambridge elements*. Cambridge University Press.
Cummins, J. (2021). Translanguaging: A critical analysis of theoretical claims. In P. Juvonen & M. Källkvist (Eds.), *Pedagogical translanguaging: Theoretical, methodological and empirical perspectives*. UK Multilingual Matters.
Dallasheh-Khatib, R., Eviatar, Z., & Kreiner, H. (In preparation). Linguistic and cultural effects on speech about emotions among Arabic and Hebrew speaking women.
Eid, M. (1990). Arabic linguistics: The current scene. *Perspectives on Arabic Linguistics I*, 3–37.
Ellis, N. C., Natsume, M., Stavropoulou, K., Hoxhallari, L., Van Daal, V. H., Polyzoe, N., ... & Petalas, M. (2004). The effects of orthographic depth on learning to read alphabetic, syllabic, and logographic scripts. *Reading Research Quarterly, 39*(4), 438–468.
Eviatar, Z. & Ibrahim, R. (2000). Bilingual is as bilingual does: Metalinguistic abilities of Arabic-speaking children. *Applied Psycholinguistics, 21*(4), 451–471.
Eviatar, Z., Ibrahim, R., Karelitz, T. M., & Simon, A. B. (2016). Speed of reading texts in Arabic and Hebrew. *Reading and Writing, 32*(3), 537–559.
Frost R. & Bentin S. (1992). Reading consonants and guessing vowels: Visual word recognition in Hebrew orthography. In R. Frost & L. Katz (Eds.), *Orthography Phonology Morphology and Meaning* (pp. 27–44). Elsevier.
Fuster, C. (2022) Lexical transfer as a resource in pedagogical translanguaging. *International Journal of Multilingualism*. 10.1080/14790718.2022.2048836
García, O. (2009). Education, multilingualism and translanguaging in the 21st century. In T. Skutnabb-Kangas, R. Phillipson, A. K. Mohanty, & M. Panda (Eds.), *Social Justice Through Multilingual Education* (pp. 140–158). Multilingual Matters.
García, O. & Kleyn, T. (2016). Translanguaging theory in education. In O. García & T. Kleyn (Eds.), *Translanguaging with Multilingual Students: Learning from Classroom Moments* (pp. 9–33). Routledge.
Geva, E. & Siegel, L. S. (2000). Orthographic and cognitive factors in the concurrent development of basic reading skills in two languages. *Reading and Writing, 12*, 1–30.
Hellmuth, S. (2022). Sentence prosody and register variation in Arabic. *Languages, 7*(2), 129.
Hoigilt, J. (2018). The contemporary politics of written Arabic. *Brown Journal of World Affairs, 25*, 41.

Hanley, R., Masterson, J., Spencer, L., & Evans, D. (2004). How long do the advantages of learning to read a transparent orthography last? An investigation of the reading skills and reading impairment of Welsh children at 10 years of age. *Quarterly Journal of Experimental Psychology*, *57A*, 1393–1410.

Ijalba, E. (2014). Effectiveness of a parent-implemented early literacy intervention in the home language. *Child Language Teaching and Therapy*, 1–14. 10.1177/0265659014548519

Ijalba, E., Bustos, A., & Romero, S. (2020a). Phonological-orthographic deficits in developmental dyslexia in three Spanish-English bilingual students. *American Journal of Speech Language Pathology*, *29*, 1133–1151.

Ijalba, E., Cuadro, A., & Ruiz, C. (Nov. 2021). Predictors of reading in Spanish-English dual-language learners. American Speech Language and Hearing Association Annual Convention, Washington DC.

Ijalba, E., Romero, S., & Lau, G. (2020b). Cultural identity and language in college students from diverse backgrounds. American Speech Language Hearing Association Annual Convention, Miami, FL.

Ijalba, E. & Obler, L. K. (2015). Grapheme-to-phoneme transparency effects in adult second language learning. *Reading in a Foreign Language*, *27*(1), 47–70. Available from: http://nflrc.hawaii.edu/rfl/April2015/articles/ijalba.pdf

Ijalba, E. & Velasco P. (2019). Political, social, and educational challenges in the struggle to develop bilingual education as a pedagogical model in the United States. In E. Ijalba, P. Velasco, & C. J. Crowley (Eds.), *Language, Culture and Education: Challenges of Diversity in the United States* (pp. 13–30). Cambridge University Press.

Khamis-Dakwar, R. (2020). Clinical linguistic research in the study of Arabic diglossia. In *Perspectives on Arabic Linguistics XXX: Papers from the annual symposium on Arabic Linguistics* (pp. 155–172). John Benjamins.

Khamis-Dakwar, R. & Froud, K. (2006). Lexical processing in two language varieties. In M. A. Mughazy (Ed.), *Perspectives on Arabic Linguistics XX: Papers from the Twentieth Annual Symposium on Arabic Linguistics, Kalamazoo* (Vol. 290). John Benjamins Publishing.

Lahoud, H., Eviatar, Z., & Kreiner, H. (2023). Eye-movement patterns in skilled Arabic readers: Effects of unique features of Arabic vs. universal factors. *Reading and Writing* 1–30.

Lallier, M. & Carreiras, M. (2018). Cross-linguistic transfer in bilinguals reading in two alphabetic orthographies: The grain size accommodation hypothesis. *Psychonomic Bulletin and Review*, *25*, 386–401. 10.3758/s13423-017-1273-0

Lang, P. J., Bradley, M. M., & Cuthbert, B. N. (1997). International affective picture system (IAPS): Technical manual and affective ratings. *NIMH Center for the Study of Emotion and Attention*, *1*(39-58), 3.

Mejdell, G. (2017). Diglossia. In *The Routledge Handbook of Arabic Linguistics* (pp. 332–344). Routledge.

Mejdell, G. (2006). *Mixed Styles in Spoken Arabic in Egypt: Somewhere Between Order and Chaos*. Brill.

NAEP Report Card. (2019). NAEP Reading Assessment. https://www.nationsreportcard.gov/highlights/reading/2019/

Office of English Language Acquisition (OELA). The top languages spoken by English Learners (ELs) in the United States (2023). https://ncela.ed.gov/files/fast_facts/olea-top-languages-fact-sheet-20191021-508.pdf

Rumbaut, R. G. & Massey, D. S. (2013). Immigration and language diversity in the United States. *Daedalus*, *142*(3), 141–154. doi: 10.1162/daed_a_00224. PMID: 25018562; PMCID: PMC4092008

Saiegh-Haddad, E. (2003). Linguistic distance and initial reading acquisition: The case of Arabic diglossia. *Applied Psycholinguistics*, *24*(3), 431–451.

Saiegh-Haddad, E. (2005). Correlates of reading fluency in Arabic: Diglossic and orthographic factors. *Reading and Writing*, *18*(6), 559–582.

Saiegh-Haddad, E. & Henkin-Roitfarb, R. (2014). The structure of Arabic language and orthography. In E. Saiegh-Haddad and M. Joshi (Eds.), *Handbook of Arabic literacy* (pp. 3–28). Springer.

Saiegh-Haddad, E. & Schiff, R. (2016). The impact of diglossia on voweled and unvoweled word reading in Arabic: A developmental study from childhood to adolescence. *Scientific Studies of Reading*, *20*(4), 311–324.

Saiegh-Haddad, E. & Spolsky, B. (2014). Acquiring literacy in a diglossic context: Problems and prospects. In *Handbook of Arabic literacy* (pp. 225–240). Springer.

Seltzer, K. & García, O. (2020). Broadening the view: Taking up a translanguaging pedagogy with all language–minoritized students. In T. Zhongfeng, L. Aghai, P. Sayer, & J. L. Schissel (Eds.), *Envisioning TESOL Through a Translanguaging Lens* (pp. 23–42). Springer.

Share, D. L. (1999). Phonological recoding and orthographic learning: A direct test of the self-teaching hypothesis. *Journal of Experimental Child Psychology*, *72*, 95–129.

Smith, P. (2020). The case for translanguaging in Black immigrant literacies. *Literacy Research: Theory, Method, and Practice*, *69*(1), 192–210.

Talebi, S. H. (2013). Cross-linguistic transfer (from L1 to L2, L2 to L1, and L2 to L3) of reading strategies in a multicompetent mind. *Journal of Language Teaching and Research*, *4*(2), 432.

Washington, J. A. & Seidenberg, M. S. (2021). Teaching reading to African American children: When home and school language differ. *American Educator*, *45*(2), 26.

Warschauer, M., Said, G. R. E., & Zohry, A. G. (2002). Language choice online: Globalization and identity in Egypt. *Journal of Computer-Mediated Communication*, *7*(4), JCMC744.

Wimmer, H. & Schurz, M. (2010). Dyslexia in regular orthographies: Manifestation and causation. *Dyslexia*, *16*, 283–299. doi: 10.1002/dys.411

Wolfram, W. (2000). Issues in Reconstructing Earlier African-American English. *World Englishes*, *19*(1), 39–58.

Wolfram, W. (2004). The grammar of urban African American vernacular English. *Handbook of Varieties of English*, *2*, 111–132.

Yaghan, M. A. (2008). "Arabizi": A contemporary style of Arabic slang. *Design Issues*, *24*(2), 39–52.

4

TRANSLANGUAGING

A Theoretical Shift Necessary for Culturally and Linguistically Responsive Practice in Speech Language Hearing Sciences

Reem Khamis and Mellissa Bortz

Introduction

The term translanguaging is borrowed from Cen Williams who used it in Welsh (i.e., trawsiethu) to name the pedagogical switching between language modes while in the same context, such as reading in one language while writing in another in a bilingual classroom setting (Bosma et al., 2022; García, 2009). The term was first translated as "translinguifying" and evolved when it was reintroduced in English by Baker in 2001 as dynamic bilingualism and then translanguaging (Bosma et al., 2022; Brooks, 2022). It currently refers to the "multiple discursive practices in which bilinguals engage in order to make sense of their bilingual world" (García, 2009, p. 45) where bilingual individuals participate in the "continuous becoming" of themselves and their language practices as they "interact and make meaning in the world" (García & Wei, 2014, p. 8).

Translanguaging is rooted in social justice and sociolinguistic equity (Brooks, 2022). Hence, translanguaging should not be understood only based on descriptive features of the phenomenon, but as a political stance aiming to challenge the national and raciolinguistic ideologies of monolingualism and to decolonize the conception of language (Wei, 2022). This process was first discussed by the African linguist, Salikoko Mufwene (for a review see Mufwene & Escobar, 2022). Translanguaging goes beyond representing languages in educational and clinical settings, "but is fundamentally reconstitutive and transformative of the power relations between the named languages in society" (Wei & García, 2022, p.10) and is considered to be a pedagogical approach that is socially just (Hurst &

DOI: 10.4324/9781003330318-5

Mona, 2017) in contrast to colonial pedagogies that are based on linguicism (Baker-Bell, 2020; Lippi-Green, 2012).

Translanguaging is not the same practice as codeswitching or codemixing. Codeswitching refers to the alternation of two languages both between and within sentences, and codemixing refers to alternation of two languages within shorter elements, commonly at word level (McCormick, 2002). Codeswitching and codemixing can be a part of translanguaging along with other bilingual languaging practices and contexts used by dual-language speakers to make sense of their bilingual worlds. These include translanguaging in communication with family members with different language profiles, translating for family members, and selecting different languages depending on modalities, social needs, and conditions.

Translanguaging and Education

Translanguaging pedagogy has been and continues to be used regularly in classrooms since the groundbreaking work of Cen Williams in the 1990s (see the state-of-the-art review by Bonacina-Pugh et al., 2021 which yielded 11,900 results for the search term "translanguaging in education"). Lopez et al. (2017) have recommended improving "existing assessments and developing new ones that are sensitive to the heterogeneous nature of bilingual students" (p. 4) due to a lack of assessment materials that are consistent with the translanguaging framework. In formative assessments, teachers need to design assessments that consider the home language practices of their students (Ascenzi-Moreno, 2018). For example, Przymus and Alvarado (2019) studied the use of translanguaging in content-based story retelling to distinguish language difference from disability, using dynamic assessment. The study was conducted with six middle school emergent special education bilingual students. In this study, the participants were asked to look at pictures and retell the stories in their own words. The explanation to the students stated that "even though English is the target language here at school, you can use your home language. If you do not know how to say something in English, use Spanish or your first language. I just want to know what you know about the story" (Przymus & Alvarado, 2019, pp. 29–30). The results indicated that the participants demonstrated more content knowledge when using translanguaging. This study highlights the importance of shifting to an assessment protocol that mixes languages in the assessment setting instead of presenting each language separately in a single mode.

Another population where the benefits of translanguaging in the classroom have been documented is the Deaf population. García and Lin

(2016) contend that deaf bilingual education indicates that integrating translanguaging with the manner that Deaf children utilize their language repertoires is a positive experience for deaf students. Translanguaging in the Deaf community is "recognized as an enabling and emancipatory framework for the use of sign language used in classrooms together with spoken and written languages" (De Meulder et al., 2019, p. 900). Therefore, these authors consider translanguaging to be central to the deaf experience (De Meulder et al., 2019).

Based on the knowledge gained from translanguaging assessment in education, we acknowledge that the metrics for guiding assessment and intervention in the multilingual population in the discipline of SLHS overlook linguistic variation and translanguaging, when it is determined by separate evaluation of language abilities spoken by those with whom we work. These metrics also approach translanguaging from a weakness-based perspective rather than a strength-based perspective and are not designed to facilitate the use of translanguaging in language assessment tools or do not tap into translanguaging as a resource for therapy. This is in contrast to the growing knowledge on the benefits of translanguaging and theoretical frameworks of culturally responsive practice. We now shift our focus to discuss and demonstrate the potential contribution of translanguaging assessment in clinical assessments in the field of SLHS.

Translanguaging in Speech Language Hearing Sciences

Speech Language Hearing Sciences (SLHS) is the fourth most white profession in the United States (82%) (Thompson, 2013) and there are a limited number (8.2%) of bi/multilingual clinicians in the discipline (ASHA, 2021). The language proficiency levels of these bi/multilingual professionals are also not known since the American Speech-Language-Hearing Association (ASHA) does not require any assessment of proficiency level from those reported to be bi/multilingual clinicians. Within this reality, an important challenge to address in attempting to adapt a translanguaging framework is the shortage of multilingual clinicians, and the range of languages that few clinicians speak (Larkman et al., 2022).

It is essential to focus on translanguaging as a method to delve into the deep values and ideologies that guide the practices of the SLHS discipline. This is important given evidence for the contemporary reality of this discipline that overlooks race (e.g., Yu et al., 2021) and research showing its complicity with racism, reliance on monolingual biased ideology, and the documented tendency to pathologize language and speech differences (e.g., Hyter & Salas Provance, 2023) that is rooted in the history of the development of the discipline (Duchan & Hewitt, 2023; St. Pierre, 2022).

The growing knowledge on language representation, processing, and use in relation to clinical work in SLHS only affirms the propriety of extending translanguaging to assessment and intervention services in SLHS. ASHA's formal definition of language highlights that "spoken language, written language, and their associated components (i.e., receptive and expressive) are each a synergistic system comprised of individual language domains (i.e., phonology, morphology, syntax, semantics, pragmatics) that form a dynamic integrative whole" (ASHA, n.d.). This dynamic defining characteristic fits within the translanguaging perspective rather than the static, monolingual biased, bordered conceptualization of languages that is triggered by nationalist and raciolinguistic ideologies of monolingualism fundamentally shaping current practice in bilingual assessment (e.g., Wei & García, 2022) that is hierarchically based with White English on top. Moreover, translanguaging in assessment and intervention is consistent with the latest research showing that multilingualism is an advantage with no risks associated with multilingual exposure (Costa, 2020; Xia et al., 2022) and that shared neural networks underlie the simultaneous activation/inhibition of all languages of a bi/multilingual individual (for a review read Sulpizio et al., 2020). The practice of conducting an assessment of each language spoken by an individual separately with no open boundaries for moving between the linguistic systems within a context is not consistent with the above findings on bilingual language processing. Lastly, translanguaging addresses several calls for change including the limitations of studying language as a property rather than focusing on its use and users (Horst, 2020) and the negative impact of Anglocentric ideologies rooted in colonialism on our understanding of language representation and processing (Levisen, 2019).

Clinically relevant inquiries of translanguaging in SLHS are still scarce. A search of the ASHA website for studies on translanguaging as a keyword reveals how marginalized research of translanguaging is in SLHS. More specifically, a search for studies on translanguaging within the ASHA website conducted in May 2022 generated only 18 articles. Further analysis of these results shows that only seven articles actually contained *translanguaging* in the text of the article. These articles were published between 2018 and 2022 and no increase in the number of studies was observed for translanguaging as a keyword: Three studies were published in 2018, three in 2021, and two until mid-2022. This is in spite of the fact that translanguaging "has become one of the most influential concepts in the field of applied linguistics and sociolinguistics" (Brooks, 2022, p. 1).

These articles fell into five categories which barely discussed the theoretical framework or the critical contribution and relevance of translanguaging to the work of clinicians in SLHS as shown in Table 4.1. Only one study

TABLE 1.1 Articles identified on ASHA website in May 2022 using *translanguaging* as keyword

Category	*Number of articles*	*Specific topic for each reference*
Literature review reference	2	Describing current use of translanguaging in education (Farran & Griffin, 2022) or future biliterate pedagogy (Squires et al., 2020)
As a substitute for dialect shifting	1	Adding a note that the term dialect shifting used by the authors can be interchangeably described as translanguaging (Diehm & Hendricks, 2021)
Codemixing in non-English-speaking communities	2	Describing language use in diverse communities outside the United States including Saint Lucia (Lindsey Nurse et al., 2021) and Jamaica (Washington et al., 2019) while interpreting observations of codemixing as translanguaging
Translanguaging as a multilingual pedagogical approach	1	Translanguaging from the framework of multilingual approaches to education (Ijalba et al., 2020)
Contribution to language assessment	1	Stating that the traditional practice in narrative analysis does not value translanguaging because it is marked as a maze (Lucero et al., 2018).

discussed translanguaging from the framework of multilingual approaches to education (Ijalba et al., 2020) and another single study highlighted its potential contribution to narrative assessment (Lucero et al., 2018).

As researchers and practitioners in SLHS, we maintain that there is an urgent need to "play catch up" in conducting much needed clinically relevant and driven research into translanguaging in the context of assessment, counseling, prevention, advocacy, and treatment services provided in SLHS. Such research should make use of already developed knowledge conducted in other related professions and domains of study such as education, critical disability theory, applied linguistics, and sociolinguistics. In addition, this analysis of available publications on translanguaging within the ASHA website search demonstrates a need to start a deeper discussion of the ideologies that shape inquiry and practice in SLHS. The reason for this is that the published research is still focused on describing language use within fixed, bounded categories which do not recognize the full repertoire of languaging exhibited by those with whom we work. Such discussion and education on translanguaging are critical to promote and implement linguistically inclusive and responsive practices. Codemixing, codeswitching, and dialect mixing need to be reexamined in SLHS in light of the learned knowledge from the study of translanguaging to highlight the risks in observing translanguaging from a "double monolingualism" perspective, of which the interconnectedness of two languages is overlooked (Wei & García, 2022, p.5). Conceiving translanguaging as codemixing prevents clinicians from holistically and functionally capturing the linguistic profile of those we work with from a strength perspective to enhance the speech and language assessment and intervention practices conducted with multilingual populations to be inclusive and ecologically appropriate. We argue that translanguaging has great potential to transform the theoretical bases and practical acts of speech language assessment and intervention services in SLHS.

The study of translanguaging assessment in education reveals that as long as language skills of multilingual individuals are assessed from a monolingual perspective, i.e., double monolingualism as the default norm set up, then the expectations and norms for language assessment of multilingual individuals are unrealistic since they are not centered on the multilingual experience in setting the norm. They would therefore miss identifying resources for multilingual individuals because the approach is monolingual at its core. Hence, evaluations of multilingual individuals that assess only the two languages separately without recognizing translanguaging as a resource for communicative and affective intentional expression and that references monolingual norms related to each language separately would be inaccurate and discriminatory. This is because this form of assessment ignores the fact that multilingual individuals do not need to exhibit the same level of proficiency across all domains in all languages compatible with monolingual speakers of these languages (García, 2009).

In the clinical discipline of SLHS in particular, assessment is questioned in general as a means to "curb the defective and reinforce class and race distinction … consistent with liberal and neoliberal governmentality … in a largely implicit manner" (St. Pierre, 2022, p. 42). This is as part of the history of speech pathology which "represents a process of purifying the voice and rendering it accelerable, compliant to market temporalities" (St. Pierre, 2022, p. 15). Developments in bilingual assessment in SLHS are still focused on highlighting the need to evaluate the two languages to inform the selection of language for intervention (e.g., Goral & Lerman, 2020; Kohnert, 2013). All these developments remain centered on separate use of the linguistic systems with growing acknowledgment of dialects and genres beyond named nation state languages. None have yet promoted exploring and designing assessments and interventions that enable translanguaging in its design, coding, or analysis, although first steps in that direction are being taken (e.g., Goral et al., under review; Ijalba et al., 2020; Luccero et al., 2018). There is a need to further examine the best ways to incorporate translanguaging into clinical assessment in SLHS in a way that acknowledges the full linguistic repertoire with permeable boundaries between the languages a bi/multilingual individual knows. As an example of how translanguaging can be applied in the field of SLHS we turn to a discussion of assessment in aphasia in multilingual people.

Translanguaging and Aphasia

Most aphasia assessments available are devised in one language (Goral & Galletta, in press; Ivanova & Hallowell, 2013) and there is a tendency to translate, adapt, and standardize these assessment tools to different languages worldwide treating them as "universal" assessment tools in the SLHS discipline (e.g., St. Pierre, 2022). This can be seen by the literature continuing to report on adaptations of several measures such as the *Comprehensive Aphasia Test* (CAT) to at least 14 languages including the recent adaptation to Turkish (e.g., Maviş et al., 2022), the *Boston Diagnostic Aphasia Examination* (BDEA) in different languages such as the latest adaptation of the BDEA in Greek (e.g., Tsapkini et al., 2009), the adaptation of *The Progressive Aphasia Language Scale* in Persian (Jafari et al., 2018) or the translations of the *Western Aphasia Battery* to 33 languages worldwide (Kertesz, 2022). These translations occur despite the majority of the world speaking more than one language (Bortz, in press; Grosjean, 2012) and such tests are not designed in their core to evaluate the languages of bi/multilinguals and bidialectal speakers.

Several developments can be observed in the field based on a review of SLHS clinical assessments for working with adults with language disorders. First, multilingualism became recognized as a resource and best practices in the assessment of aphasia clearly include evaluation of all languages spoken by an individual and potential contribution of evaluating all languages for therapy planning and dissemination (Goral et al., 2012). Moreover, linguistic dialectal and diglossic variation has gained attention in the study of aphasia recovery (e.g., Khamis-Dakwar & Froud, 2012; Khamis-Dakwar et al., 2018) and is becoming a common question for SLHS scholars to address in their assessment of language disorders in multilingual speaking adults (e.g., Scharff Rethfeldt et al., 2020). Lastly, a few tests evaluating language skills in linguistic variation that is beyond nation state languages, such as in the case of Arabic diglossia (Khamis-Dakwar et al., 2018) and Swiss German (Beierlein et al., 2021) have been developed. These assessments contribute to the expansion of language assessment to include language systems that are not defined as nation-state languages and have been marginalized in the clinical study of diglossia. The Arabic assessment includes reading and writing tasks in one variety (such as Modern Standard Arabic) and no other varieties (such as vernacular dialects) that are not commonly used for reading and writing (e.g., Khamis-Dakwar et al., 2018) consistent with the translanguaging typically observed in such diglossic situations. Most importantly the development of these tests is rooted in knowledge that highlights the interrelated nature of the linguistic profile and experiences of individuals in growing diglossic communities such as Arabic-speaking communities, and their related experiences with aphasia from a strength position and not a challenge or barrier for assessment and intervention.

As unique as these developments are in breaking the fixed boundaries of nation state languages in the assessment of aphasia, even those that are inclusive of systems of linguistic variation that have been marginalized, are still being shaped by monolingual-based ideology. This is because there is no space for evaluating translanguaging in the way these assessments are designed, and the resulting guidelines for their administration, coding, and interpretation of results.

A recent study by Bortz and Goral (under review) identified patterns of translanguaging in multilingual discourse (i.e., narrative and group conversations) of 19 younger and older adults in South Africa. The results of the study indicated that all participants made use of translanguaging in narratives with frequencies ranging from 2% to 46% with a median of 13.8%. In conversation, percentages ranged from 4% to 52% with a median of 17.9%. A focus on investigating patterns of translanguaging and ways to measure it could inform future directions in assessing the language of multilingual people with aphasia within a translanguaging approach.

Incorporating a Translanguaging Framework into Clinical Practice

The benefits of using the translanguaging framework when describing multilingual discourse are discussed in this chapter as part of a holistic framework which informs clinical treatment planning. We offer translanguaging strategies that can be incorporated in language assessments, which are applicable for educational and clinical settings. Our goal is to encourage the initiation of studies examining the best ways to implement these strategies in aphasia assessment and the evidence for its relevance, effectiveness, and efficiency in evaluating multilingual people with aphasia. We compiled a list of basic strategies that can be incorporated in clinical assessment in SLHS based on the reported literature review above on the implementation of a translanguaging assessment protocol in education (see Table 4.2).

TABLE 4.2 Suggested translanguaging strategies from education literature to consider incorporating in clinical assessments in SLHS

General central guideline: Legitimize an assessment context that is not strictly one language setting but encourages use of the whole repertoire of languages, varieties, and genres used by the individual.	
Specific suggested strategies:	
Multilingual label quests:	Plan to include cognates and non-cognates to enable identification of cognate facilitation effect and its potential use as a resource for languaging in aphasia.
Metalinguistic awareness:	Plan to evaluate the effect of incorporating metalinguistic tasks and cues on the languaging of the individual.
Multilingual reading and writing:	Plan to offer access to bi/multilingual texts as part of aphasia assessment, when appropriate.
Dynamic evaluation of the use of bi/multilingual input:	Plan to evaluate the optimal level of the range of linguistic resources available and include analysis of the translanguaging instances and the contexts in which they occurred. Make sure to highlight to the client that they may use any form of language at their disposal to connect and make meaning in the evaluation and allow requests for translation to identify its role in fulfilling a specific communicative need or a breakdown.
Linguistically inclusive scoring:	Plan to conduct scoring of performances on assessment tasks in a way that is inclusive of all languages, varieties, and genres spoken by the individual using a pool of acceptable responses
Family interview:	Plan to conduct a family interview that provides information about the entire linguistic repertoire of the client.

Conclusion and Future Directions

The paradigms and theoretical frameworks referenced in evaluating languaging have a great impact on the linguistic and communicative assessment conducted and the ability to recognize the communicative and linguistic strengths and weaknesses of the multilingual clients with whom clinicians work. The marginalization of translanguaging in SLHS research and practice limits the depth, breadth, and current relevance of the knowledge base that guides the practice in SLHS. This depth cannot be achieved without global collaboration in SLHS and related fields to languaging including not only medically oriented disciplines like neuroscience, but socially oriented fields of studies including critical disability study, sociolinguistics, applied linguistics, philosophy, sociology, computer science, and education. Interprofessional education and practice have been recognized by ASHA and the Council of Academic Programs in Communication Sciences and Disorders (CAPCSD) as important standards for educating future clinicians in the field of SLHS (Council on Academic Accreditation in Audiology and Speech Language Pathology, 2017). However, these practices can be expanded as an approach to increase collaboration and responsiveness to those with whom we actually work, i.e., individuals with communication disabilities and their families within their larger communities. This would be facilitated through deeper understanding of and learning from social studies related to power relations, language norms, and the history of the field of SLHS, which as a profession has pathologized communicative differences from ableist, classist, and/or racist norms of analysis (e.g., St. Pierre, 2022).

There is agreement that we need to move away from the traditional paradigm in multilingual assessment and dismantle the colonial hierarchy in reimagining the meaning of multilingual assessment and intervention to transcend beyond two separate systems to enabling recognition of the full linguistic repertoire of a multilingual individual and its use at all times (Wei & García, 2022). However, for the change to be efficient it needs to be based on a collective reimagination of the core goals and aims of assessment and evaluation in SLHS within the specific social, structural, geopolitical, socioeconomic, and power relations contextualizing the process itself (Hyter & Salas Provance, 2023).

The aim of assessment needs to shift from identifying communicative weakness and classifying individuals based on their language use compared to a monolingual-biased norm to scaffolding communication and provision of linguistically inclusive care that capitalizes on the full linguistic repertoire of the person we work with. It is time to extend theoretical and practical aspects of translanguaging to the assessment and intervention care provided by clinicians in SLHS and to initiate a deeper reflection on the ideologies that shape the practice of clinicians in SLHS. Hence, it is important to highlight that adopting translanguaging in the discipline of SLHS should be accompanied with core transformations to the field to enable language users with communication disabilities to have agency, rather than be pathologized and racialized for their language use (St. Pierre, 2022). Adopting translanguaging will not bring change unless it is accompanied by structural transformations and institutional commitment to social justice (Brooks, 2022). Wei (2022) states that translanguaging reconstitutes at least three senses: the sense of language, the sense of language status, and the sense of power relationships between different language users. A critical review of the work of clinicians shows that language structures are conceptualized within bordered separate systems in the assessment and intervention practices provided. Translanguaging may facilitate discipline growth toward inclusivity by addressing these fundamental theoretical and conceptual frameworks of language use that guide the practice that is called for urgently in the clinical field of SLHS (for a review see Horton, 2021). As such, we argue that overlooking translanguaging not only entails ignoring the full linguistic repertoire of those we care for, but it also strips their power to be who they are, constrains their potential growth, and constitutes a base for inequality in access to educational and clinical services.

In conclusion, this chapter provided an overview of translanguaging and its potential for the work of clinicians in SLHS, using language assessment in aphasia as an example. This approach would focus equally on empowering those we work with by acknowledging their backgrounds, from a strength position, while resisting from providing services that further marginalize or isolate them. Most of the strategies shared in this chapter for a translanguaging framework in language assessment are based on knowledge gained from the literature of translanguaging assessment in education with students at various levels, mostly students with no specific communication disabilities. There is a need for initiating clinical studies of translanguaging to determine effective and efficient best practices of translanguaging from antiracist, socially just, and a linguistically inclusive clinical approach to assessment and therapy. This chapter also highlights the educational gaps in SLHS and the need for educational programs to raise awareness of the ideological and linguistic bases of translanguaging in order to facilitate dismantling the monolingual-based assessments of multilingual populations. Such education is critical for adopting alternative, multilingual, linguistically inclusive assessment and intervention which incorporates translanguaging in its design, coding, analysis, interpretation, and intervention planning.

References

American Speech-Language-Hearing Association (ASHA) (2021). *2021 Demographic profile of ASHA members providing multilingual services.* https://www.asha.org/siteassets/surveys/demographic-profile-bilingual-spanish-service-members.pdf2021

American Speech-Language-Hearing Association (ASHA) (n.d.). *Language in brief.* https://www.asha.org/practice-portal/clinical-topics/spoken-language-disorders/language-in-brief/#:~:text=It%20is%20defined%20as%20the,e.g.%2C%20American%20Sign%20Language).

Ascenzi-Moreno, L. (2018). Translanguaging and responsive assessment adaptations. *Language Arts*, *95*(6), 355–369.

Baker-Bell, A. (2020). *Linguistic Justice: Black Language, Literacy, Identity, and Pedagogy.* Routledge.

Beierlein, S. W., Kuntner, K. P., Hemm, S., Reymond, C., García, N. F., Park, S., ... & Blechschmidt, A. (2021). *Lexical Retrieval in Diglossic Aphasia* (No. 6528). EasyChair.

Bonacina-Pugh, F., da Costa Cabral, I., & Huang, J. (2021). Translanguaging in education. *Language Teaching*, *54*(4), 439–471.

Bortz, M. A. (in press). Introduction. In M. A. Bortz (Ed.). *A Guide to Global Language Assessment: A Lifespan Approach.* Slack Publications.

Bortz, M. A. & Goral, M. (under review). Translanguaging in narratives and group conversations of South African adults. *International Journal of Multilingualism.*

Bosma, E., Bakker, A., Zenger, L., & Blom, E. (2022). Supporting the development of the bilingual lexicon through translanguaging: A realist review integrating psycholinguistics with educational sciences. *European Journal of Psychology of Education.* 10.1007/s10212-021-00586-6--

Brooks, E. (2022). Translanguaging and the shifting sands of language education. *ELT Journal*, *76*, 129–146.

Costa, A. (2020). *The Bilingual Brain: And What It Tells Us about the Science of Language.* Penguin.

Council on Academic Accreditation in Audiology and Speech Language Pathology (2017). IPE/IPP in academic and clinical curriculum. https://caa.asha.org/ask-the-caa/ipe-ipp-in-academic-and-clinical-curriculum/

De Meulder, M., Kusters, A., Moriarty, E., & Murray, J. J. (2019). Describe, don't prescribe. The practice and politics of Translanguaging in the context of deaf signers. *Journal of Multilingual and Multicultural Development*, *40*, 10, 892–906.

Diehm, E. A. & Hendricks, A. E. (2021). Teachers' content knowledge and pedagogical beliefs regarding the use of African American English. *Language, Speech, and Hearing Services in Schools*, *52*(1), 100–117.

Duchan, J. F. & Hewitt, L. E. (2023). How the charter members of ASHA responded to the social and political circumstances of their time. *American Journal of Speech-Language Pathology*, *32*(3), 1037–1049.

Farran, L. K. & Griffin, R. A. (2022). The love and science of reading: A promising instructional approach for adolescent multilingual learners. *Perspectives of the ASHA Special Interest Groups*, *7*(1), 197–208.

García, O. (2009). *Bilingual Education in the 21st Century. A Global Perspective.* Wiley, Blackwell.
García, O. & Wei L. (2014). *Translanguaging*. Palgrave Macmillan.
García, O. & Lin (2016). Translanguaging in bilingual education. In O. García & A. M. Y. Lin (Eds.), *Bilingual and Multilingual Education (Encyclopedia of Language and Education* (Vol. 5). Springer.
Goral, M., Antolovic, K., Hejazi, Z., & Schultz, F. Under review using a translanguaging framework to examining language production in a trilingual person with aphasia.
Goral, M. & Galletta, E. (in press). Assessment in aphasia: Global perspectives. In Bortz, M. (Ed.), *A Guide to Global Language Assessment: A Lifetime Approach.* Slack Publications.
Goral, M. & Lerman, A. (2020). Variables and mechanisms affecting response to language treatment in multilingual people with aphasia. *Behavioral Sciences*, 1–17
Goral, M., Rosas, J., Conner, P. S., Maul, K. K., & Obler, L. K. (2012). Effects of language proficiency and language of the environment on aphasia therapy in a multilingual. *Journal of Neurolinguistics*, 25, 538–551.
Grosjean, F. (2012). *Bilingual life and reality*. Harvard University Press.
Horton, R. (Ed.) (2021). *Critical Perspectives on Social Justice in Speech Language Pathology* (pp.130–150). IGI Global.
Horst, D. (2020). Patterns 'we 'think by? Critical cognitive linguistics between language system and language use. *Yearbook of the German Cognitive Linguistics Association*, *8*(1), 67–82.
Hurst, E. & Mona, M. (2017). "Translanguaging" as a socially just pedagogy. *Education as Change*, *21*, 126–148.
Hyter, Y. & Salas Provance, M. (2023). *Culturally Responsive Practices in Speech, Language and Hearing Sciences* (2nd ed.). Plural Publications.
Ijalba, E., Bustos, A., & Romero, S. (2020). Phonological–orthographic deficits in developmental dyslexia in three Spanish–English bilingual students. *American Journal of Speech Language Pathology*, *29*(3), 1133–1151.
Ivanova, M. V. & Hallowell, B. (2013). A tutorial on aphasia test development in any language: Key substantive and psychometric considerations. *Aphasiology*, *27*(8), 891–920.
Jafari, S., Modarresszadeh, A., Khatoonabadi, A. R., Hodges, J., Ansari, N. N., Leyton, C., & Noroozian, M. (2018). Development, cross-cultural adaptation, and psychometric characteristics of the Persian progressive aphasia language scale in patients with primary progressive aphasia: A pilot study. *Basic and Clinical Neuroscience*, *9*(1), 35.
Kertesz, A. (2022). The Western Aphasia Battery: A systematic review of research and clinical applications. *Aphasiology*, *36*(1), 21–50.
Khamis-Dakwar, R. & Froud, K. (2012). Aphasia, language, and culture: Arabs in the United States. In M. Gitterman, M. Goral, & L. K. Obler (Eds.), *Multilingual Aphasia* (pp. 275–291). Multilingual Matters.
Khamis-Dakwar, R., Ahmar, M., Farah, R., & Froud, K. (2018). Diglossic aphasia and the adaptation of the bilingual aphasia test (BAT) to Palestinian Arabic and Modern Standard Arabic. *Journal of Neurolinguistics*, *47*, 131–144.

Kohnert, K. (2013). *Language Disorders in Bilingual Children and Adults.* (2nd ed.) Plural Publishing.

Larkman, C. S., Mellahn, K., Han, W., & Rose, M. L. (2022). Aphasia rehabilitation when speech pathologists and clients do not share the same language: A scoping review. *Aphasiology*, 1–23.

Levisen, C. (2019). Biases we live by: Anglocentrism in linguistics and cognitive sciences. *Language Sciences*, *76*, 101173.

Lindsay Nurse, K. T., Gardner, K., & Brea, M. R. (2021). Operationalizing culturally responsive research practices: Documenting the communication skills of children with confirmed or possible exposure to the Zika virus in Saint Lucia, West Indies. *Perspectives of the ASHA Special Interest Groups*, *6*(1), 191–206.

Lippi-Green, R. (2012). *English with an Accent: Language, Ideology, and Discrimination in the United States.* Routledge.

Lopez, A. A., Turkan, S., & Guzman-Orth, D. (2017). Conceptualizing the Use of Translanguaging in initial content assessments. *ETS Research Report Series*, *1*, 1–12.

Lucero, A. (2018). The development of retelling among Spanish-English dual language learners Over two years. *Language, Speech, and Hearing Services in Schools*, *49*, (3), 607 -621.

Maviş, İ., Tunçer, A. M., Selvi-Balo, S., Tokaç, S. D., & Özdemir, Ş. (2022). The adaptation process of the Comprehensive Aphasia Test into CAT-Turkish: Psycholinguistic and clinical considerations. *Aphasiology*, *36*(4), 493–512.

McCormick, K. (2002). Code-switching, mixing, and convergence in Cape Town. In R. Mesthrie (Ed.), *Language in South Africa* (p. 215–233.). Cambridge University Press.

Mufwene, S. & Escobar, A. M. (Eds.). (2022). *The Cambridge Handbook of Language Contact: Volume 1: Population Movement and Language Change.* Cambridge University Press.

Pierre, J. St. (2022). *Cheap Talk: Disability and the Politics of Communication.* University of Michigan Press.

Przymus, S. D. & Alvarado, M. (2019). Advancing bilingual special education: Translanguaging in content-based story retells for distinguishing language difference from disability. *Multiple Voices for Ethnically Diverse Exceptional Learners*, *19*(1), 23–43.

Scharff Rethfeldt, W., McNeilly, L., Abutbul-Oz, H., Blumenthal, M., Garcia de Goulart, B., Hunt, E., Laasonen, M. R., Levey, S., Meir, N., Moonsamy, S., Mophosho, M., Salameh, E.-K., Smolander, S., Taiebine, M., & Thordardottir, E. (2020). *Common questions by speech and language therapists about progressive aphasia and Alzheimer's Disease in bilingual / multilingual populations and informed, evidence-based answers.* The Multilingual-Multicultural Affairs Committee of the International Association of Communication Sciences and Disorders. https://www.slh.org.tw/upload/files/Common-Questions-by-SLT-SLHS-about-Progr-Aphasia-and-Alzheimers-Disease-in-Bili-Multilingual-Pop-and-Informed-Evidence-based-Answers_2020.pdf

Sulpizio, S., Del Maschio, N., Fedeli, D., & Abutalebi, J. (2020). Bilingual language processing: A meta-analysis of functional neuroimaging studies. *Neuroscience and Biobehavioral Reviews*, *108*, 834–853.

Squires, L. R., Ohlfest, S. J., Santoro, K. E., & Roberts, J. L. (2020). Factors influencing cognate performance for young multilingual children's vocabulary: A research synthesis. *American Journal of Speech Language Pathology*, *29*(4), 2170–2188.

Thompson, D. (2013, November 6). The 33 Whitest jobs in America. Every occupation that's more than 90 percent white, according to the BLS, including vets, CEOs, and private detectives. *The Atlantic*. https://www.theatlantic.com/business/archive/2013/11/the-33-whitest-jobsin-america/281180/

Tsapkini, K., Vlahou, C. H., & Potagas, C. (2009). Adaptation and validation of standardized aphasia tests in different languages: Lessons from the Boston Diagnostic Aphasia Examination–Short Form in Greek. *Behavioral Neurology*, 22(3-4), 111–119.

Washington, K. N., Fritz, K., Crowe, K., Kelly, B., & Wright Karem, R. (2019). Bilingual preschoolers' spontaneous productions: Considering Jamaican Creole and English. *Language, Speech, and Hearing Services in Schools*, *50*(2), 179–195.

Wei, L. (2022). Translanguaging as a political stance: Implications for English language education. *ELT Journal*, *76*(2), 172–182.

Wei, L. & García, O. (2022). Not a first language but one repertoire: Translanguaging as a decolonizing project. *RELC Journal*, 00336882221092841.

Xia, L., Bak, T. H., Sorace, A., & Vega-Mendoza, M. (2022). Interference suppression in bilingualism: Stimulus-Stimulus vs. Stimulus-Response conflict. *Bilingualism: Language and Cognition*, *25*(2), 256–268.

Yu, B., Horton, R., Munson, B., Newkirk-Turner, B., Johnson, V. E., Khamis-Dakwar, R., Muñoz, M. L., & Hyter, Y. (2021). Making race visible in the speech, language & hearing sciences: A critical discourse analysis. *American Journal of Speech Language Pathology*, *3*, 1–23. 10.1044/2021_AJSLHS-20-00384

5

LANGUAGE ATTRITION

More than Just Loss of Language

Hia Datta and Zhilong Xie

Introduction

Language attrition manifests in a number of ways in individuals across various communities and ages. Although there are popular ways of thinking about what language attrition represents, for example, a loss of access to words in an immigrant's first language (L1), language attrition appears in communication in many other ways. This chapter will explore the different ways language attrition can emerge in various populations and linguistic contexts.

There is no consensus on the definition of attrition. The heterogeneous conceptualizations of the phenomenon might come from various perspectives of examining attrition, that is, linguistics, psychology, or neuroscience. One favored definition of language attrition suggests that it is a decline in a language previously acquired by an individual, due to the lack of contact with the community in which the language is spoken (Köpke & Schmid, 2004; Schmid, 2008). Köpke and Schmid (2004) refer to language attrition as a non-pathological decrease in the language processing abilities of a once proficient language. Moreover, according to Köpke (2004b), attrition is not an intra-generational process, but rather an individual change. In contrast, scholars have discussed "language shift", referring to change at the societal level, when individuals change their language use as a result of cultural and contextual adaptations. To many scholars, attrition is not a pathological process, which is the result of some form of deficit, such as a neurological disorder like dementia, though others have discussed attrition in the context of atypical aging.

DOI: 10.4324/9781003330318-6

Language Attrition in Monolingualism

The most frequent way of thinking about attrition is that it is the gradual loss of a language or its access in individuals who are no longer using that language. The popular psychological theory of "use it or lose it" is often favored by psycholinguistics and laypersons as an explanation for language attrition, especially for bilingual or multilingual individuals. However, language can erode in individuals who are monolingual, with access to a single language. Although less common, attrition has been discussed in the context of typical aging.

Natural degradation of language with age, although not often called language attrition, is the type of attrition that is associated with weakening of language processing in older individuals. Lexical retrieval, such as in picture naming (e.g., Connor et al., 2004; Higby et al., 2019; Nicholas et al., 1985) and Tip-of-the-Tongue (TOT) phenomenon (e.g., Burke et al., 1991; Huijbers et al., 2017; Shafto et al., 2007), has been extensively explored in aging. Attrition in lexical retrieval can surface as early as under 40 years of age (Goral, 2004). As demonstrated by Connor et al. (2004) lexical retrieval as measured by naming accuracy in the Boston Naming Test (BNT) decreased by 2.17 points per decade of aging. Such reports have also been corroborated by neural data. For example, in a recent study, Huijbers et al. (2017) reported that increased TOT occurrences in 73 individuals 63–90 years old were associated with increased activity in the lateral prefrontal cortex. The authors suggest that this increased activation in the prefrontal cortex could be compensatory behavior to combat TOT in the elderly. See also chapter 6, this volume.

Another area of language decline is comprehension of complex material. In a recent study, Poulisse et al. (2019) reported that older adults (71–72 years) performed poorly compared to younger adults (19–20 years) in a sentence comprehension task. Evidence suggests that the difficulty demonstrated by the elderly in sentence comprehension stems from their decline in syntactic rather than semantic processing capabilities (Taler et al., 2009), particularly since their vocabulary size is large compared to younger adults (Boxtel & Lawyer, 2021).

Language Attrition in Bilingualism

L1 attrition in bilingual individuals has been studied for approximately 50 years (De Bot & Weltens, 1995; Schmid, 2004). The first collection of papers on language attrition in bilingual individuals was published by Lambert and Freed (1982) with an increasing focus since the mid 1980s (e.g., Bettoni, 1985). In one seminal publication, Seliger and Vago (1991) edited a volume of research on language attrition that explored how L1 "disintegrates" in bilingual individuals, the various factors that lead to it, and theoretical mechanisms behind it. The study of language attrition highlighted several linguistic characteristics focused on the dynamic nature of linguistic performance and competence. Terms such as "language shift" (Köpke, 2004a) that contributed to the understanding of language processing, both at individual and societal levels, increasingly became associated with language attrition. In addition, documentation of language attrition, perhaps for the first time, spotlighted the fact that despite not being able to achieve ultimate language attainment in their second language (L2), bilingual individuals could not sustain their native-like proficiency in their L1 continually without effort.

Individual Language Attrition in Bilingual Adults

The best-known manifestation of first-language attrition in bilingual or multilingual individuals is the weakening of their L1 over time. Often, individuals who immigrate into localities where their L1 is not the primary language used in the environment are no longer able to use it as a main form of communication. Use of a language is essential for its maintenance (Park, 2018; Schmid, 2002). This becomes particularly challenging for those who live alone in environments where they are hardly able to engage in their L1. Despite their low proficiency levels in the language of the host environment, often the second language (L2) for the immigrant, such circumstances result in increased L2 interactions while confining L1 to the home environment. Over time, L1 (home language) declines while L2 (host language) becomes the more readily and frequently used language.

L1 attrition in adults can manifest within various components of language that include the phonology, lexicon, morphosyntax, syntax and pragmatics when interacting in a different language from their L1. Research on lexical attrition has identified reduced vocabulary or loss of lexical items and reduced access to one's lexicon. Studies have demonstrated lexical attrition in L1 through reduced fluency in L1 (e.g., Schmid & Fägersten, 2010), reduced comprehension of L1 words, as well as reduced lexical diversity in L1 production (e.g., Schmid & Jarvis, 2014). Phonetic attrition in L1 can also manifest as L2 accent in L1 during production and as shifted phonetic boundaries toward L2 (Hopp & Schmid, 2013). Overall, signs of L1 attrition can surface within multiple components of L1 and the extent of attrition will increase as use in L1 decreases while L2 contact increases over time.

Individual Language Attrition in Bilingual Children

L1 attrition in children is different from that in adults. Attrition in one language can occur in two ways in children. In one scenario, children begin learning L1 at home and progress in a typical fashion, achieving expected linguistic milestones until they begin school in their host community. Children in preschool (3–4 years of age) or kindergarten (4–5 years of age) are immersed in an intensive L2 environment. Now they spend substantial amounts of their "awake" and "cognitively alert" time in school, where social pressure and motivation to learn the host language (L2) as quickly as possible is high. As a result, these children never fully acquire their L1, but begin using L2 in their home environment. The second scenario is that of an older child (e.g., 10–12 years of age) who immigrates to a locality where their L1 is not a primary language. Such a child may have complete and good command over L1 upon arrival to the host culture. At this time, similar to the first scenario, impetus to learn the host language, L2, as quickly and efficiently as possible decreases their motivation to sustain L1. Although such children are able to maintain a certain level of oral proficiency in L1 initially, this may change over time as the community with which they use L1 becomes limited to immediate family.

Mechanism of L1 Attrition in Bilingualism

Language attrition has become a widespread phenomenon since most people in the world are bilingual or multilingual. There are multiple social, cognitive, linguistic, psychological, and developmental factors that influence how people learn more than one language and how their L2 affects their L1. Nevertheless, the process of L1 attrition is one of the least understood phenomena associated with L2 acquisition, leaving us with an inadequate understanding of the mechanisms that drive it and the factors that modulate it (Gallo et al., 2021). In this section, we briefly discuss the current literature on these mechanisms and factors.

The first mechanism posits that language attrition is caused by the progressive disuse of that language. This theory implicates that L1 attrition may happen even if there is no L2 learning/acquisition. Extensive research suggests that L1 attrition is the result of long-term lack of L1 use (Paradis, 2007). Some studies report that higher L1 exposure is associated with a lower degree of L1 attrition (e.g., Karayayla & Schmid, 2019), although there are inconsistencies in the literature (e.g., Schmid & Jarvis, 2014), which may result from the intrinsic difficulty of measuring the quantity and quality of L1 exposure and use (e.g., how often bilinguals switch between two languages or use a language in a single context (Gallo et al., 2021)).

The second mechanism posits that language attrition is caused by cross-language processes (e.g., L2 influence on L1). Therefore, the nature and extent of attrition may be modulated by how the two languages interact, for example, inhibiting, switching experience, and language distance between the two (Gallo et al., 2021; Schmid & Köpke, 2017). Although there are mixed results, numerous studies report that L2 plays a significant role in L1 attrition. For example, various aspects of L2 knowledge and use are correlated with the degree of L1 attrition in different linguistic components, including phonology, morphology, syntax, and semantics (e.g., Chamorro et al., 2016; De Leeuw et al., 2018; Schmid & Jarvis, 2014).

Neural Correlates of L1 Attrition in Bilingualism

The study of neural processing can be useful in understanding subtle changes associated with attrition. Gallo et al. (2021), in their review, outlined specific settings to identify neural correlates of attrition. For example, in lexico-semantics, which is one of the most susceptible domains to attrition, event-related potentials (ERPs) can be used to identify markers of L1 attrition. According to psycholinguistic models (e.g., Levelt, 1999), the first stage of language production is conceptualization, during which the semantic message is formed, which takes place from 100 to 150 ms. The second stage is formulation, taking place around 150–275 ms, which is the selection of the lemma and the phonological form to be produced (Indefrey, 2011; Indefrey & Levelt, 2004; Levelt, 1999). Participants experiencing L1 attrition will likely be slower in these two stages compared to those without attrition. Concerning brain areas activated, the anterior temporal cortex and the posterior middle temporal gyrus have been found to underlie lexico-semantics (Indefrey & Levelt, 2004). By comparing the intensity and the localization of the activated brain areas between participants with attrition and those without, researchers are able to identify brain regions associated with attrition.

As for language comprehension, the most widely recognized ERP component is the N400, which takes place in a time window of 200–400 ms post stimulus onset. This component is reported to be associated with word-processing and semantic interpretation. A higher N400 amplitude may reflect difficulty in processing incongruent/meaningless words (Kutas & Hillyard, 1980). The N400 component may serve as a neural marker for attrition in participants who tend to show a smaller N400 effect compared to controls, because individuals with attrition are not able to process semantic incongruences as efficiently as those without attrition (Kaparian et al. 2017).

In a study using N400 as the dependent variable, Datta (2010) compared Bengali L1-dominant and English L2-dominant bilingual groups in a cross-modal picture-auditory priming task. The stimuli included words that were categorized into the following four categories: a) Low familiarity L1 – Low familiarity L2, e.g., "*arrow*" and / ti:r/, b) High familiarity L1 – High familiarity L2, e.g., "*bread*" and /pauruti/, c) High familiarity L1 – Low familiarity L2, e.g., "*gourd*" and /lau/ and d) Low familiarity L1 – High familiarity L2; e.g., "*airplane*" and /biman/. Results from this study revealed that the L2-dominant group elicited the longest reaction times to L1 words in the Low familiarity L1-High familiarity L2 category. In addition, the ERP data suggested that the L2-dominant group's access to L1 words was modulated by L2 familiarity. Taken together, these data suggested that L1 attrition was impacted by L2 influence on L1, rather than L1 disuse.

L1 grammar attrition can also be detected in multiple ways. Some EEG studies have identified components related to syntax processing. For example, the Early Left Anterior Negativity (ELAN) is related to the early processing stage of syntactic structure building (Fonteneau, 2013). The N400 component is reported to be associated with sentence-level violation. Finally, the P600 component, is reported to be associated with syntactic revision and reconfiguration (Friederici & Weissenborn, 2007). A comparison between an attrition group and a control group (without attrition) showed differences in amplitude, scalp distribution, and duration of ELAN, N400, or P600 components (e.g., Kasparian et al., 2017), which has been interpreted as neural evidence of attrition.

Factors Influencing L1 Attrition in Bilingualism

A number of studies have focused on linguistic and non-linguistic factors related to the nature and the severity of language attrition. Linguistic factors include the quantity and quality of exposure to L1 as well as the nature of L2 influence on it. High exposure to L1 is generally correlated to better retention of that language (Schmid & Köpke, 2017). It has also been suggested that the age of acquisition for L2 substantially modulates L1 attrition. For example, those who move to a new language environment before puberty are more likely to experience attrition, due to the incomplete acquisition of the L1 (Schmid et al., 2013). Furthermore, it is reported that language attrition is related to L1–L2 similarity, in that topological proximity between languages facilitates the retention of L1 knowledge and skills (e.g., Hansen, 2011). Non-linguistic factors that influence L1 attrition involve individuals' attitude and motivation toward their native language, which is much understudied for both individuals and societies (Kik et al., 2021). For example, German Jewish refugees who fled to other countries before or during World War II, reported being hateful of the German language and retained it less than those who moved from Germany to other countries under less oppressive circumstances (Schmid, 2002).

Language Attrition in the Society

Change in languages (in multiple components of a language, e.g., phonetic, lexical, morphosyntactic, syntactic, pragmatic) in societies and across generations may eventually lead to the erosion and death of languages. In this section we begin to scratch the surface of how attrition in the L1s of individuals and then across generations (Köpke & Schmid, 2004) may lead to changes in identities of communities and languages and how this process is alarmingly linked to biodiversity.

The process of change and erosion in languages within communities begins with L1 attrition at the individual level. There is long standing research in bilingual acquisition that has established links between language input and language output (e.g., De Houwer, 2007). In a world where media and telecommunications have globalized language and culture to predominantly English, urban and suburban communities across the world already operate more bilingually than they used to prior to internet and cable. Hence it follows that when individuals leave their linguistic communities such that they are now surrounded by a different language than their home language or L1, no matter how intensely they try to keep themselves immersed in L1, changes in both quality and quantity to L1 input tend to prevail. This is where the process of L1 attrition begins, followed by interference from the host language, L2, via increased frequency and amount of L2 language contact. These individuals that are now within environments that provide minimal or no L1 input then have children but are not in the position to provide this next generation the same quality and quantity of L1 input they had enjoyed. This creates a generation of L1 speakers who are now labeled heritage speakers of a language, a term that originated in Canada (Kagan & Dillon, 2008).

Heritage Speakers of L1

Heritage speakers are non-proficient speakers of a language (typically L1), usually learned at home, while dominant in another language of the environment (typically L2) (Montrul & Polinsky, 2011). Often, heritage speakers do not acquire their L1 completely (in contrast to their immigrant parents or grandparents) and present substantial differences in their L1 from native L1 speakers. These differences manifest in phonology, morphosyntax, syntax, and lexicon. A good example of how heritage languages operate is the use of Spanish in second-generation speakers in the United States. Despite Spanish being the most popular language other than English used in the U.S. (American Community Survey, 2019 as cited in Dietrich & Hernandez, 2022) with 44,742,305 speakers, studies show that the Spanish used by second generation speakers is different from that used by native speakers in lexical access (Montrul & Foote, 2014), phonology (Colantoni et al., 2016), morphosyntax, and grammar (Cabo, 2020; Montrul, 2009). Therefore, it is expected that languages other than English in the U.S. that do not comprise large groups of speakers (e.g., Native American indigenous languages such as Oneida and Mohawk) will become extinct unless we make a collective effort to preserve them. Language attrition in communities and societies is intimately linked to the cultures that they are tied to. Linguistic structures and labels are intimately connected with cultural identities, artifacts, and practices, and with language loss these practices and artifacts no longer occupy social space.

Language Attrition and its Effects on Linguistic Diversity and Biodiversity

A recent study of the linguistic communities in Papua New Guinea (PNG) by Kik et al. (2021) highlights the decline in linguistic diversity in extraordinary detail. The investigators set out to study "drivers of language attrition" in the world's most linguistically diverse nation, PNG, which is located northeast of Australia and boasts of more than nine million people speaking more than 840 languages from 33 language families or more. Through extensive questionnaires and language tests, Kik and his colleagues documented the language skills of 6,190 secondary school students in PNG. This survey recorded 392 languages of which at least 110 were reported by over 10 students each. The investigators uncovered a steep decline in language skills reported by these students as compared to their parents. While 90.8% of the parents were reported as speaking an indigenous language fluently, only 57.7% of the students taking the survey reported being able to do so, and 2% of the students reported that they spoke no indigenous language at all. Remarkably, the investigators found that this decline in linguistic diversity, leading to alarming rates of language attrition at the societal level, was a result of economic and social growth in the country driven by globalization. They attributed this dramatic decline in language skills across a single generation to changes in home language input, socioeconomic conditions, language traits, and urbanization. Sixty-six percent within the 30% of the families that used indigenous languages at home experienced competition from both English and Tok-Pisin (a creole language, one of the official languages of PNG, and the most widely used language in PNG). In addition, mixed-language families have reduced language input in indigenous languages (16%) compared to same-language families (38%). Unsurprisingly, urbanization showed a negative impact on indigenous language skills in the participants such that skills such as hunting, fishing, house building, farming, and medicinal plant use correlated positively with indigenous language skills while technical skills in computers and mobile-phone use correlated negatively with indigenous language skills.

Kik and colleagues also investigated ethnobiographical knowledge and the impact that language attrition has on it in PNG. Ethnobiographical knowledge is societies' understanding and knowledge of natural systems that surround them and is documented as a strength in indigenous communities (Zarger, 2011). PNG is rich in natural resources and is known to be the most diverse island in the world in terms of flora, accounting for approximately 5% of biodiversity of the world. The indigenous communities living in PNG have historically been closely connected with this biodiversity, with rich ethnobiographical knowledge of its ecological systems. However, this study demonstrated that not only linguistic diversity, but ethnobiographical knowledge in the participants also declined across a single generation. In fact, the investigators found that the participants' indigenous language skills were a predictor of their knowledge of bird species and plant use. This was an expected finding as much of the ethnobiographical knowledge is coded in indigenous languages with no translations in English or Tok Pisin, demonstrating the connection between language and ethnobiology. PNG has been known to be a rich source of both biological and linguistic diversity, with these two variables interconnected via ethnobiological knowledge of the many indigenous peoples who inhabit this rich land. Today, urbanization, mobility, and socioeconomic opportunities threaten both linguistic and ethnobiographical knowledge in the current generation of young indigenous people in PNG, posing questions and concerns about the relationship between reduced linguistic diversity and biodiversity in the world.

A number of studies are beginning to document the link between protection of biodiversity and preservation of cultures and languages (Frainer et al., 2020; Gorenflo et al., 2012; Upadhyay & Hasnain, 2017). Frainer and colleagues highlight the importance of linguistic diversity and how language attrition can negatively impact biodiversity, endangering the survival of humanity. They too cite examples of indigenous cultures and how their linguistic knowledge and interpretation of the local ecological systems is the bridge to preserved biodiversity, as an important tool to healthy and diverse ecosystems. In fact, Frainer et al. (2020) provide many examples of how such languages can be maintained and preserved while taking advantage of economic expansion and opportunities. One such example is from the Mangagoulak community of the Casamance region of Senegal, Africa. Fishing communities in the villages of the Casamance region were able to register their fishing territories as Indigenous and Community-Conserved Area (ICCA) in 2009 as "Kawawana" through non-government organizations operating in this region. These organizations helped the ICCA Kawawana establish and preserve their rights to culturally unique fishing practices along with their unique linguistic coding. As a result of this, the Kawawana ICCA is able to continue healthy fishing practices to produce thrice as much fish as before, conserve the dolphin populations in the region, and gain enough economic strength for better schooling and supplies for the local educational systems. Such examples are important to understand and study, so that we can not only help other indigenous communities, but minority cultures and languages at large.

Conclusion and Future Directions

In this chapter, we have talked about definitions of attrition, its mechanisms, its influencing factors, and finally its effect on social diversity, linguistic diversity, and biodiversity. It is only natural that humans should connect with others, linguistically and culturally different from them (Park, 2018). Such connections lead to language and cultural contacts, new opportunities, and potential birth of new languages and cultural practices. Early studies of language attrition opened the doorway to understanding how languages are changing both within and across generations, perhaps connecting these branches of research for the first time (Schmid & Köpke, 2019). This work began to shed light on the notion that languages that were not passed down to the next generation due to poor input could lead to "language death" over a few generations. So, what is our responsibility toward L1 attrition as researchers, consumers, and clinicians in our respective fields? It is imperative that we continue to examine the nature, extent, and mechanisms of language attrition in individuals and how they affect generations and societies in order to prioritize linguistic diversity and preserve biodiversity, so that we can support individuals and communities in this process.

References

Bettoni, C. (1985). Italian language attrition: a Sydney case study. In *Australia, Meeting Place of Languages*. Pacific Linguistics.

Boxtel, W. V. & Lawyer, L. (2021). Sentence comprehension in ageing and Alzheimer's disease. *Language and Linguistics Compass*, *15*(6), e12430.

Burke, D. M., MacKay, D. G., Worthley, J. S., & Wade, E. (1991). On the tip of the tongue: What causes word finding failures in young and older adults?. *Journal of Memory and Language*, *30*(5), 542–579.

Cabo, D. P. (2020). Examining the role of cross-generational attrition in the development of Spanish as a heritage language: Evidence from gustar-like verbs. *Linguistic Approaches to Bilingualism*, *10*(1), 86–108.

Chamorro, G., Sorace, A., & Sturt, P. (2016). What is the source of L1 attrition? The effect of recent L1 re-exposure on Spanish speakers under L1 attrition. *Bilingualism 19*, 520–532. 10.1017/S1366728915000152

Colantoni, L., Cuza, A., & Mazzaro, N. (2016). Task-related effects in the prosody of Spanish heritage speakers and long-term immigrants. *Intonational Grammar in Ibero-Romance: Approaches across Linguistic Subfields*, 3–23.

Connor, L. T., Spiro III, A., Obler, L. K., & Albert, M. L. (2004). Change in object naming ability during adulthood. *The Journals of Gerontology Series B: Psychological Sciences and Social Sciences*, *59*(5), 203–209.

Datta, H. (2010). *Brain bases for first language lexical attrition in Bengali-English speakers* [Unpublished doctoral dissertation]. City University of New York.

De Bot, K. & Weltens, B. (1995). Foreign language attrition. *Annual Review of Applied Linguistics*, *15*, 151–164.

De Leeuw, E., Tusha, A. & Schmid, M. S. (2018). Individual phonological attrition in Albanian-English late bilinguals. *Bilingualism 21*, 278–295. 10.1017/S1366728917000025

De Houwer, A. (2007). Parental language input patterns and children's bilingual use. *Applied Psycholinguistics*, *28*(3), 411–424.

Dietrich, S. & Hernandez, E. (2022). Language use in the United States: 2019. American Community Survey Reports. Retrieved from https://www.census.gov/library/publications/2022/acs/acs-50.html

Fonteneau, E. (2013). Structural syntactic prediction measured with ELAN: Evidence from ERPs. *Neuroscience Letters*, *534*, 211–216. 10.1016/j.neulet.2012. 11.055

Frainer, A., Mustonen, T., Hugu, S., Andreeva, T., Arttijeff, E. M., Arttijeff, I. S., ... & Pecl, G. (2020). Cultural and linguistic diversities are underappreciated pillars of biodiversity. *Proceedings of the National Academy of Sciences*, *117*(43), 26539–26543.

Friederici, A. D. & Weissenborn, J. (2007). Mapping sentence form onto meaning: the syntax-semantic interface. *Brain Research*, *1146*, 50–58. 10.1016/j.brainres.2006.08.038

Gallo, F., Bermudez-Margaretto, B., Shtyrov, Y., Abutalebi, J., Kreiner, H., Chitaya, T., ... & Myachykov, A. (2021). First language attrition: What it is, what it isn't, and what it can be. *Frontiers in Human Neuroscience*, *15*, 686388. 10.3389/fnhum.2021.686388

Goral, M. (2004). First-language decline in healthy aging: Implications for attrition in bilingualism. *Journal of Neurolinguistics*, *17*(1), 31–52.

Gorenflo, L. J., Romaine, S., Mittermeier, R. A., & Walker-Painemilla, K. (2012). Co-occurrence of linguistic and biological diversity in biodiversity hotspots and high biodiversity wilderness areas. *Proceedings of the National Academy of Sciences*, *109*(21), 8032–8037.

Hansen, L. (2011). The acquisition, attrition, and relearning of mission vocabulary. *Modeling Bilingualism: From Structure to Chaos*, 115–134.

Higby, E., Cahana-Amitay, D., Vogel-Eyny, A., Spiro III, A., Albert, M. L., & Obler, L. K. (2019). The role of executive functions in object-and action-naming among older adults. *Experimental Aging Research*, *45*(4), 306–330.

Hopp, H. & Schmid, M. S. (2013). Perceived foreign accent in first language attrition and second language acquisition: The impact of age of acquisition and bilingualism. *Applied Psycholinguistics*, *34*(2), 361–394.

Huijbers, W., Papp, K. V., LaPoint, M., Wigman, S. E., Dagley, A., Hedden, T., ... & Sperling, R. A. (2017). Age-related increases in tip-of-the-tongue are distinct from decreases in remembering names: A functional MRI study. *Cerebral Cortex*, *27*(9), 4339–4349.

Indefrey, P. (2011). The spatial and temporal signatures of word production components: A critical update. *Frontiers in Psychology*, 2, 255. 10.3389/fpsyg.2011.00255

Indefrey, P. & Levelt, W. J. M. (2004). The spatial and temporal signatures of word production components. *Cognition*, 92, 101–144. 10.1016/j.cognition. 2002.06.001

Kagan, O. & Dillon, K. (2008). Issues in heritage language learning in the United States. *Encyclopedia of Language and Education*, *4*, 143–156.

Karayayla, T. & Schmid, M. S. (2019). First language attrition as a function of age at onset of bilingualism: First language attainment of Turkish-English Bilinguals in the United Kingdom. *Language Learning*, *69*, 106–142. 10.1111/lang.12316

Kasparian, K., Vespignani, F. & Steinhauer, K. (2017). First language attrition induces changes in online morphosyntactic processing and re-analysis: An ERP study of number agreement in complex Italian sentences. *Cognitive Science*, *41*, 1760–1803. 10.1111/cogs.12450

Kik, A., Adamec, M., Aikhenvald, A. Y., Bajzekova, J., Baro, N., Bowern, C., ... & Novotny, V. (2021). Language and ethnobiological skills decline precipitously in Papua New Guinea, the world's most linguistically diverse nation. *Proceedings of the National Academy of Sciences*, *118*(22), e2100096118.

Köpke, B. (2004a). Neurolinguistic aspects of attrition. *Journal of Neurolinguistics*, *17*(1), 3–30.

Köpke, B. (2004b). Attrition is not a unitary phenomenon: On different possible outcomes of language contact situations. In Proceedings from the Second International Symposium on Bilingualism, Bilingual Socialization and Bilingual Language Acquisition, Vigo, pp. 1331–1347.

Köpke, B. & Schmid, M. S. (2004). Language attrition: The next phase. In M. S. Schmid, B. Köpke, M. Keijzer, and L. Weilemar (Eds.), *First Language Attrition: Interdisciplinary Perspectives on Methodological Issues*. John Benjamins Publishing. 10.1075/sibil.28.02kop

Kutas, M. & Hillyard, S. A. (1980). Reading senseless sentences: Brain potentials reflect semantic incongruity. *Science*, *207*, 203–205. 10.1126/science. 7350657

Lambert, R. D. & Freed, B. F. (1982). *The Loss of Language Skills*. Newbury House Publishers, Inc.

Levelt, W. J. M. (1999). Language production: A blueprint of the speaker. In C. Brown and P. Hagoort (Eds.), *Neurocognition of Language* (pp. 83–122). Oxford University Press.

Montrul, S. (2009). Knowledge of tense-aspect and mood in Spanish heritage speakers. *International Journal of Bilingualism*, *13*(2), 239–269.
Montrul, S. & Foote, R. (2014). Age of acquisition interactions in bilingual lexical access: A study of the weaker language of L2 learners and heritage speakers. *International Journal of Bilingualism*, *18*(3), 274–303.
Montrul, S. & Polinsky, M. (2011). Why not heritage speakers? *Linguistic Approaches to Bilingualism*, *1*(1), 58–62.
Nicholas, M., Obler, L., Albert, M., & Goodglass, H. (1985). Lexical retrieval in healthy aging. *Cortex*, *21*(4), 595–606.
Paradis, M. (2007). L1 attrition features predicted by a neurolinguistic theory of bilingualism. Language attrition: *Theoretical Perspectives*, *33*, 121–133.
Park, E. S. (2018). Language attrition. *The TESOL Encyclopedia of English language teaching* (pp. 1–12). John Wiley & Sons.
Poulisse, C., Wheeldon, L., & Segaert, K. (2019). Evidence against preserved syntactic comprehension in healthy aging. *Journal of Experimental Psychology: Learning, Memory, and Cognition*, *45*(12), 2290–2308.
Shafto, M. A., Burke, D. M., Stamatakis, E. A., Tam, P. P., & Tyler, L. K. (2007). On the tip-of-the-tongue: Neural correlates of increased word-finding failures in normal aging. *Journal of Cognitive Neuroscience*, *19*(12), 2060–2070.
Schmid, M. S. (2002). *First language attrition, Use and maintenance: The case of German Jews in anglophone countries*, Vol. 24. Benjamins Publishing Company. 10.1075/sibil.24
Schmid, M. S. (2004). First language attrition: The methodology revised. *International Journal of Bilingualism*, *8*(3), 239–255.
Schmid, M. S. (2008). Defining language attrition. *Babylonia*, *2*, 9–12.
Schmid, M. S., Köpke, B., & De Bot, K. (2013). Language attrition as a complex, non-linear development. *International Journal of Bilingualism*, *17*(6), 675–682.
Schmid, M. S. & Fägersten, K. B. (2010). Disfluency markers in L1 attrition. *Language Learning*, *60*(4), 753–791.
Schmid, M. S. & Jarvis, S. (2014). Lexical access and lexical diversity in first language attrition. *Bilingualism: Language and Cognition*, *17*(4), 729–748.
Schmid, M. S. & Köpke, B. (2017). The relevance of first language attrition to theories of bilingual development. *Linguistic Approaches to Bilingualism* *7*(6), 637–667. 10.1075/lab.17058.sch
Schmid, M. S. & Köpke, B. (Eds.). (2019). *The Oxford Handbook of Language Attrition*. Oxford University Press.
Seliger, H. W. & Vago, R. M. (Eds.). (1991). *First Language Attrition*. Cambridge University Press.
Taler, V., Klepousniotou, E., & Phillips, N. A. (2009). Comprehension of lexical ambiguity in healthy aging, mild cognitive impairment, and mild Alzheimer's disease. *Neuropsychologia*, *47*(5), 1332–1343.
Upadhyay, R. K. & Hasnain, S. I. (2017). Linguistic diversity and biodiversity. *Lingua*, *195*, 110–123.
Zarger, R. K. (2011). Learning ethnobiology: Creating knowledge and skills about the living world. *Ethnobiology*. Willey-Blackwell. https://cis.org/Report/673-Million-United-States-Spoke-Foreign-Language-Home-2018

6

NEUROANATOMICAL PREDICTORS OF LANGUAGE AND COGNITIVE FUNCTIONS IN AGING

JungMoon Hyun and Alexandre Nikolaev

Introduction

The world population is aging. As of 2020, the number of Americans aged 65 and older is about 55 million, or 16.8% of the total population; this number is expected to reach 95 million by 2060 (United States Census Bureau, 2022). The effects of aging on cognitive function and brain health are not homogeneous. Some older adults experience neurodegenerative diseases accompanied with cognitive disorders, whereas others do not experience those diseases and stay on the track of "normal cognitive aging", which can also be highly heterogeneous. Some people report subjective cognitive decline, in which they perceive a depreciation in their cognitive functioning despite objective testing performance remaining within a normal range, while others do not report unusual cognitive deterioration. Additionally, there are individuals known as *Superagers* who are over the age of 80 yet still have a sharp memory similar to that of people in their 60s. Therefore, understanding older adults' cognitive functioning is important to differentiate normal aging from pathological aging. In this chapter, we discuss the characteristics of language and cognitive changes in older adults, and how those changes are related to structural and functional brain changes.

Language Changes in Aging

Some language functions remain stable, while others decline early in the cognitively normal aging population. Accumulated general knowledge, such as vocabulary, continuously increases and remains stable until age

DOI: 10.4324/9781003330318-7

70–80 (Ben-David et al., 2015; Goral et al., 2007). Additionally, the accuracy of older adults' written word recognition is parallel to that of younger adults, with maintained morphological knowledge in word inflection (Nikolaev et al., 2019). To investigate how mental grammar is influenced by age, Nikolaev et al. (2019) employed a word recognition test and found that inflectional morphology (part of our mental grammar) seems to be unaffected by age. This study utilized Finnish nouns with different degrees of stem allomorphy some words had more complex inflectional paradigms (greater stem allomorphy) while other words had less complex inflectional paradigms. The complexity effect of stem allomorphs was not modulated by age; younger and older adults showed a similar pattern of recognition: faster reaction times to words with more stem allomorphs in their inflectional paradigms compared with words with fewer stem allomorphs. Thus, the maintenance of word knowledge, recognition ability, and some morphological awareness is resilient in advanced age among cognitively healthy older adults.

It appears that older adults' sentence comprehension is also relatively well retained unless there are challenging circumstances. Older adults face greater challenges than younger adults when it comes to perceiving sentences in degraded listening environments, particularly when the audio signal is disrupted by competing background noise, such as multi-talker babble (Füllgrabe et al., 2015). Also, older adults are much slower and less accurate than younger adults in comprehending syntactically complex sentences, and this difficulty increases as the length of the sentence increases (Wingfield et al., 2006). Nonetheless, older adults' comprehension of words and simple sentences is generally well preserved (Tyler et al., 2010).

Compared to well-maintained comprehension abilities, language production skills, such as word retrieval abilities decline early in the aging process. Most cross-sectional and longitudinal studies have used noun confrontation naming tasks and found that for these tasks, word retrieval abilities peak at 30–40 years then gradually decline, with steeper deterioration beginning in the mid-60s for cognitively healthy adults (Goral et al., 2007; Zec et al., 2005). While younger adults can name known items immediately, older adults are less accurate, with more frequent "tip-of-the-tongue" states, in which a person is confident that she knows the target word (e.g., "hammock") but unable to retrieve the sound information (Brown, 2012; Burke et al., 1991; James & Burke, 2000). This decline in word retrieval ability tested in noun naming has been also observed in action/verb naming (Goral et al., 2007; Ramsay et al., 1999).

In addition to naming tests, verbal fluency tests are frequently used in neuropsychological evaluations. These tests measure an individual's ability to produce words belonging to a specific semantic category (e.g., animal) or letter/sound category (e.g., words beginning with the letter "F" or /f/ sound) in a fixed amount of time. Performance on these tests indicates word retrieval efficiency as well as executive functioning. Studies generally find that older adults produce fewer words on semantic than letter fluency tests, as well as fewer words than younger adults within semantic fluency tests only (Crossley et al., 1997; Tombaugh et al., 1999; Tomer & Levin, 1993). Thus, semantic fluency is considered more sensitive to aging than letter fluency to aging than letter fluency, and performance on semantic fluency tasks can distinguish normal aging from mild cognitive impairment or dementia (Henry et al., 2004).

Due to their high sensitivity to aging effects, both word retrieval and verbal fluency tests are frequently included in neuropsychological batteries to detect language and cognitive deterioration. These tests have often been normed on large sample sizes that include diverse languages and countries. However, when assessing language, it is also important to consider gender and education level, as these have been implicated in performance on some language tests (Goral et al., 2007, Tombaugh et al., 1999; Zec et al., 2007).

Overall, compared to relatively well-maintained comprehension abilities, older adults experience declines in language production abilities earlier (Goral et al., 2007; Zec et al., 2005), even at the level of a single word. These declines vary among individuals and are influenced by a variety of factors, including cognitive changes associated with aging.

Cognitive Changes in Aging

Along with age-associated language changes, other cognitive domains, such as memory (e.g., working memory, episodic memory), attention (e.g., selective attention), processing speed, and executive functions (EFs; e.g., inhibition, shifting) are frequently investigated. Individuals who experience a marked decline in these multiple cognitive domains usually exhibit difficulties in their activities of daily living (ADLs) indicating early-stage cognitive impairment (Ferguson et al., 2021). The ability to independently perform ADLs, including both complex and basic activities, is an index of distinguishing cognitively healthy adults from pathological aging because the diagnosis of dementia requires symptoms that "interfere with the ability to function at work or at usual activities" (McKhann et al., 2011, p. 236). Thus, it is important to monitor changes in cognitive functions that are susceptible to aging to promote the maintenance of independent life.

Older adults who experience simple forgetfulness or slowness in problem-solving may still be able to handle their ADLs if their EFs are preserved. EFs involve a variety of cognitive processes, such as cognitive flexibility, inhibitory control, working memory, planning, attention allocation, monitoring, and reasoning (Lezak et al., 2004). The most frequently used neuropsychological tests for EFs include the *Stroop Test*, *Trail Making Test*, *Wisconsin Card Sorting Test*, *Verbal Fluency Test*, *Digit Span Test*, and *Tower of London*. These tests tap into different but overlapping sub-domains of EFs and a lower performance in one test does not imply a deficit in one specific cognitive process. While some studies of EFs found no difference between younger and older adults (e.g., Rey-Mermet & Gade, 2018; Sebastian et al., 2013; Vallesi et al., 2021), or a non-linear, U-shaped trajectory of decline with age (Cepeda et al., 2001), advancing age has been linked to poor performance on EF tests suggesting reduced efficiency. Compared to younger adults, older adults show significantly lower performance in working memory (Salthouse & Meinz, 1995), inhibition (Hasher & Zacks, 1988), and cognitive flexibility (Richard's et al., 2021). Also, selective attention seems to decline early, as opposed to sustained attention which appears to be relatively well preserved (Carriere et al., 2010; Staub et al., 2013, but also see Fortenbaugh et al.'s study, 2015, reporting the early decline of sustained attention after the age of 40). A decline in selective attention with age can be attributed to the difficulties in selectively allocating attention or inhibition, which is a controlled ability to actively ignore or suppress irrelevant information in order to focus on more appropriate, goal-oriented stimuli, a crucial component of EFs (Logan, 1994).

Older adults' reduced efficiency in multiple cognitive functions has been associated with many factors, such as target salience (Humphrey & Kramer, 1997), perception load (Maylor & Lavie, 1998), stimulus modality (e.g., visual vs. auditory), and task demands (Isingrini et al., 2015; Zhuravleva et al., 2014), as well as biological brain changes (Pettemeridou et al., 2021). These complex considerations warrant further investigation in order to develop a comprehensive cognitive profile of healthy aging.

Brain Changes in Aging

Structural Changes

During adult life, the aging process affects brain structure and function, similar to its effects on physical shape and strength. The most salient structural brain changes are reduced volume and thickness of gray and white matter, and enlargement of the ventricles. These changes have been documented in post-mortem autopsy since the early history of brain research, and now magnetic resonance imaging (MRI) offers *pre-mortem, in vivo* images to evaluate brain structures.

Decreased cortical volume and thickness are associated with the shrinkage of neuronal cells and dendrites with increasing age. This gray matter atrophy begins around age 30–40 and more rapidly increases after age 70 in adults without dementia (Scahill et al., 2003). Longitudinal and cross-sectional studies of cognitively normal aging have documented reductions of brain volume and thickness in almost the entire cerebral cortex, including diffuse and mild atrophy in the parietal, temporal, and frontal lobes. The prefrontal cortex, associated with higher-level cognitive processes, is especially susceptible to atrophy, while the occipital lobes are least affected (e.g., Fotenos et al., 2005). Overall, frontal and temporal lobes experience the highest rate of reduction compared to other brain regions, and researchers have connected these brain changes to cognitive function changes. For example, medial orbitofrontal lobe degeneration has been associated with EF decline, and temporal lobe degeneration has been associated with memory decline in the elderly (Gunning-Dixon & Raz, 2003; Head et al., 2009).

White matter volume changes are also observed in older adults due to degeneration of the myelin sheath and reduction in axonal length. In addition to volumetric changes, the integrity of white matter tracts has been vigorously investigated with diffusion tensor imaging (DTI), an MRI technique that relies on the unique characteristics of water diffusion in different types of molecules (e.g., bones and brain tissues) to detect subtle changes in the brain's microstructure. This technique has been widely implemented to study age-related brain changes, including in clinical populations such as dementia and stroke. Commonly implemented DTI measures serve as proxies for white matter integrity (i.e., fractional anisotropy [FA]) or weaker or disrupted white matter tracts (i.e., mean diffusivity [MD]; radial diffusivity [RD]). Studies have found lower FA in the frontal, temporal, and parietal (but not occipital) white matter of older adults (Grieve et al., 2007). Generally, DTI studies have found lower FA, and higher MD and RD in normal aging compared to younger adults (e.g., Head et al., 2004; Yoon et al., 2008). These findings indicate that white matter tracts in the brain undergo various structural changes as part of the aging process, resulting in decreased connectivity between brain regions and alteration of cognitive functioning. For instance, reduced naming ability has been correlated with decreased FA within the left superior longitudinal fasciculus (e.g., Houston et al., 2019), and poorer EF has been associated with lower FA in the bilateral frontal lobes (e.g., Grieve et al., 2007).

Functional Changes

The focus on finding the relationship between specific cognitive functions and brain areas has moved from individual regions to multi-region networks functionally working together as large-scale systems (Damoiseaux, 2017). Major networks include the default mode network (DMN), which is more active during a resting state without external stimulation and less active during a task-oriented process, as well as other networks, including sensorimotor, attention, visual, and executive control networks (Deery et al., 2023). Aging research investigating differences in functional brain connectivity within and between networks has found that older adults show lower intrinsic DMN connectivity compared to younger adults, which has been associated with poorer performance on various cognitive tasks (Damoiseaux et al., 2008; Grady et al., 2016). In addition to the DMN, the salience, executive control, and sensorimotor networks also show age-related changes in functional connectivity (Doucet et al., 2021; Geerligs et al., 2015). These findings suggest that aging affects the integration of both local and global brain networks.

One pervasive characteristic of age-associated neural changes is *bilateral* brain activation. While younger adults typically activate specific regions in either the left or right hemisphere during a task, older adults frequently activate the same regions in both hemispheres (Cabeza, 2002; Reuter-Lorenz et al., 2000). This hemispheric asymmetry reduction in older adults, or HAROLD model (Cabeza, 2002), highlights increased bilaterality in the aging brain. This bilateral, or less-specific brain recruitment pattern has been interpreted as a *compensatory* mechanism. That is, by enlisting the help of the contralateral hemisphere, older adults can utilize more cognitive resources to perform better on a task. However, it is controversial whether these bilateral brain activations lead to better performance, or whether they are only an attempt to make up for the decline of function. Studies comparing high- versus low-performers generally support the idea that aging-related increases in bilateral activation are compensatory (e.g., Gutchess et al., 2005), but other studies also reported that not all activations in the contralateral hemisphere are beneficial; some bilateral activities show no correlation with cognitive task performance, or have a negative correlation with performance (e.g., Martins et al., 2012). Thus, it has been suggested that regional specificity within each hemisphere should also be considered (e.g., Wierenga et al., 2008).

Neural Correlates of Language and Cognitive Tasks in Aging

The classical views of language areas in the brain, which were supported by data from stroke patients, have been challenged in the past decades (e.g., Mesulam et al., 2019; Tremblay & Dick, 2016). Traditionally, it is widely considered that language functions are heavily left lateralized within perisylvian areas. Thus, the involvement of the right hemisphere and the regions outside of the perisylvian areas in the left hemisphere has been largely neglected. However, studies have shown that the contribution of brain regions beyond the perisylvian areas to language is not negligible in aging populations (e.g., Stern et al., 2008; Wingfield & Grossman, 2006). In a study that investigated the relationship between naming performance and gray matter volume among cognitively normal older adults, better action naming (ANT) performance was associated with higher volumes of the left middle frontal, right inferior parietal (angular lobule), and right middle temporal gyri (Obler et al., 2010). The authors also found a correlation between better object naming performance (as measured by the Boston Naming Test (BNT)) and higher volumes in the left middle frontal and superior temporal gyri (planum temporale). This study highlights the importance of the frontal lobe and bihemispheric involvement in older adults' naming. The right hemisphere's involvement in word retrieval has also been found in other studies with aging brains, such as Wierenga et al. (2008), which found larger, bilateral activation in the frontal network in older adults compared to younger adults. These findings suggest that older adults have less lateralized brain activities for a given task than younger adults, and additional activities in some right hemisphere regions might be recruited for a compensatory function.

Multiple studies have investigated age-related changes in sentence processing and brain response (Antonenko et al., 2013; Karimi & Diaz, 2021; Peelle et al., 2010; Tyler et al., 2010). Tyler et al. (2010) found that older adults employed similar brain networks to younger adults during a sentence comprehension task, but with differing activation levels among frontal and temporal regions. Older adults showed activity in broad frontal areas and the middle temporal gyrus, suggesting that, though weakened with age, frontotemporal connections were compensated by strong connectivity between functionally related regions (Tyler et al., 2010). Similarly, Peelle et al. (2010) found older adults' decreased brain responses in the primary sentence-processing network (i.e., left middle frontal gyrus and right superior frontal gyrus), but increased responses outside of this network, suggestive of a compensatory role. Conversely, Antonenko et al. (2013) found different intra- and inter-hemispheric connectivity within the syntax network in older adults compared to younger adults. Older adults exhibited difficulty in syntactic processing associated with weaker functional connectivity within the left-lateralized fronto-temporal syntax network and stronger functional connectivity outside of the primary syntax network (in the angular gyrus bilaterally and left middle frontal gyrus). The authors propose that older adults' difficulties in syntactic processing could be explained by their weaker ability to deactivate the DMN during task performance, leading to more diffuse and less distinct activation of task-relevant brain networks. Taken together, these results suggest that older adults tend to display less coherent brain activation patterns than younger adults, with over- or under-recruitment of brain regions creating altered functional connectivity between- and within-networks.

Conclusion and Future Directions

Understanding the intricate connections among aging, language ability, and brain involvement presents a formidable challenge. However, a close investigation of older adults' characteristics may provide a more solid and convincing explanation for why, as we grow older, we acquire more communication skills and knowledge, but we become slower, more laborious, and less efficient language users. Neuroimaging studies suggest that older adults use compensatory strategies to perform better on language and cognitive tasks. These compensation mechanisms include older adults' greater neural activation or additional recruitment of brain regions to match similar levels of performance compared to younger adults, as well as age-associated neural reorganization. To fully comprehend the cognitive functions and neural changes in the aging brain, many factors, including task demand, modality, and individual differences, must also be considered, and further research is required to evaluate the influence of these factors. A better understanding of the aging process will enable us to detect cognitive dysfunction early, offer the appropriate services, and advance our knowledge so that we can lead cognitively healthier lives.

References

Antonenko, D., Brauer, J., Meinzer, M., Fengler, A., Kerti, L., Friederici, A. D., & Flöel, A. (2013). Functional and structural syntax networks in aging. *NeuroImage*, *83*, 513–523.

Ben-David, B. M., Erel, H., Goy, H., & Schneider, B. A. (2015). "Older is always better": Age-related differences in vocabulary scores across 16 years. *Psychology and Aging*, *30*(4), 856–862.

Brown, A. S. (2012). *The tip of the tongue state*. Psychology Press.

Burke, D. M., MacKay, D. G., Worthley, J. S., & Wade, E. (1991). On the tip of the tongue: What causes word finding failures in young and older adults? *Journal of Memory and Language*, *30*(5), 542–579.

Cabeza, R. (2002). Hemispheric asymmetry reduction in older adults: The HAROLD model. *Psychology and Aging*, *17*, 85–100.

Carriere, J. S., Cheyne, J. A., Solman, G. J., & Smilek, D. (2010). Age trends for failures of sustained attention. *Psychology and Aging*, *25*(3), 569–574.

Cepeda, N. J., Kramer, A. F., & Gonzalez de Sather, J. C. M.(2001). Changes in executive control across the life span: Examination of task-switching performance. *Developmental Psychology*, *37*, 715–730.

Crossley, M., D'Arcy, C., & Rawson, N. S. (1997). Letter and category fluency in community-dwelling Canadian seniors: A comparison of normal participants to those with dementia of the Alzheimer or vascular type. *Journal of Clinical and Experimental Neuropsychology*, *19*, 52–62.

Damoiseaux, J. S. (2017). Effects of aging on functional and structural brain connectivity. *NeuroImage*, *160*, 32–40.

Damoiseaux, J. S., Beckmann, C. F., Arigita, E. J., Barkhof, F., Scheltens, P., Stam, C. J., Smith, S. M., & Rombouts, S. A. (2008). Reduced resting-state brain activity in the "default network" in normal aging. *Cerebral Cortex*, *18*(8), 1856–1864.

Deery, H. A., Paolo, R. D., Moran, C., Egan, G. F., & Jamada, S. D. (2023). The older adult brain is less modular, more integrated, and less efficient at rest. *Psychophysiology*, *60*, e14159

Doucet, G. E., Labache, L., Thompson, P. M., Joliot, M., & Frangou, S., Alzheimer's Disease Neuroimaging Initiative (2021). Atlas55+: Brain functional atlas of resting-state networks for late adulthood. *Cerebral Cortex*, *31*(3), 1719–1731.

Ferguson, H. J., Brunsdon, V. E. A. & Bradford, E. E. F. (2021). The developmental trajectories of executive function from adolescence to old age. *Scientific Reports*, *11*, 1382.

Fortenbaugh, F. C., DeGutis, J., Germine, L., Wilmer, J. B., Grosso, M., Russo, K., & Esterman, M. (2015). Sustained attention across the life span in a sample of 10,000: Dissociating ability and strategy. *Psychological Science*, *26*(9), 1497–1510.

Fotenos, A. F., Snyder, A., Girton, L., Morris, J., & Buckner, R. (2005). Normative estimates of cross-sectional and longitudinal brain volume decline in aging and AD. *Neurology*, *64*(6), 1032–1039.

Füllgrabe, C., Moore, B. C., & Stone, M. A. (2015). Age-group differences in speech identification despite matched audiometrically normal hearing: Contributions from auditory temporal processing and cognition. *Frontiers in Aging Neuroscience*, *6*, 347.

Geerligs, L., Renken, R. J., Saliasi, E., Maurits, N. M., & Lorist, M. M. (2015). A brain-wide study of age-related changes in functional connectivity. *Cerebral Cortex*, *25*(7), 1987–1999.

Goral, M., Spiro, A. III, Albert, M. L., Obler, L. K., & Connor, L. (2007). Change in lexical retrieval skills in adulthood. *The Mental Lexicon*, *2*(2), 215–238.

Grady, C., Sarraf, S., Saverino, C., & Campbell, K. (2016). Age differences in the functional interactions among the default, frontoparietal control, and dorsal attention networks. *Neurobiology of Aging*, *41*, 159–172.

Grieve, S. M., Williams, L. M., Paul, R. H., Clark, C. R. & Gordon, E. (2007) Cognitive aging, executive function, and fractional anisotropy: A diffusion tensor MR imaging study. *American Journal of Neuroradiology*, *28*, 226–235.

Gunning-Dixon, F. M., & Raz, N. (2003). Neuroanatomical correlates of selected executive functions in middle-aged and older adults: a prospective MRI study. *Neuropsychologia*, *41*, 1929–1941.

Gutchess, A. H., Welsh, R. C., Hedden, T., Bangert, A., Minear, M., Liu, L. L., & Park, D. C. (2005). Aging and the neural correlates of successful picture encoding: Frontal activations compensate for decreased medial-temporal activity. *Journal of Cognitive Neuroscience*, *17*(1), 84–96.

Hasher, L. & Zacks, R. T. (1988). Working memory, comprehension, and aging: A review and a new view. *Psychology of Learning and Motivation*, *22*, 193–225.

Head, D., Buckner, R. L., Shimony, J. S., Williams, L. E., Akbudak, E., Conturo, T. E., McAvoy, M., Morris, J. C., & Snyder, A. Z. (2004). Differential vulnerability of anterior white matter in nondemented aging with minimal acceleration in dementia of the Alzheimer type: Evidence from diffusion tensor imaging. *Cerebral Cortex*, *14*, 410–423.

Head, D., Kennedy, K. M., Rodrigue, K. M., & Raz, N. (2009). Age differences in perseveration: Cognitive and neuroanatomical mediators of performance on the Wisconsin Card Sorting Test. *Neuropsychologia*, *47*, 1200–1203.

Henry, J. D., Crawford, J. R., & Phillips, L. H. (2004). Verbal fluency performance in dementia of the Alzheimer's type: A meta-analysis. *Neuropsychologia*, *42*, 1212–1222.

Houston, J., Allendorfer, J., Nenert, R., Goodman, A. M., & Szaflarski, J. P. (2019). White matter language pathways and language performance in healthy adults across ages. *Frontiers in Neuroscience*, *13*, 1185.

Humphrey, D. G. & Kramer, A. F. (1997). Age differences in visual search for feature, conjunction and triple-conjunction targets. *Psychology and Aging*, *12*, 704–717.

Isingrini, M., Angel, L., Fay, S., Taconnat, L., Lemaire, P., & Bouazzaoui, B. (2015) Age-related differences in the reliance on executive control in working memory: Role of task demand. *PLoS One*, *10*(12), e0145361.

James, L. E. & Burke, D. M. (2000). Phonological priming effects on word retrieval and tip-of-the-tongue experiences in young and older adults. *Journal of Experimental Psychology: Learning, Memory, and Cognition*, *26*(6), 1378–1391.

Karimi, H. & Diaz, M. (2021). Age-related differences in the retrieval of phonologically similar words during sentence processing: Evidence from ERPs. *Brain and Language*, *220*, 104982.

Lezak, M., Howieson, D., & Loring, D. (2004). *Neuropsychological Assessment* (4th ed), Oxford University Press.

Logan, G. D. (1994). On the ability to inhibit thought and action: A users' guide to the stop signal paradigm. In D. Dagenbach & T. H. Carr (Eds.), *Inhibitory processes in attention, memory, and language* (pp. 189–239). Academic Press.

Martins, R., Simard, F., Provost, J. S., & Monchi, O. (2012). Changes in regional and temporal patterns of activity associated with aging during the performance of a lexical set-shifting task. *Cerebral Cortex*, *22*, 1395–1406.

Maylor, E. A. & Lavie, N. (1998). The influence of perceptual load on age differences in selective attention. *Psychology and Aging*, *13*, 563–573.

McKhann, G. M., Knopman, D. S., Chertkow, H., Hyman, B. T., Jack, C. R., Jr, Kawas, C. H., Klunk, W. E., Koroshetz, ... & Phelps, C. H. (2011). The diagnosis of dementia due to Alzheimer's disease: recommendations from the National Institute on Aging-Alzheimer's Association workgroups on diagnostic guidelines for Alzheimer's disease. *Alzheimer's and Dementia: The Journal of the Alzheimer's Association*, *7*(3), 263–269.

Mesulam, M. M., Rader, B. M., Sridhar, J., Nelson, M. J., Hyun, J., Rademaker, A., Geula, C., Bigio, E. H., Thompson, C. K., Gefen, T. D., Weintraub, S., &

Rogalski, E. J. (2019). Word comprehension in temporal cortex and Wernicke area: A PPA perspective. *Neurology*, *92*(3), e224–e233.
Nikolaev, A., Ashaie, S., Hallikainen, M., Hänninen, T., Higby, E., Hyun, J., Lehtonen, M., & Soininen, H. (2019). Effects of morphological family on word recognition in normal aging, mild cognitive impairment, and Alzheimer's disease. *Cortex*, *116*, 91–103.
Obler, L. K., Rykhlevskaia, E., Schnyer, D., Clark-Cotton, M. R., Spiro, A., III, Hyun, J., Kim, D. S., Goral, M., & Albert, M. L. (2010). Bilateral brain regions associated with naming in older adults. *Brain and Language*, *113*(3), 113–123.
Peelle, J. E., Troiani, V., Wingfield, A., & Grossman, M. (2010). Neural processing during older adults' comprehension of spoken sentences, age differences in resource allocation and connectivity. *Cerebral Cortex*, *20*(4), 773–782.
Pettemeridou, E., Kallousia, E., & Constantinidou, F. (2021). Regional brain volume, brain reserve and MMSE performance in healthy aging from the NEUROAGE cohort. *Frontiers in Aging Neuroscience*, *13*, 711301.
Ramsay, C. B., Nicholas, M., Au, R., Obler, L. K., & Albert, M. L. (1999). Verb naming in normal aging. *Applied Neuropsychology*, *6*(2), 57–67.
Reuter-Lorenz, P. A., Jonides, J., Smith, E. E., Hartley, A., Miller, A., Marshuetz, C., & Koeppe, R. A. (2000). Age differences in the frontal lateralization of verbal and spatial working memory revealed by PET. *Journal of Cognitive Neuroscience*, *12*(1), 174–187.
Rey-Mermet, A., & Gade, M. (2018). Inhibition in aging: What is preserved? What declines? A meta-analysis. *Psychonomic Bulletin and Review*, *25*(5), 1695–1716.
Richard's, M. M., Krzemien, D., Valentina, V., Vernucci, S., Zamora, E. V., Comesaña, A., García Coni, A., & Introzzi, I. (2021). Cognitive flexibility in adulthood and advanced age: Evidence of internal and external validity. *Applied Neuropsychology: Adult*, *28*(4), 464–478.
Salthouse, T. A. & Meinz, E. J. (1995). Aging, inhibition, working memory, and speed. *The Journals of Gerontology: Series B, Psychological Sciences and Social Sciences*, *50*(6), 297–306.
Scahill, R. I., Frost, C., Jenkins, R., Whitwell, J. L., Rossor, M. N., & Fox, N. C. (2003). A longitudinal study of brain volume changes in normal aging using serial registered magnetic resonance imaging. *Archives of Neurology*, *60*(7), 989–994.
Sebastian, A., Baldermann, C., Feige, B., Katzev, M., Scheller, E., Hellwig, B., ... & Klöppel, S. (2013). Differential effects of age on subcomponents of response inhibition. *Neurobiology of Aging*, *34*(9), 2183–2193.
Staub, B., Doignon-Camus, N., Després, O., & Bonnefond, A. (2013). Sustained attention in the elderly: What do we know and what does it tell us about cognitive aging? *Ageing Research Reviews*, *12*(2), 459–468.
Stern, Y., Zarahn, E., Habeck, C., Holtzer, R., Rakitin, B. C., Kumar, A., & Flynn, J. (2008). A common neural network for cognitive reserve in verbal and object working memory in young but not old. *Cerebral Cortex*, *18*(4), 959–967.
Tombaugh, T. N., Kozak, J., & Rees, L. (1999). Normative data stratified by age and education for two measures of verbal fluency: FAS and animal naming. *Archives of Clinical Neuropsychology*, *14*(2), 167–177.

Tomer, R. & Levin, B. E. (1993). Differential effects of aging on two verbal fluency tasks. *Perceptual and Motor Skills*, *76*(2), 465–466.

Tremblay, P. & Dick, A. S. (2016). Broca and Wernicke are dead, or moving past the classic model of language neurobiology. *Brain and Language*, *162*, 60–71.

Tyler, L. K., Shafto, M. A., Randall, B., Wright, P., Marslen-Wilson, W. D., & Stamatakis, E. A. (2010). Preserving syntactic processing across the adult life span: the modulation of the frontotemporal language system in the context of age-related atrophy. *Cerebral Cortex*, *20*(2), 352–364.

United States Census Bureau (2022). *QuickFacts-United States*. www.census.gov/quickfacts/

Vallesi, A., Tronelli, V., Lomi, F., & Pezzetta, R. (2021). Age differences in sustained attention tasks: A meta-analysis. *Psychonomic Bulletin and Review*, *28*(6), 1755–1775.

Wierenga, C. E., Benjamin, M., Gopinath, K., Perlstein, W. M., Leonard, C. M., Rothi, L. J. G., Conway, T., Cato, M. A., Briggs, R., & Crosson, B. (2008). Age-related changes in word retrieval: Role of bilateral frontal and subcortical networks. *Neurobiology of Aging*, *29*(3), 436–451.

Wingfield, A. & Grossman, M. (2006). Language and the aging brain: Patterns of neural compensation revealed by functional brain imaging. *Journal of Neurophysiology*, *96*, 2830–2839.

Wingfield, A., McCoy, S. L., Peelle, J. E., Tun, P. A., & Cox, L. C. (2006). Effects of adult aging and hearing loss on comprehension of rapid speech varying in syntactic complexity. *Journal of the American Academy of Audiology*, *17*(7), 487–497.

Yoon, B., Shim, Y. S., Lee, K. S., Shon, Y. M., & Yang, D. W. (2008). Region-specific changes of cerebral white matter during normal aging: a diffusion-tensor analysis. *Archives of Gerontology and Geriatrics*, *47*(1), 129–138.

Zec, R. F., Burkett, N. R., Markwell, S. J., & Larsen, D. L. (2007). Normative data stratified for age, education, and gender on the Boston Naming Test. *The Clinical Neuropsychologist*, *21*(4), 617–637.

Zec, R. F., Markwell, S. J., Burkett, N. R., & Larsen, D. L. (2005). A longitudinal study of confrontation naming in the "normal" elderly. *Journal of the International Neuropsychological Society: JINS*, *11*(6), 716–726.

Zhuravleva, T. Y., Alperin, B. R., Haring, A. E., Rentz, D. M., Holcomb, P. J., & Daffner, K. R. (2014). Age-related decline in bottom-up processing and selective attention in the very old. *Journal of Clinical Neurophysiology: Official Publication of the American Electroencephalographic Society*, *31*(3), 261–271.

PART II

Language Processing in Multilingual and Monolingual Adults with Dementia

7

DIFFERENTIATING NEUROPATHOLOGY, BIOMARKERS, AND CLINICAL SYMPTOMS IN DEMENTIA DUE TO ALZHEIMER'S DISEASE VS. PRIMARY PROGRESSIVE APHASIA

Taryn R. Malcolm and Susan De Santi

Introduction

Alzheimer's disease (AD), the most common cause of dementia, is a progressive and irreversible neurodegenerative brain disease with an insidious onset, usually affecting people over the age of 65 (Kumar et al., 2021). According to DSM-V, dementia due to AD involves memory decline plus at least one of the following: aphasia, apraxia, agnosia, or disturbance in executive function (APA, 2013). These cognitive deficits cause significant impairment in activities of daily living and social or occupational capabilities compared to previous functioning. Other forms of dementia may be difficult to distinguish from dementia due to AD. For example, those dementias subsumed under frontotemporal lobar dementia (FTLD), which include the primary progressive aphasias (PPA), have a heterogeneous clinical presentation which may be misdiagnosed as dementia due to AD, Parkinson's disease, or a psychiatric disorder. Unlike other dementia types, PPA has a primary deficit in language that later may also include deficits in cognition (e.g., memory, executive function, spatial abilities), behavior, and motor function. Clinically, it can be challenging to accurately diagnose the cause of dementia, as brain abnormalities associated with more than one type of dementia may coexist (Schneider et al., 2009). Due to overlapping clinical presentations of some dementia types, the use of biomarkers to determine the underlying neuropathology is crucial for accurate diagnosis and management. This chapter will review the clinical profiles of PPA and dementia due to AD, the underlying pathologies (with a focus on AD), and imaging techniques for differential diagnosis of these

DOI: 10.4324/9781003330318-9

disorders. We will also review how language is affected and discuss both behavioral treatment methods for PPA and dementia due to AD as well as pharmacological treatments (symptomatic and disease modifying).

Clinical Profiles

Dementia due to Alzheimer's Disease

According to the updated diagnostic criteria for dementia due to AD (McKhann et al., 2011) core clinical criteria must be present with either an amnestic or a non-amnestic presentation. An amnestic presentation is most common, with primary deficits in learning and recalling recent information, and decline in one other area of cognition (reasoning, visuospatial, language, or behavior). In the non-amnestic presentation, the primary deficit is in language, visuospatial abilities, or executive function, all co-occurring with other cognitive dysfunction (McKhann et al., 2011).

Though language decline in dementia due to AD is highly variable, some patterns consistently emerge, including deficits in verbal fluency, narrative production, and comprehension ability (e.g., Stopford et al., 2008; Tsantali et al., 2013). Language functions that rely heavily on working memory become more impaired as working memory declines, impacting language processing such as sentence comprehension (e.g., Tsantali et al., 2013). Lexico-semantics and pragmatics show decline more than syntax or phonology, resulting in impaired retrieval, overuse of pronouns, and semantic paraphasias (e.g., Kempler & Goral, 2008). Cognitive impairment and decline in memory may result in shorter utterances, phonological and grammatical errors, with complex syntactic constructions being impaired due to the cognitive load required for processing (e.g., Kempler & Goral, 2008).

Primary Progressive Aphasia

Primary progressive aphasia (PPA) is a complex neurodegenerative disorder that expresses itself with three clinical variants: semantic (svPPA), nonfluent (nfvPPA; sometimes referred to as nonfluent/agrammatic naPPA), and logopenic (lvPPA), all characterized by a primary speech and language impairment, in the absence of episodic and nonverbal memory loss and visuospatial impairments (Tee & Gorno-Tempini, 2019). SvPPA presents with impaired confrontation naming, single-word comprehension, object knowledge (particularly for low-frequency items), dyslexia or dysgraphia, and intact repetition abilities (Gorno-Tempini et al., 2011). NfvPPA[1] presents with agrammatic language production, effortful or halting speech, mild auditory comprehension deficits for syntactically complex sentences, and spared single-word comprehension and object knowledge (Gorno-Tempini et al., 2011; Mesulam et al., 2014). LvPPA presents with impaired single-word retrieval, decreased repetition ability for phrases and sentences, phonological errors in spontaneous speech and naming, with spared single-word comprehension, object knowledge, motor speech production, and an absence of frank agrammatism (distinguishing it from nfvPPA) (Gorno-Tempini et al., 2011).

Differentiating Language Changes in PPA and Dementia due to AD

Severity of language deficits in dementia due to AD depends on disease progression, as language impairment is different at each stage (e.g., Muslant & Zubenko, 1994). Conversely, in PPA, language changes occur in the initial stages in the absence of non-linguistic impairments, potentially distinguishing it from dementia due to AD. However, while nfvPPA and lvPPA can be easily differentiated from dementia due to AD, particularly in the early stages before more advanced cognitive decline, svPPA has been more difficult to differentiate because semantic memory is central to both cognition and language processing. Thus, reduced access to semantic information can interrupt language production, comprehension, reading, writing, and object recognition (Hodges & Graham, 2001). This disruption of semantic access can result in similarly-presenting language deficits for svPPA and dementia due to AD.

To crucially differentiate these dementia subtypes, clinicians must examine the broader scope of linguistic deficits and other cognitive symptoms, such as the presence of reasoning or visuospatial impairment in dementia due to AD. For example, in dementia due to AD, hippocampal atrophy usually spares autobiographical memory for the individual's early life compared with more recent events (e.g., Hodges & Graham, 2001), while patients with svPPA show the opposite pattern (Snowden et al., 1996). While separate memory stores for autobiographical and semantic memory is unlikely, Hodges and Graham (2001) suggest that autobiographical memory may be dependent, to an extent, on functioning semantic memory, while autobiographical memory loss does not necessarily directly impact semantic access.

Although sophisticated diagnostic criteria for dementia due to AD and for PPA have been developed, the diagnostic paradigms in clinical practice today continue to assess clinical features and symptoms (i.e., cognition, behavior, and function) and primarily use cognitive testing for diagnosis and staging (Hampel et al., 2022). Moreover, many patients with dementia due to AD and with PPA are not diagnosed in a timely manner (Barnett et al., 2014). With new treatments available for AD, the diagnostic pathway needs to change for dementia due to AD and potentially PPA too, consistently incorporating biomarkers to better support screening, diagnosis, and treatment (Hampel et al., 2022).

Neuropathology, Imaging, and Fluid Biomarker Measures

Alzheimer's Disease

The classic neuropathological changes associated with AD are neuritic plaques and neurofibrillary tangles identified by Alois Alzheimer in 1906 in a case with pre-senile dementia (Maurer et al., 1997) and by Oskar Fisher in a case of senile dementia (Goedert, 2009). Beta amyloid (Aβ) was identified as the component of neuritic plaques and cerebral amyloid angiopathy (CAA) (Glenner & Wong, 1984) and tau, a microtubule binding protein, was identified as the major component of neurofibrillary tangles (Cleveland et al., 1977). Six isoforms of tau have been identified and the intracellular neurofibrillary tangles in AD pathology are composed of equal ratios of 3R and 4R tau (Irwin, 2016). Until recently, AD was diagnosed based on clinical presentation, categorized as possible or probable, with histopathological evidence from biopsy or autopsy required for definite AD (McKhann et al., 1984). With the advancement of biomarkers (e.g., imaging and fluid), pathophysiological features of AD can now be detected in-vivo, becoming part of the continually evolving diagnostic recommendations.

Structural imaging (CT or MRI) plays an important role in the differential diagnosis of AD and is recommended to rule out structural explanations for cognitive impairment (e.g., tumor, stroke) (Hampel et al., 2022). With AD, there is extensive atrophy throughout the cortex. Patterns of cortical atrophy track disease progression and are associated with white matter track changes (Pini et al., 2016). MRI hippocampal formation volumetric measurements significantly correlate with neurons from postmortem AD brains, suggesting the anatomical validity of this measurement (Bobinski et al., 1999). Furthermore, hippocampal formation (entorhinal cortex and hippocampus) becomes atrophic in Mild Cognitive Impairment (MCI), which correlates to memory functioning and thus may be an early indication of AD pathology (de Leon et al., 1997).

Positron emission tomography (PET) with radioligands (i.e., Aβ and tau) provide the visualization of AD pathology in-vivo. Fluorodeoxyglucose (FDG) PET measures cerebral metabolic rate of glucose and has been used clinically to differentiate dementia due to AD from Lewy body dementia and FTLD (Minoshima et al., 2021). Cerebral spinal fluid (CSF) obtained through lumbar puncture also measures AD pathology (Zetterberg & Blennow, 2021). Both PET and CSF are important for an accurate diagnosis, however their clinical application is limited due to availability, cost, and perceived invasiveness. Blood-based biomarkers (BBBm) using plasma may provide a more accessible assessment of AD pathology. BBBm show high correlations with amyloid and tau PET and CSF (Leuzy et al., 2022).

In 2011, the National Institute on Aging (NIA) along with the Alzheimer's Association published diagnostic/research criteria for three phases of the disease: preclinical stage of AD (Sperling et al., 2011), (MCI) due to AD (Albert et al., 2011), and dementia due to AD (McKhann et al., 2011). These criteria incorporated biomarkers and formalized different stages of disease in the diagnostic criteria (Jack et al., 2011). An updated recommendation defines and stages AD as a continuum of six stages (Jack et al., 2018). Furthermore, the International Working Group purports that a diagnosis of dementia due to AD should include positive biomarkers (Aβ and tau) and AD clinical phenotypes (Dubois et al., 2021). Indeed, AD pathology has been shown to be present up to 20 years before clinical symptom presentation (e.g., Aizenstein et al., 2008; Quiroz et al., 2018). Key biomarkers are summarized in Tables 7.1 and 7.2.

Primary Progressive Aphasia

In PPA there is no clearly defined lesion, and, unlike in AD, there is no diffuse cortical atrophy. Rather, there is progressive atrophy, initially to a confined region of the brain (Gorno-Tempini et al., 2011). Diagnosis of PPA must incorporate the clinical features described above as well as imaging showing volume loss or hypoperfusion in specific cortical regions, with atrophy being mostly confined to the left hemisphere for nfvPPA and lvPPA (e.g., Gorno-Tempini et al., 2011). SvPPA has bilateral atrophy, which in most cases is more pronounced in the left than the right hemisphere (Mion et al., 2010; Rogalski et al., 2011). Each variant has a typical epicenter, and with disease progression atrophy can spread to other regions, resulting in extensive degeneration, yet the course of this degeneration may depend on the specific neuropathology.

PPA is associated with three classes of pathology: tau-positive immunoreactivity, AD pathology, and FTLD that is negative for tau immunoreactivity but positive for ubiquitin immunoreactivity (FTLD-U), mostly with TDP-43 (e.g., Grossman, 2010). LvPPA has been linked to AD pathology (the most common), FTLD, and Lewy body dementia. PET studies in lvPPA confirm amyloid deposition in 90% of cases, similar to dementia due to AD (e.g., Bergeron et al., 2018). SvPPA has been linked to FTLD-TDP-43 type C disorder (e.g., Tee & Gorno-Tempini, 2019), with typically negative amyloid deposition and tau, particularly for individuals under the age of 60 (Bergeron et al., 2018).

TABLE 7.1 Imaging biomarkers for Alzheimer's disease

	Imaging Biomarkers: Positron Emission Tomography (PET)		
Radiotracer	Neuraceq[1] Amyvid[2] Vizamyl[3]	Tauvid[4]	[^{18}F] fluorodeoxyglucose (FDG)[5]
Research Compounds	[^{11}C] Pittsburgh compound B (PIB)[6] [^{18}F]-NAV4694[7]	[^{18}F]MK6240 [^{18}F] RO948 [^{18}F]PI2620 [^{18}F]JNJ067[8]	
Use	Estimate Aβ- neuritic plaque density in adult patients with cognitive impairment who are being evaluated for AD and other causes of cognitive decline[1,2,3]	Estimate density and distribution of aggregated tau neurofibrillary tangles in adult with cognitive impairment who are being evaluated for AD[4]	Measures cerebral metabolic rate of glucose; marker of neuronal activity, neuronal injury and synaptic function[5]
Hallmark of AD	Moderate to frequent Aβ neuritic plaques; - noted in AD, other neurologic conditions and with normal cognition[1,2,3]	Increased neocortical activity in posterolateral temporal (PLT), occipital, or parietal/precuneus region(s), + or - frontal activity[4]	Decreased FDG uptake in parieto-temporal, frontal and posterior cingulate reductions in AD[5]

Inconsistent with AD	Sparse to no neuritic plaques - inconsistent with the neuropathological diagnosis of AD[1,2,3]	No increased neocortical activity, or increased neocortical activity isolated to the mesial temporal, anterolateral temporal, and/or frontal regions[4]	Normal glucose metabolism; Decreased FDG uptake in occipital and primary visual cortex in DLB; Decreased FDG uptake in anterior temporal lobe bilaterally, left temporal lobe more severe than right in svPPA[5]

Note: [1]Neuraceq (florbetaben) 2014; [2]Amyvid (florbetapir) 2013; [3]Vizamyl (flutemetamol) 2013; [4]Tauvid (flortaucipir) 2020; [5]Minoshima et al., 2021; [6]Klunk et al. 2004; [7]Rowe et al. 2016; [8]Yap et al. 2021. Aβ = beta amyloid, DLB = dementia with Lewy bodies, svPPA = semantic variant of primary progressive aphasia.

TABLE 7.2 Fluid biomarkers for Alzheimer's disease

Fluid Biomarkers: Cerebral Spinal Fluid (CSF) and Blood Based (BBBm) Biomarkers [9,10,11]		
Assays	Aβ40 Aβ42 (brain amyloid deposition) Aβ42/Aβ40 (ratio compensates for individual variation)	p-tau (tau pathology) p-tau 181 (axonal loss & tau pathology) p-tau 217 (tau pathology) p-tau 231 (early marker of tau pathology) t-tau (neurodegeneration)
Changes in AD	Aβ40 (no change) Aβ42 (low levels) Aβ42/Aβ40 (low ratio)	p-tau (high levels) p-tau 181 (high levels) p-tau 217 (high levels) p-tau 231 (high levels) t-tau (high levels)

Note: [9]Blennow, 2017; [10]Zetterberg and Blennow, 2021; [11]Leuzy et al., 2022. Aβ = beta amyloid, p-tau – phosphorylated tau, t-tau – total tau.

FTLD-Tau is the most common cause of nfvPPA (e.g., Josephs et al., 2006; Spinelli et al., 2017), although nfvPPA has also been linked to AD pathology (e.g., Grossman, 2010), FTLD-U (e.g., Josephs et al., 2006), FTLD-TDP (e.g., Bergeron et al., 2018), dementia with Pick bodies, and corticobulbar degeneration (e.g., Josephs et al., 2006). The importance of identifying the underlying neuropathology in PPA is critical; the uncertainty can have serious implications in the treatment of PPA subtypes, particularly when developing pharmacological intervention. A summary of the neuropathology, brain regions impacted, and resulting language impairments can be found in Table 7.3.

Treatment

Treatment in Dementia due to AD

Historically, the pharmacological treatment options for AD mostly addressed the symptoms using cholinergic and glutamatergic modulators. Acetylcholine is a neurotransmitter that is important for cognition (Hasselmo, 2006). Cholinergic neurons deteriorate in AD and reduce acetylcholine synthesis (Bartus et al., 1982). Acetylcholinesterase inhibitors (AChEIs) slow the breakdown of acetylcholine and may increase its

TABLE 7.3 Neuropathy, impacted brain regions, and resulting language impairments in PPA

PPA Type	*lvPPA*	*svPPA*	*nfvPPA*
Common Pathology	Aβ and tau deposition	FTLD-TDP-43 type C, negative for Aβ and tau deposition	FTLD-Tau
Other Pathologies	FTLD, DLB		Aβ and tau, FTLD-U, FTLD-TDP, corticobulbar degeneration, dementia with Pick bodies
Brain areas initially affected	Left superior and midtemporal gyrus, angular gyrus, and midfrontal gyrus	Anterior temporal lobe	Left posterior fronto-insular region
Brain areas affected later	Diffuse atrophy	Posterior temporal and orbital regions	Varied frontal regions
Resulting language impairments	Initial phonological errors; later global aphasia with episodic memory impairment	Semantic deficits with periods of fluency; later pronounced behavioral and motor symptoms	Agrammatic language production, effortful or halting speech, mild auditory comprehension deficits; later becoming minimally verbal

Note. FTLD = fronto-temporal lobe dementia; DLB = dementia with Lewy bodies; TDP = TAR DNA-binding protein; U = ubiquitin-positive inclusions; Aβ = beta amyloid.

availability and compensate for cholinergic neuronal loss (Hasselmo, 2006). However, to date, AChEIs including donepezil (Aricept), rivastigmine (Exelon) and galantamine (Razadyne), show limited efficacy and dose-dependent side-effects, especially with higher doses (Sharma, 2019). Memantine (Namenda), a treatment for moderate to severe dementia due to AD, received U.S. Food and Drug Administration (FDA) approval in 2003. It modulates glutamate (an excitatory neurotransmitter important in memory and learning) at the N-methyl-D-aspartate (NMDA) receptor (Reisberg et al., 2003), thus reducing the excitotoxic effects which can cause neuronal damage (Reisberg et al., 2003). Memantine and donepezil in combination (Namzaric) was FDA approved for moderate to severe dementia due to AD in 2014; it may improve memory, awareness, and activities of daily living.

A new wave of pharmacological compounds targeting AD pathophysiological hallmarks are under development, including passive immunotherapy antibodies targeting different forms of Aβ, tau, and neuroinflammation. Aβ immunotherapy treatments such as Aduhelm (2022) and Leqembi (2023) aim to reduce Aβ plaque and thus maintain cognition and function in both mild dementia and MCI, potentially allowing the individual to function at a higher level for longer.

Other treatments, specifically non-pharmacological interventions, have shown promise in preventing or delaying cognitive decline. Physical exercise has been shown to delay cognitive decline in people with dementia due to AD (Ribarič, 2022) while combining cognitive training with physical exercise may even promote small improvements to certain cognitive functions (Rodakowski et al., 2015). Programs such as the FINGER study (Finnish Geriatric Intervention Study to Prevent Cognitive Impairment and Disability) and MAKS (a German acronym for Motor, Activities of daily living, Cognitive, Social) use multidomain approaches to prevent or delay cognitive decline. For example, FINGER provides nutritional guidance, exercise, cognitive training, and social activities (Kivipelto et al., 2006). It also manages metabolic and vascular risk factors associated with an increased risk of AD (Etgen et al., 2011). MAKS targets social interaction, sensorimotor activities, cognitive activation, and activation of activities of daily living in people with dementia who visit daycare centers or live in nursing homes (Straubmeier et al., 2017).

Treatment in PPA

Pharmacological treatments shown to be effective with dementia due to AD have also been explored for their potential in mitigating symptoms of PPA, for example dopamine receptor agonists such as Bromocriptine (Reed et al.,

2004), glutamate modulators such as memantine (Johnson et al., 2010), and AChEIs such as galantamine and rivastigmine (Birks et al., 2006). Little effect on PPA symptoms have been observed in these studies, and no improvement to cognitive deficits has been observed (e.g., Mouton et al., 2022; Shigaeff et al., 2017). Furthermore, cholinesterase inhibitors are not recommended for FTLD pathology as they have been suspected to worsen the outcomes for FTLD (Kerchner et al., 2011). As this field continues to develop, it will be critical to identify the specific neuropathology underlying the clinical symptoms of PPA to determine whether treatment is likely to be potentially beneficial or detrimental (Grossman, 2010).

Evidence for the efficacy of targeted speech and language treatment has been well-documented for PPA, dependent on the subtype and underlying neuropathology. For example, nfvPPA typically presents with agrammatism, thus structured treatments such as script training have had positive effects on these patients (Henry et al., 2013, 2018). In all PPA subtypes, treatments targeting lexical retrieval have been most frequently studied (Croot, 2018). However, understanding variant-specific deficits can maximize efficacy of treatment, such as building on the phonological strengths of individuals with svPPA (Tee & Gorno-Tempini, 2019). The basis for planning treatment will depend on the severity and progression of the disease, influencing the decision to provide restorative or prophylactic therapy. Some treatments have been shown to be effective regardless of the individual differences in variants, such as verb-based treatments, because verbs will eventually be compromised in all variants (Meyer et al., 2020). Other treatment interventions and modalities have also been shown to have a positive effect on all PPA variants, such as transcranial direct current stimulation (tDCS; see also chapter 10, this volume), when coupled with targeted language therapies (Cotelli et al., 2014; Tsapkini et al., 2018).

Conclusion and Future Directions

While much is known about the clinical presentations and neurodegeneration in dementia due to AD and in PPA, the use of imaging and blood-based tests to examine the underlying neuropathology is an emerging diagnostic tool for these conditions that can inform both pharmacological and non-pharmacological treatments. Early and accurate diagnosis is the best course for a successful treatment plan, yet how to determine the most accurate course of the neurodegeneration in both dementia due to AD and in PPA has evaded researchers and healthcare providers until recently. Using specialized imaging techniques or fluid-based testing may be the key to obtaining the most accurate diagnosis and will guide pharmacological intervention to potentially slow the progression of dementia due to AD and of PPA. Use of clinical features, neuroimaging, and biomarkers continues to be crucial to understand how an individual may change cognitively, linguistically, or functionally with dementia due to AD or with PPA, as well as to understand the treatment types that will be most beneficial. As research continues to move forward in the development of successful treatments, the ability to treat dementia due to AD and to treat PPA long-term is within reach.

Note

1 While we recognize the heterogeneity of nfvPPA encompassing both language and motor speech symptoms, this chapter focuses on the nonfluent agrammatic variant and associated language deficits.

References

Aduhelm [Prescribing Information]. (2022). Cambridge, (MA). Biogen Inc.

Aizenstein, H. J., Nebes, R. D., Saxton, J. A., Price, J. C., Mathis, C. A., Tsopelas, N. D., ... & Klunk, W. E. (2008). Frequent amyloid deposition without significant cognitive impairment among the elderly. *Archives of Neurology*, *65*(11), 1509–1517.

Albert, M. S., DeKosky, S. T., Dickson, D., Dubois, B., Feldman, H. H., Fox, N. C., ... & Phelps, C. H. (2011). The diagnosis of mild cognitive impairment due to Alzheimer's disease: Recommendations from the National Institute on Aging-Alzheimer's Association workgroups on diagnostic guidelines for Alzheimer's disease. *Alzheimer's and Dementia*, 7(3), 270–279.

American Psychiatric Association. (2013). *Diagnostic and Statistical Manual of Mental Disorders, Fifth Edition (DSM-5)*. American Psychiatric Association.

Amyvid (florbetapir) [Prescribing Information]. (2013). Indianapolis, (IN): Eli Lilly and Co.

Barnett, J. H., Lewis, L., Blackwell, A. D., & Taylor, M. (2014). Early intervention in Alzheimer's disease: A health economic study of the effects of diagnostic timing. *BMC Neurology*, *14*(1), 1–9.

Bartus, R. T., Dean III, R. L., Beer, B., & Lippa, A. S. (1982). The cholinergic hypothesis of geriatric memory dysfunction. *Science*, *217*(4558), 408–414.

Bergeron, D., Gorno-Tempini, M. L., Rabinovici, G. D., Santos-Santos, M. A., Seeley, W., Miller, B. L., ... & Ossenkoppele, R. (2018). Prevalence of amyloid-β pathology in distinct variants of primary progressive aphasia. *Annals of Neurology*, *84*(5), 729–740.

Birks, J. & Craig, D. (2006). Galantamine for vascular cognitive impairment. *Cochrane Database of Systematic Reviews*, (1).

Blennow, K. (2017). A review of fluid biomarkers for Alzheimer's disease: Moving from CSF to blood. *Neurology and Therapy*, 6, 15–24.

Bobinski, M., De Leon, M. J., Wegiel, J., Desanti, S., Convit, A., Saint Louis, L. A., ... & Wisniewski, H. M. (1999). The histological validation of postmortem magnetic resonance imaging-determined hippocampal volume in Alzheimer's disease. *Neuroscience*, *95*(3), 721–725.

Cleveland, D. W., Hwo, S. Y., & Kirschner, M. W. (1977). Purification of tau, a microtubule-associated protein that induces assembly of microtubules from purified tubulin. *Journal of Molecular Biology*, *116*(2), 207–225.
Cotelli, M., Manenti, R., Brambilla, M., Petesi, M., Rosini, S., Ferrari, C., ... & Miniussi, C. (2014). Anodal tDCS during face-name associations memory training in Alzheimer's patients. *Frontiers in Aging Neuroscience*, 6, 38.
Croot, K. (2018). Treatment for lexical retrieval impairments in primary progressive aphasia: A research update with implications for clinical practice. In *Seminars in Speech and Language* (Vol. 39, No. 03, pp. 242–256). Thieme Medical Publishers.
de Leon, M. J., Convit, A., DeSanti, S., Bobinski, M., George, A. E., Wisniewski, H. M., ... & Saint Louis, L. A. (1997). Contribution of structural neuroimaging to the early diagnosis of Alzheimer's disease. *International Psychogeriatrics*, *9*(S1), 183–190.
Dubois, B., Villain, N., Frisoni, G. B., Rabinovici, G. D., Sabbagh, M., Cappa, S., ... & Feldman, H. H. (2021). Clinical diagnosis of Alzheimer's disease: Recommendations of the International Working Group. *The Lancet Neurology*, *20*(6), 484–49s6.
Etgen, T., Sander, D., Bickel, H., & Förstl, H. (2011). Mild cognitive impairment and dementia: The importance of modifiable risk factors. *Deutsches Ärzteblatt International*, *108*(44), 743.
Glenner, G. G. & Wong, C. W. (1984). Alzheimer's disease: Initial report of the purification and characterization of a novel cerebrovascular amyloid protein. *Biochemical and Biophysical Research Communications*, *120*(3), 885–890.
Goedert, M. (2009). Oskar Fischer and the study of dementia. *Brain*, *132*(4), 1102–1111.
Gorno-Tempini, M. L., Hillis, A. E., Weintraub, S., Kertesz, A., Mendez, M., Cappa, S. F., ... & Grossman, M. (2011). Classification of primary progressive aphasia and its variants. *Neurology*, *76*(11), 1006–1014.
Grossman, M. (2010). Primary progressive aphasia: clinicopathological correlations. *Nature Reviews Neurology*, *6*(2), 88–97.
Hampel, H., Au, R., Mattke, S., van der Flier, W. J., Aisen P., Apostolova, L., ... & Cummings, J. (2022). Designing the next-generation clinical care pathway for Alzheimer's disease. *Nature Aging*, *2*, 692–703.
Hasselmo, M. E. (2006). The role of acetylcholine in learning and memory. *Current Opinion in Neurobiology*, *16*(6), 710–715.
Henry, M. L., Meese, M. V., Truong, S., Babiak, M. C., Miller, B. L., & Gorno-Tempini, M. L. (2013). Treatment for apraxia of speech in nonfluent variant primary progressive aphasia. *Behavioral Neurology*, *26*(1-2), 77–88.
Henry, M. L., Hubbard, H. I., Grasso, S. M., Mandelli, M. L., Wilson, S. M., Sathishkumar, M. T., ... & Gorno-Tempini, M. L. (2018). Retraining speech production and fluency in non-fluent/agrammatic primary progressive aphasia. *Brain*, *141*(6), 1799–1814.
Hodges, J. R. & Graham, K. S. (2001). Episodic memory: Insights from semantic dementia. *Philosophical Transactions of the Royal Society of London. Series B: Biological Sciences*, *356*(1413), 1423–1434.
Irwin, D. J. (2016). Tauopathies as clinicopathological entities. *Parkinsonism and Related Disorders*, *22*, S29–S33.

Jack Jr, C. R., Albert, M. S., Knopman, D. S., McKhann, G. M., Sperling, R. A., Carrillo, M. C., ... & Phelps, C. H. (2011). Introduction to the recommendations from the National Institute on Aging-Alzheimer's Association workgroups on diagnostic guidelines for Alzheimer's disease. *Alzheimer's and Dementia*, 7(3), 257–262.

Jack Jr, C. R., Bennett, D. A., Blennow, K., Carrillo, M. C., Dunn, B., Haeberlein, S. B., ... & Silverberg, N. (2018). NIA-AA research framework: Toward a biological definition of Alzheimer's disease. *Alzheimer's and Dementia*, *14*(4), 535–562.

Johnson, N. A., Rademaker, A., Weintraub, S., Gitelman, D., Wienecke, C., & Mesulam, M. (2010). Pilot trial of memantine in primary progressive aphasia. *Alzheimer Disease and Associated Disorders*, *24*(3), 308.

Josephs, K. A., Duffy, J. R., Strand, E. A., Whitwell, J. L., Layton, K. F., Parisi, J. E., ... & Petersen, R. C. (2006). Clinicopathological and imaging correlates of progressive aphasia and apraxia of speech. *Brain*, *129*(6), 1385–1398.

Kempler, D. & Goral, M. (2008). Language and dementia: Neuropsychological aspects. *Annual Review of Applied Linguistics*, *28*, 73–90.

Kerchner, G. A., Tartaglia, M. C., & Boxer, A. L. (2011). Abhorring the vacuum: Use of Alzheimer's disease medications in frontotemporal dementia. *Expert Review of Neurotherapeutics*, *11*(5), 709–717.

Kivipelto, M., Ngandu, T., Laatikainen, T., Winblad, B., Soininen, H., & Tuomilehto, J. (2006). Risk score for the prediction of dementia risk in 20 years among middle aged people: A longitudinal, population-based study. *The Lancet Neurology*, *5*(9), 735–741.

Klunk, W. E., Engler, H., Nordberg, A., Wang, Y., Blomqvist, G., Holt, D. P., ... & Långström, B. (2004). Imaging brain amyloid in Alzheimer's disease with Pittsburgh Compound-B. *Annals of Neurology*, *55*(3), 306–319.

Kumar A., Sidhu J., Goyal A., & Tsao J. W. (2021). *Alzheimer Disease*. StatPearls: StatPearls Publishing.

Leqembi (lecanemab) [Prescribing Information]. (2023). Nutley, NJ. Eisai Inc.

Leuzy, A., Mattsson-Carlgren, N., Palmqvist, S., Janelidze, S., Dage, J. L., & Hansson, O. (2022). Blood-based biomarkers for Alzheimer's disease. *EMBO Molecular Medicine*, *14*(1), e14408.

Maurer, K., Volk, S., & Gerbaldo, H. (1997). Auguste D and Alzheimer's disease. *The Lancet*, *349*(9064), 1546–1549.

McKhann, G., Drachman, D., Folstein, M., Katzman, R., Price, D., & Stadlan, E. M. (1984). Clinical diagnosis of Alzheimer's disease: Report of the NINCDS-ADRDA Work Group under the auspices of Department of Health and Human Services Task Force on Alzheimer's Disease. *Neurology*, *34*(7), 939–939.

McKhann, G. M., Knopman, D. S., Chertkow, H., Hyman, B. T., Jack Jr, C. R., Kawas, C. H., ... & Phelps, C. H. (2011). The diagnosis of dementia due to Alzheimer's disease: Recommendations from the National Institute on Aging-Alzheimer's Association workgroups on diagnostic guidelines for Alzheimer's disease. *Alzheimer's and Dementia*, 7(3), 263–269.

Mesulam, M. M., Rogalski, E. J., Wieneke, C., Hurley, R. S., Geula, C., Bigio, E. H., ... & Weintraub, S. (2014). Primary progressive aphasia and the evolving neurology of the language network. *Nature Reviews Neurology*, *10*(10), 554–569.

Meyer, A. M., Snider, S. F., McGowan, S. A., Tippett, D. C., Hillis, A. E., & Friedman, R. B. (2020). Grammatical ability predicts relative action naming impairment in primary progressive aphasia. *Aphasiology*, *34*(6), 664–674.

Minoshima, S., Mosci, K., Cross, D., & Thientunyakit, T. (2021). Brain [F-18] FDG PET for clinical dementia workup: Differential diagnosis of Alzheimer's disease and other types of dementing disorders. In *Seminars in Nuclear Medicine*, *51*(3), 230–240.

Mion, M., Patterson, K., Acosta-Cabronero, J., Pengas, G., Izquierdo-Garcia, D., Hong, Y. T., ... & Nestor, P. J. (2010). What the left and right anterior fusiform gyri tell us about semantic memory. *Brain*, *133*(11), 3256–3268.

Mouton, A., Plonka, A., Fabre, R., Tran, T. M., Robert, P., Macoir, J., ... & Gros, A. (2022). The course of primary progressive aphasia diagnosis: a cross-sectional study. *Alzheimer's Research and Therapy*, *14*(1), 1–10.

Muslant, B., & Zubenko, G. S. (1994). Clinical, neuropathologic, and neurochemical correlates of depression and psychosis in primary dementia. In V. O. B. Emery & T. E. Oxman (Eds.), *Dementia: Presentations, differential diagnosis, and nosology* (pp. 336–352). Johns Hopkins.

Neuraceq (florbetaben) [Prescribing Information]. (2014). Matran, Switzerland: Life Molecular Imaging.

Pini, L., Pievani, M., Bocchetta, M., Altomare, D., Bosco, P., Cavedo, E., ... & Frisoni, G. B. (2016). Brain atrophy in Alzheimer's disease and aging. *Ageing Research Reviews*, *30*, 25–48.

Quiroz, Y. T., Sperling, R. A., Norton, D. J., Baena, A., Arboleda-Velasquez, J. F., Cosio, D., ... & Johnson, K. A. (2018). Association between amyloid and tau accumulation in young adults with autosomal dominant Alzheimer disease. *JAMA Neurology*, *75*(5), 548–556.

Reed, D. A., Johnson, N. A., Thompson, C., Weintraub, S., & Mesulam, M. M. (2004). A clinical trial of bromocriptine for treatment of primary progressive aphasia. *Annals of Neurology: Official Journal of the American Neurological Association and the Child Neurology Society*, *56*(5), 750–750.

Reisberg, B., Doody, R., Stöffler, A., Schmitt, F., Ferris, S., & Möbius, H. J. (2003). Memantine in moderate-to-severe Alzheimer's disease. *New England Journal of Medicine*, *348*(14), 1333–1341.

Ribarič, S. (2022). Physical exercise, a potential non-pharmacological intervention for attenuating neuroinflammation and cognitive decline in Alzheimer's disease patients. *International Journal of Molecular Sciences*, *23*(6), 3245.

Rodakowski, J., Saghafi, E., Butters, M. A., & Skidmore, E. R. (2015). Non-pharmacological interventions for adults with mild cognitive impairment and early stage dementia: An updated scoping review. *Molecular Aspects of Medicine*, *43*, 38–53.

Rogalski, E., Cobia, D., Harrison, T. M., Wieneke, C., Weintraub, S., & Mesulam, M. M. (2011). Progression of language decline and cortical atrophy in subtypes of primary progressive aphasia. *Neurology*, *76*(21), 1804–1810.

Rowe, C. C., Jones, G., Doré, V., Pejoska, S., Margison, L., Mulligan, R. S., ... & Villemagne, V. L. (2016). Standardized expression of 18F-NAV4694 and 11C-PiB β-amyloid PET results with the Centiloid scale. *Journal of Nuclear Medicine*, *57*(8), 1233–1237.

Schneider, J. A., Arvanitakis, Z., Leurgans, S. E., & Bennett, D. A. (2009). The neuropathology of probable Alzheimer disease and mild cognitive impairment. *Annals of Neurology: Official Journal of the American Neurological Association and the Child Neurology Society*, *66*(2), 200–208.

Sharma, K. (2019). Cholinesterase inhibitors as Alzheimer's therapeutics. *Molecular Medicine Reports*, *20*(2), 1479–1487.

Shigaeff, N., Amaro, E., Franco, F. G., Jacinto, A. F., Chiochetta, G., Cendoroglo, M. S., & Citero, V. A. (2017). Functional magnetic resonance imaging response as an early biomarker of cognitive decline in elderly patients with metabolic syndrome. *Archives of Gerontology and Geriatrics*, *73*, 1–7.

Snowden, J. S., Griffiths, H. L., & Neary, D. (1996). Semantic-episodic memory interactions in semantic dementia: Implications for retrograde memory function. *Cognitive Neuropsychology*, *13*(8), 1101–1139.

Sperling, R. A., Aisen, P. S., Beckett, L. A., Bennett, D. A., Craft, S., Fagan, A. M., ... & Phelps, C. H. (2011). Toward defining the preclinical stages of Alzheimer's disease: Recommendations from the National Institute on Aging-Alzheimer's Association workgroups on diagnostic guidelines for Alzheimer's disease. *Alzheimer's and Dementia*, *7*(3), 280–292.

Spinelli, E. G., Mandelli, M. L., Miller, Z. A., Santos-Santos, M. A., Wilson, S. M., Agosta, F., ... & Gorno-Tempini, M. L. (2017). Typical and atypical pathology in primary progressive aphasia variants. *Annals of Neurology*, *81*(3), 430–443.

Stopford, C. L., Snowden, J. S., Thompson, J. C., & Neary, D. (2008). Variability in cognitive presentation of Alzheimer's disease. *Cortex*, *44*, 185–195.

Straubmeier, M., Behrndt, E. M., Seidl, H., Özbe, D., Luttenberger, K., & Graessel, E. (2017). Non-pharmacological treatment in people with cognitive impairment: Results from the randomized controlled German day care study. *Deutsches Ärzteblatt International*, *114*(48), 815.

Tauvid (flortaucipir) [Prescribing Information]. (2020). Indianapolis, (IN): Eli Lilly and Co.

Tee, B. L. & Gorno-Tempini, M. L. (2019). Primary progressive aphasia: A model for neurodegenerative disease. *Current Opinion in Neurology*, *32*(2), 255.

Tsantali, E., Economidis, D., & Tsolaki, M. (2013). Could language deficits really differentiate Mild Cognitive Impairment (MCI) from mild Alzheimer's disease? *Archives of Gerontology and Geriatrics*, *57*(3), 263–270.

Tsapkini, K., Webster, K. T., Ficek, B. N., Desmond, J. E., Onyike, C. U., Rapp, B., ... & Hillis, A. E. (2018). Electrical brain stimulation in different variants of primary progressive aphasia: A randomized clinical trial. *Alzheimer's and Dementia: Translational Research and Clinical Interventions*, *4*, 461–472.

Vizamyl (flutemetamol) [Prescribing Information]. (2013). Arlington Heights, (IL): GE Healthcare, Medi-Physics Inc.

Yap, S. Y., Frias, B., Wren, M. C., Schöll, M., Fox, N. C., Årstad, E., ... & Sander, K. (2021). Discriminatory ability of next-generation tau PET tracers for Alzheimer's disease. *Brain*, *144*(8), 2284–2290.

Zetterberg, H. & Blennow, K. (2021). Moving fluid biomarkers for Alzheimer's disease from research tools to routine clinical diagnostics. *Molecular Neurodegeneration*, *16*(1), 1–7.

8

BEYOND NAMING

Narrative Production in L1 and L2 in Multilingual Individuals with and without Dementia

Monica I. Norvik, Ingeborg Sophie Ribu, Pernille Bonnevie Hansen, and Hanne Gram Simonsen

Introduction

Language deficits are central to several types of dementia. For instance, they are recognized as the first indications of Primary Progressive Aphasia (PPA) and also pronounced in dementia of the Alzheimer's type (DAT; sometimes referred to as dementia due to Alzheimer's disease), in addition to a decline in memory and other cognitive domains. In particular, problems with lexical retrieval are prominent symptoms in PPA (Gorno-Tempini et al., 2011), and in both earlier and later stages of DAT (Chen et al., 2001; Nicholas & Brookshire, 1995; Salmon et al., 1999). Such problems are also found in healthy aging, but to a lesser degree (Connor et al., 2004; Goral et al., 2007; Nicholas et al., 1985; Vogel-Eyny et al., 2016). A recurring question is what lies behind difficulties with word-retrieval: Are they an artifact of deficient semantic representations, or mainly an issue of lexical access? While this question is still under debate, evidence indicates that in the healthy aging population, the main problem lies in lexical access, while in persons with DAT or PPA, both lexical access and semantic deterioration may play a role (Slegers et al., 2018).

Many studies have found a "bilingual disadvantage" in lexical production: Multilingual individuals take longer time to retrieve words while naming than monolingual individuals, in particular for low-frequency words (Gollan et al., 2008, 2011; Ivanova & Costa, 2008). This has been attributed to the fact that although multilingual persons may have smaller vocabularies in each of their languages, their total vocabularies are generally larger, so that word search becomes less efficient, and more so in

DOI: 10.4324/9781003330318-10

their non-dominant, than in their dominant language (the so-called frequency-lag hypothesis; Gollan et al., 2008, 2011). In addition, assuming that all languages of a multilingual person are activated during production, in a larger vocabulary more words must be inhibited to reach the target word (Abutalebi & Green, 2007).

Cognitive abilities of multilingual individuals are affected by dementia in much the same way as in monolingual individuals, but their languages may be affected in different ways. In the literature, the first acquired language is usually found to be better preserved throughout the course of the disease (Ardila & Ramos, 2008; Mendez et al., 2004). The pattern of language preservation in dementia in multilingual persons is not clear but appears to depend on several factors relating to language balance, use, and dominance (see discussion in de Bot et al., 2020, p. 55). The fact that several languages are affected, often to different degrees, complicates the language assessment of multilingual persons with dementia (PWD). Such assessment is particularly challenging due to a lack of appropriate tools for persons who speak several languages (Norvik & Goral, 2021).

Word retrieval in dementia has commonly been assessed through standard language tests like word fluency and single-word naming tasks, but word-retrieval problems are found also in connected speech (Boschi et al., 2017; Kavé & Dassa, 2018; Kavé & Goral, 2016), and single-word tasks do not capture the full spectrum of either performance or difficulties in real communication in dementia. As evidenced in several recent review articles (Boschi et al., 2017; Mueller et al., 2018; Slegers et al., 2018), tasks eliciting connected speech (e.g., picture descriptions, story narrations, and structured interviews) are valuable tools for investigating language impairment in neurodegenerative diseases, facilitating differential diagnosis and revealing the multidimensional nature of linguistic and communicative breakdown in dementia.

Assessment of connected speech has several advantages. It makes it possible to detect the interaction between different processes – in addition to semantic storage and retrieval, which is also assessed in single-word tasks, connected-speech production puts a heavier load on working memory and executive functions (Mueller et al., 2018). Connected speech also offers the possibility of a broader analysis of a variety of linguistic domains (Ahmed et al., 2013) and although it is not as ecologically valid as natural conversations (Clarke et al., 2021), it is clearly more so than single-word naming. Finally, it is a relatively easy task for the participant (Mueller et al., 2018). The reviews above (Boschi et al., 2017; Mueller et al., 2018; Slegers et al., 2018) mention a range of communication difficulties found in persons with dementia through connected speech samples. The difficulties vary substantially between different dementia types.

Some examples, at different linguistic levels, are phonology (e.g., slower speech rate, hesitations, pauses), lexico-semantics (e.g., word-finding difficulties, increased use of pronouns, overuse of high-frequency words, "empty speech", low idea density), morphosyntactics (e.g., reduced syntactic complexity, shorter sentences), and discourse and pragmatics (e.g., compromised coherence, failure to mention key components) (Ahmed et al., 2013; Boschi et al., 2017).

The above-mentioned reviews only refer to studies of dementia in monolingual participants, as studies of multilingualism and dementia are scarce. A search for studies on assessment of connected speech in multilingual persons with dementia returned only three published papers; Kambanaros and Grohmann (2012), Lerman et al. (2023), and Lind et al. (2018). All are case studies of multilingual persons with PPA, assessed with several linguistic measures, including assessment of connected-speech production through the cartoon description from the Bilingual Aphasia Test (BAT; Paradis & Libben, 1987).[1] We only report the Bird story results here. In all three studies, the impairment initially observed aligned with pre-onset proficiency levels.

Kambanaros and Grohmann (2012) present a Greek-English-Czech trilingual person with PPA. Premorbidly, the participant (SG), a 60-year-old right-handed male, used all three languages on a regular basis, and had high proficiency in all three languages. SG (only assessed in Greek and English) was unable to produce sentences and connected speech in English, and his Greek sentence production was characterized as poor and limited to shorter sentences. The Bird story in Greek was scored in accordance with the BAT scoring system; amount of speech (nothing, very little, less than normal, normal), whether he produced a connected story or only described the cartoon picture-by-picture, and whether he finished the story in the end. According to these criteria, there is no indication of impairment in SG's performance.

However, when we inspected the transcript more thoroughly, it was evident that SG often used pronouns incorrectly (*I* instead of *he*) and showed an overuse of pronouns (failing to introduce the main characters). In addition, he demonstrated empty speech (e.g., "(…) they took him to the hospital *and they found it there*") and morpho-syntactic errors; both in possessive marking and in agreement ("I [1st person] went to find [correctly inflected for 3rd person] them"). With regard to which language was best preserved, Kambanaros and Grohmann (2012) concluded that SG showed a parallel deterioration, since they found similar impairment in comprehension and lexical access in Greek and English. But in the remaining linguistic areas differential deterioration was found, with worse performance in English than in Greek.

Lerman et al. (2023) is an intervention study with a 70-year-old English-Hebrew speaking female with lvPPA. The participant was dominant in English, her first language (L1), but had high proficiency in both languages in all modalities. Following treatment in Hebrew, her non-native language (L2) (VNeST; Edmonds et al., 2009), the Bird story results showed similar patterns of decline in the treated and untreated languages. This is in contrast to what was reported for word production, sentence production, and written narratives, where no decline in either language was found measured by the REHAB (Revised English-Hebrew Aphasia Battery; Lerman & Goral, unpublished).

Lind et al. (2018) present a case study of a 69-year-old bilingual English-Norwegian male with a PPA diagnosis (this person, JJ, is also included in the dataset for the present study). Premorbidly, JJ had higher proficiency and more frequent use of English, his L1, but was very proficient in Norwegian (L2) prior to his illness. His performance in oral language production was analyzed across three language contexts (confrontation naming, the Bird story, and conversation), at two different testing points (12 and 30 months post diagnosis). Overall, the connected-speech results were better for English (L1) than for Norwegian, conforming with JJ's premorbid proficiency and use of the languages, and indicating a better preserved L1 in line with much previous research. However, along the duration of the progression of the disease, the difference between the languages decreased. In the cartoon description, his performance was low both in L1 and L2, with relatively low lexical density, and he produced very few of the key components of the story.

Connected-speech production tasks (conversation/interview, story narrative, and picture description) are closely connected to functional communication skills, and more so than other standardized language tests (Boschi et al., 2017; Mueller et al., 2018; Slegers et al., 2018). While conversation/interview is most similar to everyday conversation, in that the speech is relatively spontaneous without predefined goals, and also that the person tested can lean on his/her conversation partner, the lack of set goals makes comparison across individuals more difficult. Semi-spontaneous tasks like picture descriptions and story narratives on the other hand, allow for comparison.

In this study, we therefore investigate differences in connected speech elicited through a cartoon description in L1 and L2 speakers of Norwegian with DAT and the logopenic subtype of PPA (lvPPA),[2] and neurologically healthy controls. Connected speech data are elicited through a cartoon description and analyzed by combining established lexical analysis with a new bottom-up analysis of the components that make up the story. Based on previous findings, we expected the L1 participants to exhibit fewer word-finding problems than the L2 participants. Furthermore, based mainly on the research on monolingual persons with dementia, we expected to find more word-finding problems, lower lexical density, and more empty speech among the participants with dementia than among the control participants. Finally, we expected failure to mention or fewer key components in their stories.

Methods

Participants

A total of 44 participants took part in the study. Twenty-six participants were L1 speakers of Norwegian, of whom eight had a clinical diagnosis of DAT and two PPA. Eighteen participants spoke Norwegian as an additional language. Five of them had a clinical diagnosis of DAT and one had lvPPA. An overview of the participant groups can be found in Table 8.1.

The L2 participants were all immigrants to Norway who had learned Norwegian in early adulthood (ranging between ages 17 and 33). All of them had used Norwegian in their daily lives, mainly in professional settings and reported that they were highly proficient. Their L1s varied, and among the persons with dementia there were two who spoke English as their L1, and one each whose L1 was an African Creole, Japanese, Swedish (Finland), and Urdu. Among the neurologically healthy participants, two spoke English as their L1, two Hindi, two Spanish and one each from the following languages: Dutch (Belgium), Greek, Japanese, Portuguese, Russian, and Swedish (Finland). All the L2 participants spoke at least one other language in addition to their L1 and Norwegian. Similarly, all the L1 Norwegian individuals reported that they were proficient in two to three additional languages.

The project was approved by the Norwegian Center for Research data (NSD), having met appropriate ethical standards (project number 809562).

TABLE 8.1 Participants

	Norwegian L1 (n=26)	*Norwegian L2 (n=18)*
Dementia (n=16)	10	6
Neurologically healthy (n=28)	16	12

Materials

The participants described the cartoon The participants described the Bird story cartoon from the BAT (Paradis & Libben, 1987), with the following instruction: "I am going to show you a set of six pictures. All together the pictures make a little story. Look at the pictures and tell me the story". The cartoon is constructed around two parallel storylines. The first revolves around the human characters, starting with the introduction of the man and the woman and the motivations for climbing the tree, and ending at the hospital with the man's leg in plaster. The second storyline concerns the birds, starting with the introduction of the mother bird and nest, and ending with her crying over her dead baby chicks (see Figure 8.1).

The L2 individuals with dementia described the story in all their languages, including Norwegian, whereas the neurologically healthy participants only described the story in Norwegian. In the current study, only the descriptions in L2 (Norwegian) were analyzed. The descriptions were recorded digitally and subsequently transcribed orthographically, including all words and attempts at words (i.e., false starts, interruptions, and neologisms) and dysfluencies, such as repetitions. Incomprehensible words, hesitations, and pauses were marked in the transcripts, but not included in the subsequent analysis.

Analyses

Lexical Analysis

We calculated the total number of words, including repetitions but excluding false starts and hesitations, for all participants. From the total word count, we extracted the total number of content words, including nouns, verbs (excluding auxiliaries and semantic light verbs), adjectives, and pronouns (all pronouns, e.g., personal, possessive, demonstrative pronouns, and repetitions). Lexical density was calculated by dividing the total number of content word tokens by the total number of words, following the description in Gordon (2008). Furthermore, we calculated pronoun ratio by dividing the number of pronouns by the total number of nouns and pronouns together (Kavé & Dassa, 2018). We also calculated percentages of nouns out of all words, since these have been found to differ significantly between persons with dementia and control participants in monolingual persons (Kavé & Dassa, 2018; Kavé & Goral, 2016). Differences between the groups were explored by visual inspection as well as Wilcoxon rank sum tests, which is well suited for comparing small samples with unequal numbers of participants.

FIGURE 8.1 The Bird story from the BAT (Paradis & Libben, 1987).[3]

Key Components

Rather than using predefined story units, key components were defined bottom-up by examining the content of the narratives from all participants. In each transcription, all central elements in the narrative were described (e.g., *the man is introduced; the woman is introduced*) and schematized into the ten key components (e.g., *the main characters are introduced*) included in the narratives by at least 70 % of the neurologically healthy L1 and L2 speakers of Norwegian.

Results

Lexical Analysis

The means and standard deviations of each lexical variable per group are presented in Table 8.2.

The PWD did not produce more words in their cartoon descriptions than the control participants: Among the participants with Norwegian as L2, the persons without dementia produced significantly more words in their narratives than did PWD ($W = 7$, $p = 0.007$); between the L1 individuals, there was no difference. The neurologically healthy individuals used more nouns than the PWD (L1 PWD vs. L1 control $W = 41.5$, $p = 0.04$; L2 PWD vs. L2 control $W = 5.5$, $p = 0.004$), but the difference in proportion of nouns to all words was only significant between the L2 individuals (L2 PWD vs. L2 control $W = 13$, $p = 0.03$). Furthermore, the L2 PWD produced significantly fewer verbs ($W = 4$, $p = 0.003$) and adjectives ($W = 10$, $p = 0.016$) than the L2 individuals without dementia.

In addition, when looking at differences between L1 and L2 individuals, there was a significant difference in the total number of verbs used between the L1 and L2 PWD ($W = 9$, $p = 0.02$), where the L1 speakers produced more verbs in their narratives than the L2 PWD did. There was no difference between L1 and L2 PWD or L1 and L2 control participants in any of the other word classes (see Figure 8.2).

There were no significant differences in the number of pronouns between any of the participant groups. However, while the L2 PWD had a higher pronoun ratio than the L2 persons without dementia ($W = 64$, $p = 0.006$), there were no significant differences between the L1 individuals with and without dementia in this respect. Furthermore, we found a lower lexical density among the PWD relative to control participants (L1 PWD vs. L1 control: $W = 39$, $p = 0.03$; L2 PWD vs. L2 control: $W = 4$, $p = 0.001$) (see Figure 8.3).

TABLE 8.2 Means and standard deviations of each lexical variable for each participant group

	Norwegian L2 Dementia (n=6) Mean (SD)	*Norwegian L1 Dementia (n=10) Mean (SD)*	*Norwegian L2 Control (n=12) Mean (SD)*	*Norwegian L1 Control (n=16) Mean (SD)*
Total number of words	85.5 (36.7)	135.1 (54.7)	171 (62.2)	153.2 (61.1)
Total number of nouns	11 (7.9)	16.8 (9.0)	30.8 (11.6)	25 (11.1)
Percentage of nouns to all words	12% (4%)	13% (4%)	18% (4%)	16% (3%)
Total number of verbs	8 (5.2)	15.4 (5)	21.4 (6.8)	18.6 (6.1)
Total number of adjectives	2.2 (1.7)	4.1 (3.9)	7.3 (4.4)	6.1 (3.2)
Total number of pronouns	13.3 (4.7)	17.7 (9.2)	15.8 (5.3)	15 (6.5)
Pronoun ratio	0.6 (0.1)	0.5 (0.1)	0.4 (0.1)	0.4 (0.1)
Lexical density	0.2 (0.1)	0.3 (0.1)	0.3 (0.1)	0.3 (0.1)

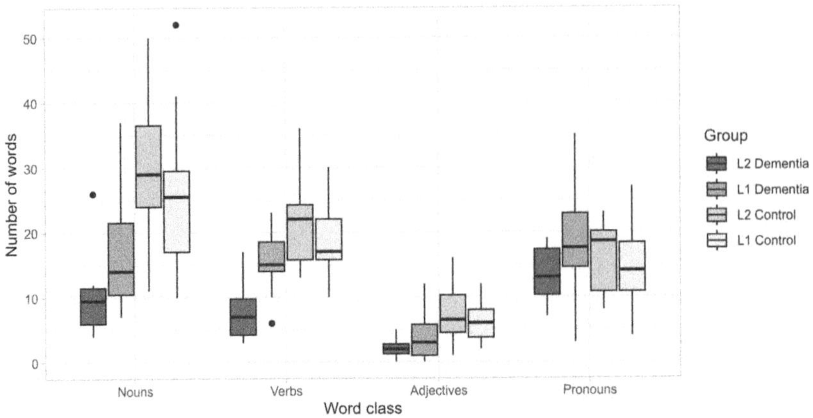

FIGURE 8.2 Number of words per word class.

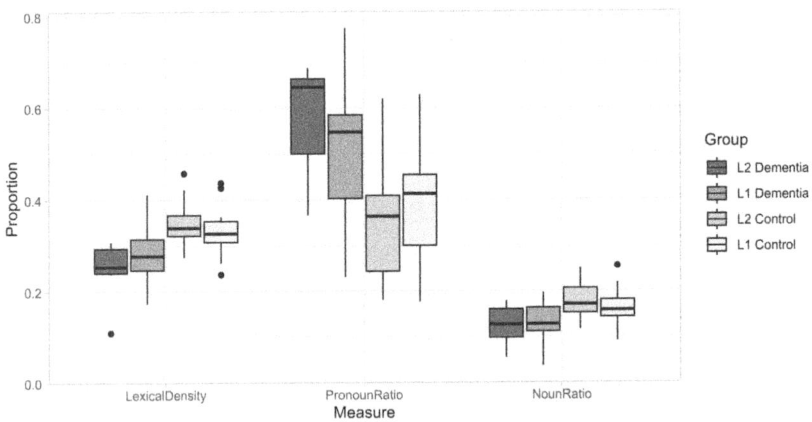

FIGURE 8.3 Lexical density, pronoun ratio, and noun ratio.

Key Components

As mentioned, our bottom-up analysis of the narrative production of the healthy controls resulted in ten key components.

Figure 8.4 shows the number of key components used by each group. There were significantly fewer key components among the PWD (L1 PWD vs. L1 control $W = 145$, $p<0.001$; L2 PWD vs. L2 control $W = 64.5$, $p = 0.008$), but no significant difference between L1 and L2 speakers, neither among PWD nor among control participants. These ten key components are shown in Table 8.3, listed with the percentage of participants within the four groups that included the component in their narrative.

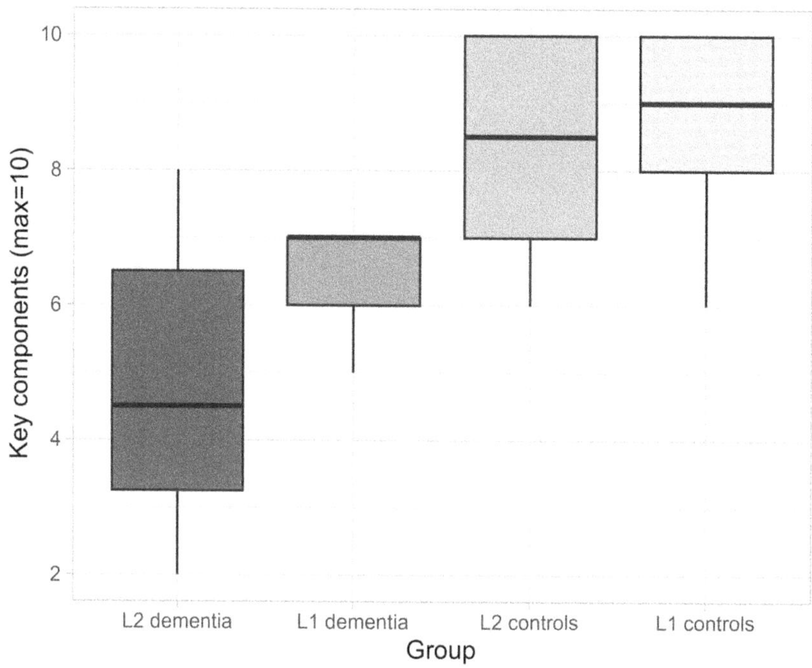

FIGURE 8.4 Number of key components within the four groups.

For some of the key components with low prevalence among the PWD, they tended to offer a less specific content component instead. For instance, only two of the six participants with dementia and Norwegian as an L2 mentioned the *man* falling, but two more included the event of *falling* without mentioning the man specifically. For instance, JJ says *det det kom ned begge to* "it it came down both of them". A closer look at Table 8.3 indicates that some of the L2 participants with dementia focus on the human storyline and pay less attention to the key components relating to the bird storyline in their narratives. Overall, there is no difference in the number of key components produced by the L1 and L2 PWD.

Discussion

A few studies have explored connected speech in multilingual individuals with dementia, three of which (Kambanaros & Grohmann, 2012; Lerman et al., 2023; Lind et al., 2018) used the cartoon description task from the BAT (Paradis & Libben, 1987). In this study we have used the same task,

TABLE 8.3 Ten key components and their prevalence in the four participant groups

	Key components	*Picture*	*Norwegian L2 Dementia (n=6)*	*Norwegian L1 Dementia (n=10)*	*Norwegian L2 Control (n=12)*	*Norwegian L1 Control (n=16)*
A	Man/woman intro	1	67 %	60 %	75 %	69 %
B	Birds/nest intro	1	67 %	80 %	100 %	88 %
C	Intention: get birds	1	50 %	20 %	75 %	88 %
D	Climb/disturb	2	50 %	80 %	100 %	88 %
E	Branch breaks	3	17 %	60 %	83 %	100 %
F	Man falling	3	33 %	70 %	83 %	75 %
G	Man hurt	4	83 %	80 %	83 %	100 %
H	Ambulance	5	67 %	90 %	100 %	100 %
I	Man in hospital	6	33 %	50 %	75 %	81 %
J	Birds hurt/dead	6	17 %	60 %	67 %	88%

the Bird story, to investigate connected speech in L1 and L2 users of Norwegian, with and without dementia.

There are many ways to analyze and score connected speech, as shown in the recent reviews mentioned previously (e.g., Boschi et al., 2017; Mueller et al., 2018; Slegers et al., 2018). Many of these analyses are time consuming and complex to perform in a clinical setting. We selected lexical variables that are relatively easily extracted from connected speech, and that have been shown to distinguish between persons with and without dementia (e.g., Kavé & Dassa, 2018; Kavé & Goral, 2016). Furthermore, we have explored an alternative scoring system to analyze the cartoon description task in the BAT. The BAT suggests scoring the narratives by the amount of speech (nothing, very little, less than normal, normal), whether the narrative makes up a connected story or if each picture is described individually, and finally whether the participant finishes the story (as performed by Kambanaros & Grohmann, 2012). In the alternative proposed in the current study, we investigate semantic and pragmatic aspects, that is, whether the participants identify specific key components of the Bird story.

Lexical Retrieval

Regarding lexical retrieval, based on results from picture naming we expected that both dementia (e.g., Chen et al., 2001; Kavé & Goral, 2016; Nicholas & Brookshire, 1995; Salmon et al., 1999) and being an L2 user of a language (e.g., Gollan et al., 2008, 2011; Ivanova & Costa, 2008) could make it more difficult to find relevant words for describing the cartoon. Furthermore, especially for the participants with dementia, we expected a higher pronoun ratio and lower lexical density than for the healthy persons.

For all lexical variables, the results indicate, as expected, that the combination of being an L2 user and having dementia amplifies the word finding difficulties; the PWD tested in L2 scored lower than the other participant groups on all lexical variables tested, with fewer nouns, verbs, and adjectives. In contrast to our predictions, the L2 control participants did not differ from the L1 control participants on any of the lexical measures. Possibly, the task of describing a story based on a cartoon is not complex enough to reveal any differences in connected speech production between L1 and highly proficient L2 speakers of a language. Looking at the length of the narratives, the participants with dementia did not produce more words than the healthy controls. This is in accordance with several previous studies (e.g., Kavé & Goral, 2016; Nicholas et al., 1985), but in contrast to Kavé and Dassa (2018).

Both L1 and L2 PWD had a significantly lower lexical density and a lower number of nouns than control participants, in line with earlier research (e.g., Kavé & Dassa, 2018; Kavé & Goral, 2016; Nicholas et al., 1985). In addition, all PWD had a higher pronoun ratio than control participants, but this was significant for L2 PWD only. Our findings show that PWD produce more empty speech, with less specific reference than healthy participants, indicative of word retrieval difficulty in connected speech, which can be explained by either an impairment in lexical access or deterioration of the semantic representations, or both.

Semantic and Pragmatic Aspects

Looking at the content of the narratives, based on the literature on dementia in monolingual individuals (Boschi et al., 2017; Mueller et al., 2018; Slegers et al., 2018), we expected the PWD to produce fewer and different key components than the control participants. Since producing a coherent narrative, including speech planning, and identifying the components that compose a story, is not solely dependent on the language domain, and more on domain-general cognitive abilities (Runnqvist et al., 2013), we expected less difference between L1 and L2 users, but rather an effect of dementia.

As predicted, our results show that the participants with dementia produce fewer of the key components in their stories than do the neurologically healthy individuals, whereas there was no difference between the L1 and L2 participants. While the dataset is not large enough for statistical analyses, Table 8.3 indicates group patterns in the individual key components, attributable to great individual variation between the L1 and L2 PWD and few participants in each group. For example, control participants and PWD appear to follow somewhat different paths in terms of the key components C (Intention: get birds), I (Man in hospital) and J (Birds hurt/dead). These patterns may be related to semantic and pragmatic aspects, such as the relative salience of the key components in each picture, the concreteness of the components and/or the narrator's identification of the two different storylines, the human storyline and the bird storyline.

The key components produced by healthy controls differ in salience in the cartoon pictures, in concreteness and in relation to the two storylines. These aspects influence cognitive abilities like attention, executive functions, and the ability to identify the characters' intentions and emotions: The more concrete and salient, the less demands on cognitive abilities. We note that Component G (Man hurt) is described by all participant groups equally. This component is salient in several pictures in the cartoon, and therefore receives much attention and focus throughout. Salience in each picture may also contribute to focus on one specific aspect taking away focus on other actions or events in the picture, for example that the man is hurt in picture 4, or the arrival of the ambulance in picture 5. We also find that the PWD are less likely to include key components that assign intention/emotion to the characters (Components C and J), and more likely to include key components that include concrete things or events (Components A, B, and H).

Finally, keeping track of two storylines in parallel is challenging for PWD. It is clear that what happens to the birds receives less focus, illustrated by the fact that the components related to the birds are often left out in the narratives produced by the PWD (Components C and J).

This type of analysis gives a more comprehensive overview of the differences in narrative descriptions in individuals with and without dementia, compared to the suggested analysis in the BAT. In line with earlier literature, PWD have a lower lexical density and higher pronoun ratio compared to healthy individuals, which cannot be found in naming tasks alone (e.g., Kavé & Dassa, 2018; Kavé & Goral, 2016; Nicholas et al., 1985). Furthermore, we see no difference between L1 and L2 PWD when it comes to semantic and pragmatic abilities, which indicates that these differences are not specific to language, but rather related to domain-general processes. We find that the PWD include fewer of the key components in their narratives compared to the control participants, specifically with regard to the components' salience, concreteness, and relation to the storylines.

Conclusion and Future Directions

The results confirm that connected speech production can reveal not only word-retrieval difficulties, but also difficulties beyond the single-word level. The BAT, and thus also the Bird story, is developed for assessing two or more languages in a comparable manner. Although developed for aphasia, it seems to be a suitable tool for other kinds of language impairments. Combining a lexical and a content analysis can provide a broader understanding of the multifaceted impairments associated with dementia. However, for the tool to be clinically relevant, there is a need to establish norms for typical performance. In addition, the tool needs a scoring system that is feasible in clinical practice. Ideally, one would aim for multilingual norms for multilingual people. This is, however, far from an easy task, and is not included in the BAT. This study is a starting point in this regard.

We have collected data from L1 and L2 users of Norwegian, with and without dementia, piloting a method for creating lexical and content norms for Norwegian for the Bird story narratives. The lexical variables used in studies of monolingual participants with dementia also seem to differentiate between L1 and L2 users of Norwegian, with and without dementia. Additionally, the analysis of the key components reveals problems that the original Bird story analysis does not detect. Establishing norms would require data from more L1 and L2 control participants. For clinical practice, we thus advocate for this combination of lexical, more form-based analysis and an analysis of content, based on the presented key components.

Acknowledgments

We thank all participants who contributed to this study. This work was supported by the Research Council of Norway [223265] and [250093].

Notes

1 The cartoon-description task in the BAT is referred to as the Nest story, the 6-picture story, and the Bird story in different studies (Kambanaros & Grohmann, 2012; Lerman et al., 2023; Lind et al., 2018). In this chapter, we refer to it as the Bird story.
2 We included lvPPA with the DAT group since their language characteristics and the underlying pathologies are similar (Gorno-Tempini et al., 2011).
3 Downloaded from: https://www.mcgill.ca/linguistics/files/linguistics/english_stimulus_book.pdf

References

Abutalebi, J. & Green, D. (2007). Bilingual language production: The neurocognition of language representation and control. *Journal of Neurolinguistics*, *20*(3), 242–275.

Ahmed, S., Haigh, A.-M. F., de Jager, C. A., & Garrard, P. (2013). Connected speech as a marker of disease progression in autopsy-proven Alzheimer's disease. *Brain*, *136*(12), 3727–3737. doi: 10.1093/brain/awt269

Ardila, A. & Ramos, E. (2008). Normal and abnormal aging in bilinguals. *Dementia and Neuropsychologia*, 2(4), 242–247. 10.1590/s1980-57642009dn20400002

Boschi, V., Catricalà, E., Consonni, M., Chesi, C., Moro, A., & Cappa, S. F. (2017). Connected speech in neurodegenerative language disorders: A review. *Frontiers in Psychology*, *8*. 10.3389/fpsyg.2017.00269

Chen, P., Ratcliff, G., Belle, S. H., Cauley, J. A., DeKosky, S. T., & Ganguli, M. (2001). Patterns of cognitive decline in presymptomatic Alzheimer Disease: A prospective community study. *Archives of General Psychiatry*, *58*(9), 853–858. 10.1001/archpsyc.58.9.853

Clarke, N., Barrick, T. R., & Garrard, P. (2021). A comparison of connected speech tasks for detecting early Alzheimer's Disease and Mild Cognitive Impairment using natural language processing and machine learning. *Frontiers in Computer Science*, *44*. 10.3389/fcomp.2021.634360

Connor, L. T., Spiro, A., III, Obler, L. K., & Albert, M. L. (2004). Change in object naming ability during adulthood. *The Journals of Gerontology: Series B*, *59*(5), P203–P209. 10.1093/geronb/59.5.P203

de Bot, K., Plejert, C., Simonsen, H. G., Fyndanis, V., Hansen, P., Norvik, M. I., Svendsen, B. A., & Svennevig, J. (2020). Multilingualism and ageing: An overview. *Brill Research Perspectives in Multilingualism and Second Language Acquisition*, *1*(4), 1–98. 10.1163/9789004445802

Edmonds, L. A., Nadeau, S. E., & Kiran, S., et al. (2009). Effect of verb network strengthening treatment (VNeST) on lexical retrieval of content words in sentences in persons with aphasia. *Aphasiology*, *23*(3), 402–424. 10.1080/02687030802291339

Gollan, T. H., Montoya, R. I., Cera, C., & Sandoval, T. C. (2008). More use almost always means a smaller frequency effect: Aging, bilingualism, and the weaker links hypothesis. *Journal of Memory and Language*, *58*(3), 787–814.

Gollan, T. H., Slattery, T. J., Goldenberg, D., Van Assche, E., Duyck, W., & Rayner, K. (2011). Frequency drives lexical access in reading but not in speaking: The frequency-lag hypothesis. *Journal of Experimental Psychology: General*, *140*(2), 186.

Goral, M., Spiro III, A., Obler, L. K., & Connor, L. T. (2007). Change in lexical retrieval skills in adulthood. *The Mental Lexicon*, *2*(2), 215–238. 10.1075/ml.2.2.05gor

Gordon, J. K. (2008). Measuring the lexical semantics of picture description in aphasia. *Aphasiology*, *22*(7-8), 839–852. 10.1080/02687030701820063

Gorno-Tempini, M. L., Hillis, A. E., Weintraub, S., Kertesz, A., Mendez, M., Cappa, S. F., Ogar, J. M., Rohrer, J. D., Black, S., Boeve, B. F., Manes, F., Dronkers, N. F., Vandenberghe, R., Rascovsky, K., Patterson, K., Miller, B. L., Knopman, D. S., Hodges, J. R., Mesulam, M. M., & Grossman, M. (2011). Classification of primary progressive aphasia and its variants. *Neurology*, *76*(11), 1006–1014. 10.1212/WNL.0b013e31821103e6

Ivanova, I. & Costa, A. (2008). Does bilingualism hamper lexical access in speech production? *Acta psychologica*, *127*(2), 277–288.

Kambanaros, M. & Grohmann, K. K. (2012). BATting multilingual primary progressive aphasia for Greek, English, and Czech. *Journal of Neurolinguistics*, *25*(6), 520–537. 10.1016/j.jneuroling.2011.01.006

Kavé, G. & Dassa, A. (2018). Severity of Alzheimer's disease and language features in picture descriptions. *Aphasiology*, *32*(1), 27–40. 10.1080/02687038.2017.1303441

Kavé, G. & Goral, M. (2016). Word retrieval in picture descriptions produced by individuals with Alzheimer's disease. *Journal of Clinical and Experimental Neuropsychology*, *38*(9), 958–966. 10.1080/13803395.2016.1179266

Lerman, A. & Goral, M. (unpublished). Revised English-Hebrew Aphasia Battery.

Lerman, A., Mais, D., Nissani, Y., & Malcolm, T. (2023). Preserving lexical retrieval skills across languages in a bilingual person with logopenic primary progressive aphasia. *Aphasiology*, *37*(3), 432–455.

Lind, M., Simonsen, H. G., Ribu, I. S. B., Svendsen, B. A., Svennevig, J., & de Bot, K. (2018). Lexical access in a bilingual speaker with dementia: Changes over time. *Clinical Linguistics and Phonetics*, *32*(4), 353–377. 10.1080/02699206.2017.1381168

Mendez, M. F., Saghafi, S., & Clark, D. G. (2004). Semantic dementia in multilingual patients. *The Journal of Neuropsychiatry and Clinical Neurosciences*, *16*(3), 381–381.

Mueller, K. D., Hermann, B., Mecollari, J., & Turkstra, L. S. (2018). Connected speech and language in mild cognitive impairment and Alzheimer's disease: A review of picture description tasks. *Journal of Clinical and Experimental Neuropsychology*, *40*(9), 917–939. 10.1080/13803395.2018.1446513

Nicholas, L. E. & Brookshire, R. H. (1995). Presence, completeness, and accuracy of main concepts in the connected speech of non-brain-damaged adults and adults with aphasia. *Journal of Speech, Language, and Hearing Research*, *38*, 145–156. 10.1044/jshr.3801.145

Nicholas, M., Obler, L., Albert, M., & Goodglass, H. (1985). Lexical retrieval in healthy aging. *Cortex*, *21*(4), 595–606. 10.1016/S0010-9452(58)80007-6

Norvik, M. & Goral, M. (2021). Assessment challenges in acquired aphasia in multilingual individuals. In U. Røyneland & R. Blackwood (Eds.), *Multilingualism across the Lifespan* (pp. 189–208). Routledge.

Paradis, M. & Libben, G. (1987). *The assessment of bilingual aphasia*. Lawrence Erlbaum Associates.

Runnqvist, E., Gollan, T. H., Costa, A., & Ferreira, V. S. (2013). A disadvantage in bilingual sentence production modulated by syntactic frequency and similarity across languages. *Cognition*, *129*(2), 256–263.

Salmon, D. P., Heindel, W. C., & Lange, K. L. (1999). Differential decline in word generation from phonemic and semantic categories during the course of Alzheimer's disease: Implications for the integrity of semantic memory. *Journal of the International Neuropsychological Society*, *5*(7), 692–703. 10.1017/S1355617799577126

Slegers, A., Filiou, R. P., Montembeault, M., & Brambati, S. M. (2018). Connected speech features from picture description in Alzheimer's Disease: A systematic review. *Journal of Alzheimer's Disease*, *65*(2), 519–542. 10.3233/jad-170881

Vogel-Eyny, A., Galletta, E. E., Gitterman, M. R., & Obler, L. K. (2016). Lexical retrieval in healthy aging. In H.-O. Enger, M. I. K. Knoph, K. E. Kristoffersen, & M. Lind (Eds.), *Helt fabelaktig! Festskrift til Hanne Gram Simonsen på 70-årsdagen* (pp. 275–289). Novus.

9

BILINGUALISM AND LINGUISTIC DIVERSITY

Dementia Practice and Research in India

Avanthi Paplikar and Suvarna Alladi

Introduction

Dementia is a syndrome in which there is deterioration in cognitive functions such as memory, language, thinking, reasoning, and judgement that impairs an individual's ability to perform functions of daily living. In 2016, 47 million people were living with dementia worldwide. With increasing aging populations globally, this number is projected to rise to 131 million by 2050 (Prince et al., 2016). India's population in 2018 was estimated to be around 1.35 billion, the majority of whom were in the working age-group with only 10% of the population above 60 years. This proportion is projected to rise to 19% by 2050 indicative of an aging population. By 2050, 13.3 million people over 60 years of age are predicted to be living with dementia (Ravindranath & Sundarakumar, 2021) suggestive of a significant burden of dementia in India (Nulkar et al., 2019). Cognitive decline has a significant social, emotional, and financial burden, as well as an associated impact on the health care system, individuals with dementia, families with dementia, and societies. There is also a huge treatment gap that exists in India with only 10% of the population receiving medical treatment and care (Nulkar et al., 2019).

Dementia is a public health problem and there is a need to emphasize public health-based prevention models (Kumar et al., 2019; Sathianathan & Kantipudi, 2018). Prevention emphasizes reducing the incidence of dementia by addressing various risk factors such as minimal education, hypertension, hearing impairment, smoking, physical inactivity, diabetes, low social contact, and excessive alcohol consumption, among others (Livingston et al., 2020). These modifiable risk factors and various

DOI: 10.4324/9781003330318-11

recommendations toward keeping a cognitively, physically, and socially active lifestyle through midlife and late life have been found to have a greater potential for prevention in low-middle income countries where dementia prevalence is higher (Livingston et al., 2020).

The low-middle income countries including India are typically linguistically diverse with many scheduled[1] and local languages spoken (Bauer et al., 2022). India is one of the most socio-demographically diverse countries in the world. It is ranked fourth in terms of number of languages spoken (Eberhard et al., 2022), with 122 major languages and 1,599 other languages spoken in the country. The multiplicity of Indian languages can be divided into language families: a) Indo-Aryan: approximately 78% of the Indian population speak languages belonging to this family (e.g., Hindi, Bengali, Marathi, Punjabi); b) Dravidian: 19.6% speak Dravidian languages (e.g., Telugu, Tamil, Kannada, and Malayalam); and c) Austroasiatic and Sino-Tibetan: approximately 2.31% of the population speak languages belonging to this family (e.g., Manipuri, Bodo, Burmese) (Census of India, 2011). The spread of these languages across India has led to bi/multilingualism (Bhattacharya, 2018) which is considered a normal societal phenomenon in India. Twenty six percent of the Indian population are bilingual speakers and 7% are multilingual speakers (Census of India, 2011). In this context of linguistic heterogeneity, it is crucial to have culturally appropriate cognitive tests standardized across multiple languages that can accurately diagnose dementia.

Non-pharmacological intervention strategies (such as speech-language therapy, cognitive training) remain an important step toward management and care for dementia. These strategies target reducing the symptoms and overall impact of the disease on the individual and the community. Patients with dementia and their caregivers need multi-disciplinary treatment and support services involving cognitive, environmental, speech and language, and behavioral interventions. Speech and language therapy by speech-language pathologists (SLPs) is especially helpful for treating language and cognitive impairments in dementia (Volkmer, 2013). World Alzheimer's Report (2011) has recommended the global adaptation of non-pharmacological therapy strategies that can be used effectively in developing countries (ADI, 2011). It is therefore crucial to develop appropriate protocols to provide speech and language therapy to persons with dementia in linguistically diverse contexts and in bilingual communities as well.

Dementia Practice and Research in India

Bilingualism and Cognitive Reserve/Resilience

It is essential to identify and study various factors that contribute towards cognitive resilience i.e., ability of the brain to cope with neuropathology and neurodegeneration, for instance, in people with dementia (PWD) (Voits et al., 2022). As mentioned above, engaging in cognitively stimulating activities, physical exercise, social interaction, and certain lifestyle choices contribute to cognitive resilience (Livingston et al., 2020). Life-course experiences such as bilingualism is one such protective factor that is associated with improving cognitive reserve and resilience (Antoniou et al., 2013; Bialystok et al., 2007; Wilson et al., 2013) and has contributed to delayed onset of dementia symptoms leading to preserved quality of life throughout aging (Mendis et al., 2021; Vega-Mendoza et al., 2019). There is also evidence suggesting better cognitive performance and decreased pathology in bilingual people than for comparable levels of dementia in monolingual people (Bialystok, 2021).

Based on the first report on bilingualism and its connection with delayed dementia symptom onset (Bialystok et al., 2007), a series of studies investigating the relationship between bilingualism and dementia symptoms was conducted by Alladi and colleagues in India (Alladi et al., 2013, 2016, 2017). For example, bilingualism was examined in connection with dementia syndromes using case records of 648 patients with dementia (391 bilingual and 257 monolingual) from a memory clinic in India (Alladi et al., 2013). The authors found a bilingual advantage – where there was a 4.5-year delay in the onset of dementia symptoms in bilingual individuals with Alzheimer's disease (AD), fronto-temporal dementia (FTD), and vascular dementia compared to monolingual individuals, which was independent of education, sex, occupation, and place of dwelling of the participants. Alladi et al. (2017) compared the effects of bilingualism on different subtypes of FTD and found that bilingualism delayed the age at onset in the behavioral variant of FTD but not in the aphasic forms of FTD (i.e., primary progressive aphasia) by 6 years. In a different study from the same group, 115 patients with mild cognitive impairment (MCI) were recruited to investigate the association between MCI, bilingualism, and education (Ramakrishnan et al., 2017). Age at onset of symptoms in bilingual MCI patients was delayed by 7.4 years compared to monolingual MCI patients. Apart from MCI, AD, and FTD, bilingual people have been found to have less severe cognitive and language symptoms after a stroke than monolingual people (Alladi et al., 2016; Paplikar et al., 2019).

Furthermore, protective effects of bilingualism in delaying the onset of dementia have been reported in at least four multicultural cohorts from four different locales: Toronto (Bialystok et al., 2007), Montreal (Chertkow et al., 2010), Hyderabad (Alladi et al., 2013), and Belgium (Woumans et al., 2015). These studies reported an association between language use history and delay in the onset of dementia (Freedman et al., 2014). Future cross-cultural studies are essential to study the effect of bilingualism and its interaction with other associated contextual factors.

Bilingual speakers with AD and FTD have demonstrated preserved cognitive functioning in the presence of atrophy supporting the cognitive reserve hypothesis (Perani et al., 2017; Placek et al., 2016). Furthermore, there is a growing body of research showing greater cortical thickness in bilingual speakers with AD and MCI than their monolingual counterparts in areas related to language and executive control (Duncan et al., 2018). As India is characterized by socio-cultural diversity and bilingualism, it makes the population distinctively suitable to study cognitive resilience. A study conducted by Arshad et al. (2021) on 45 patients with FTD (27 bilingual and 18 monolingual) matched for various demographic factors and disease severity, found that the neural substrates underlying the protective effects of bilingualism are different from the neural substrates underlying the effects of education in FTD. Bilingual patients with FTD had greater cortical thickness and reduced surface area in bilateral dorsolateral and medial frontal areas, and right parietotemporal cortex, regions associated with executive control. Bilingual speakers also demonstrated lesser cortical thickness in the language processing areas of left superior temporal, inferior parietal, and lateral occipital regions compared to monolingual speakers.

Many studies on dementia have suggested cognitive reserve may be enhanced by life-long bilingualism. Research on cognitive reserve should diversify to bilingual populations with other disorders beyond AD and FTD. It would be interesting to explore cognitive reserve in other conditions exhibiting both linguistic (e.g., primary progressive aphasia) and non-linguistic (e.g., amyotrophic lateral sclerosis) features. This would pave the way for a better understanding of the impact of bilingualism on enhancing cognitive reserve.

Linguistic Diversity and Diagnosis of Dementia

In the context of linguistic heterogeneity that prevails in India, it is crucial to have clinical instruments and neuropsychological test batteries to measure various cognitive domains that are standardized across multiple languages to detect dementia and its subtypes. Few validation studies of cognitive screening instruments, naming tests, and neuropsychological test batteries have addressed linguistic, cultural, and educational diversity in India. Cognitive screening instruments such as the Addenbrooke's Cognitive Examination (ACE; Mekala et al., 2020), the Mini Mental State Examination (MMSE; Mathuranath et al., 2007), and the Montreal Cognitive Assessment (MoCA; Kaul et al., 2022) have been adapted and validated in many Indo Aryan and Dravidian languages including for the low-educated population (Ganguli et al., 1995). Furthermore, culturally appropriate pictures for native speakers of Urdu/Kashmiri and Malayalam have been developed (Ashaie & Obler, 2014; George & Mathuranath, 2007). Also, a reliable common test to assess naming abilities in mild-moderate dementia across five Indian languages was developed following cross-cultural adaptation guidelines and by establishing correlations using item-wise factor analysis (Paplikar et al., 2022).

In a multi-center study across six institutions, a cognitive test battery, the Indian Council of Medical Research – Neuro-Cognitive Tool-Box (ICMR-NCTB) was adapted and validated in Hindi, Bengali, Telugu, Kannada, and Malayalam (Iyer et al., 2020). The ICMR-NCTB can be used to characterize, quantify, and diagnose MCI and dementia (Menon et al., 2020; Verma et al., 2021). Furthermore, the Cambridge Semantic Memory (CSM) test battery was adapted and validated to the Indian cultural context and is known as the Indian Semantic Memory battery (ISM-B). The ISM-B will aid in early and accurate identification of semantic memory impairment in dementia and its subtypes (Paplikar et al., 2022). A few functional scales for activities of daily living and life course factors that enable diagnosis and help in devising intervention strategies in dementia have also been adapted to the Indian cultural context (Mathuranath et al., 2005; Paplikar et al., 2020).

Appropriate guidelines should be followed for language and neuropsychological evaluation in a linguistically diverse bilingual context: a) evaluating language proficiency of the patient and the clinician is necessary to select the appropriate language for testing; b) due to frequent language-mixing and language-switching encountered in daily communication in the Indian cultural context, responses from non-target languages should be accounted for in scoring; and c) the effect of bilingualism on language and cognitive test scores should be carefully interpreted (Paplikar et al., 2021). In the Indian cultural context, there were no significant differences on neuropsychological tests between monolingual and bilingual cohorts, suggesting separate normative data for monolingual and bilingual speakers may not be required. These recommendations, however, may vary in other bilingual communities. Many initiatives have been undertaken globally to improve the neuropsychological assessments of culturally, educationally, and linguistically diverse groups (e.g., Franzen et al., 2021; Nielsen et al., 2011). Franzen and colleagues (2021) developed the TULIPA battery (Towards a Universal Language: Intervention and Psychodiagnostic Assessment) to assess culturally diverse populations. Furthermore, Nielsen et al. (2011) found assessment of ethnic minority patients to be difficult as there is a considerable need to develop specific tests to assess ethnic minority groups. The current practice of assessment of dementia in India is suboptimal. Specialized dementia services are lacking and the care system should be prepared for an increase in demand for dementia assessment from different cultural and linguistic backgrounds in India.

Speech and Language Therapy for Dementia

Speech and language deficits are frequent in dementia. The language impairment patterns vary in each subtype of dementia depending on the distribution of neuropathology and the associated cognitive deficits. Some of the commonly reported speech and language deficits include articulatory errors, agrammatism, impaired comprehension of complex utterances, reduced word output, word retrieval difficulty, lexical and semantic impairment, and impaired repetition. While the literature on intervention strategies in stroke-induced aphasia is abundant, evidence-based research targeting PWD has been slowly emerging globally. Speech and language therapy for PWD include training basic communication needs, word relearning and retrieval, spaced retrieval training, thematic based language training, and planning care needs and routines for patients (Jokel et al., 2014; Rangarajan et al., 2022).

Existing language and cognitive therapy approaches offered for non-progressive communication disorders (e.g., post-stroke aphasia) are also feasible for treating language and cognitive impairments in dementia (Henry et al., 2019; Lerman et al., 2023; Rangarajan et al., 2022; Volkmer, 2013). However, there is little evidence on the treatment for bilingual speakers with aphasia caused by neurodegenerative conditions (Lerman et al., 2023; Meyer et al., 2015). A study by Meyer and colleagues (2015), investigated the effects of naming intervention in a Norwegian-English bilingual speaker with the logopenic variant of primary progressive aphasia (lvPPA). The intervention was provided in English for eight sessions and the patient showed improvement in the written naming for the trained items. Although treatment was provided only in English, cross-language transfer was observed in oral naming and naming-to-definition in Norwegian as well. More recently, Lerman et al. (2023) studied the effects of Verb Network Strengthening Training (VNeST) in an English-Hebrew bilingual speaker with lvPPA. VNeST was provided in Hebrew for 20 sessions over 10 weeks. The authors found that during the 10 weeks of treatment, lexical retrieval skills in both English and Hebrew did not decline in single-word naming tasks, sentence production, and/or written narratives but did continue to decline during oral narrative production. The results of these studies suggest that cross-language transfer is possible in bilingual speakers with PPA, despite progressive worsening. To date, the speech and language intervention strategies targeting PWD in linguistically and culturally diverse bilingual contexts (such as India) are less known. Therefore, culturally tailored treatment approaches should be considered for culturally diverse settings (Grasso et al., 2021).

Conclusion and Future Directions

Assessment, Prevention, and Intervention of Language in Dementia

Bi/multilingualism, new language learning, and language use promote a physical and mental active lifestyle geared towards healthy aging. Most of the Indian population are either sequential or simultaneous bilingual speakers, however, due to globalization the English language is given much prominence and the native language is losing its status in some parts of the country. Bi/multilingual speakers should be encouraged to use more than one language within the family and/or community, as a part of a healthy lifestyle (Mehmedbegovic & Bak, 2017). As the evidence suggests, if in fact, bilingualism modulates the relationship between cognitive performance and neuropathology, learning a new language or practicing the use of two or more languages might help build cognitive reserve (Antoniou et al., 2013).

According to the American Speech-Language-Hearing Association (ASHA, 2017), SLP intervention results in improvements in communication function and the well-being of PWD and their caregivers. Recently, positive communication outcomes have been reported for direct and indirect cognitive communication interventions that includes cognition training (spaced retrieval training), speech and language training (functional communication, Schuell's stimulation approach), cognitive stimulation approaches, mindfulness-based intervention (meditation and yoga), and caregiver communication techniques (Swan et al., 2018). Despite the recognition of the role of SLPs in the treatment of communication in PWD throughout the disease progression, they are rarely part of the intervention team in highly specialized services like memory clinics (Mehrani & Sachdev, 2022). Although there is a sizeable body of research on cognitive and communication difficulties in dementia from India, there are no concrete guidelines towards SLP intervention. Therefore, there is a need to develop socio-culturally appropriate communication and cognitive strategies addressing the functional communication needs of PWD in the Indian cultural context (Ojha & Moharana, 2020).

Family caregivers are one of the most reliable resources available to provide care and support for people with cognitive impairment. As the disease progresses, the caregiver transforms into a decision maker that changes the roles of partners and/or children (Bunn et al., 2017; Livingston et al., 2020). Studies from India and elsewhere have reported increasing psychological and physical demands for caregivers which leads to poorer physical health, lower quality of life, and poorer social relationships than non-caregivers (Goren et al., 2016; Jathanna et al., 2010; Srivastava et al., 2016). In the Indian cultural context, studies on individualized multi-component support for caregivers and extended family should be conducted in collaboration with social workers and psychologists to improve caregivers' mental and physical health.

Many researchers have suggested inter-disciplinary collaborative work on bilingualism between neuroscientific and medical fields (Voits et al., 2022). Future large-scale population studies on language experiences and bilingual language use patterns together with other predictive factors and experiences will be helpful to understand the complex effects of lifestyle factors on cognitive reserve and resilience in PWD.

Conclusion

Many linguists, SLPs, psychologists, behavioral neurologists, and experts from related fields have come together to contribute toward the role of bilingualism in healthy and degenerating pathological conditions such as dementia, MCI, and PPA. Various measures have been developed for screening and diagnostic assessment of non-English speaking communities globally and in India that will aid in the early identification and diagnosis of cognitive impairment. There is a great need to develop protocols and recommendations for providing speech, language, and cognitive interventions to PWD in bilingual and linguistically diverse contexts.

Note

1 Scheduled languages are any languages other than the official languages of a country. They are generally regional languages.

References

Alladi, S., Bak, T. H., Duggirala, V., Surampudi, B., Shailaja, M., Shukla, A. K., ... & Kaul, S. (2013). Bilingualism delays age at onset of dementia, independent of education and immigration status. *Neurology*, *81*(22), 1938–1944.

Alladi, S., Bak, T. H., Shailaja, M., Gollahalli, D., Rajan, A., Surampudi, B., ... & Kaul, S. (2017). Bilingualism delays the onset of behavioral but not aphasic forms of frontotemporal dementia. *Neuropsychologia*, *99*, 207–212.

Alladi, S., Bak, T. H., Mekala, S., Rajan, A., Chaudhuri, J. R., Mioshi, E., ... & Kaul, S. (2016). Impact of bilingualism on cognitive outcome after stroke. *Stroke*, *47*(1), 258–261.

Alzheimer's Disease International (ADI). (2011). *World Alzheimer Report 2011: Benefits of Early Diagnosis and Intervention*. London: International Alzheimer's Disease.

American Speech-Language-Hearing Association (ASHA). (2017). Dementia. Retrieved from http://www.asha.org/PRPSpecificTopic.aspx?folderid=8589935289&section=References

Antoniou, M., Gunasekera, G. M., & Wong, P. C. (2013). Foreign language training as cognitive therapy for age-related cognitive decline: A hypothesis for future research. *Neuroscience and Biobehavioral Reviews*, *37*(10), 2689–2698.

Arshad, F., Alladi, S., Kenchaiah, R., Thanissery, N., Khokhar, S., Paplikar, A., ... & Surampudi, B. R. (2021). Neural correlates of cognitive resilience differ between experiences of bilingualism and education: A cortical based morphometry study in Frontotemporal dementia. *American Academy of Neurology*, *96* (15 supplement).

Ashaie, S. & Obler, L. (2014). Effect of age, education, and bilingualism on confrontation naming in older illiterate and low-educated populations. *Behavioural Neurology*, Article ID 970520.

Bauer, K., Morin, K. L., Renz III, T. E., & Zungu, S. (2022). Autism assessment in low-and middle-income countries: Feasibility and usability of western tools. *Focus on Autism and Other Developmental Disabilities*, *37*(3), 179–188 10883576211073691.

Bhattacharya, S. S. (2018). Languages, mother tongues and bilingualism in India: An overview. Workshop of field linguistic. Tezpur University, Assam.

Bialystok, E., Craik, F. I., & Freedman, M. (2007). Bilingualism as a protection against the onset of symptoms of dementia. *Neuropsychologia*, *45*(2), 459–464.

Bialystok, E. (2021). Bilingualism: Pathway to cognitive reserve. *Trends in Cognitive Sciences*, *25*(5), 355–364.

Bunn, F., Goodman, C., Reece Jones, P., Russell, B., Trivedi, D., Sinclair, A., ... & Burton, C. (2017). What works for whom in the management of diabetes in people living with dementia: A realist review. *BMC Medicine*, *15*(1), 1–18.

Census of India. (2011). *Language: India, States and Union territories*. New Delhi, India: Office of the Registrar General.

Chertkow, H., Whitehead, V., Phillips, N., Wolfson, C., Atherton, J., & Bergman, H. (2010). Multilingualism (but not always bilingualism) delays the onset of Alzheimer disease: Evidence from a bilingual community. *Alzheimer Disease and Associated Disorders*, *24*(2), 118–125.

Duncan, H. D., Nikelski, J., Pilon, R., Steffener, J., Chertkow, H., & Phillips, N. A. (2018). Structural brain differences between monolingual and multilingual patients with mild cognitive impairment and Alzheimer disease: Evidence for cognitive reserve. *Neuropsychologia*, *109*, 270–282.

Eberhard, D. M., Simons, F. F., & Fennig, C. D. (eds.). (2022). *Ethnologue: Languages of the World*. Twenty-fifth edition. SIL International.

Franzen, S., Papma, J. M., van den Berg, E., & Nielsen, T. R. (2021). Cross-cultural neuropsychological assessment in the European Union: A Delphi expert study. *Archives of Clinical Neuropsychology*, *36*(5), 815–830.

Freedman, M., Alladi, S., Chertkow, H., Bialystok, E., Craik, F. I., Phillips, N. A., ... & Bak, T. H. (2014). Delaying onset of dementia: are two languages enough? *Behavioural Neurology*, 2014:808137.

Ganguli, M., Ratcliff, G., Chandra, V., Sharma, S., Gilby, J., Pandav, R., ... & Dekosky, S. (1995). A Hindi version of the MMSE: The development of a cognitive screening instrument for a largely illiterate rural elderly population in India. *International Journal of Geriatric Psychiatry*, *10*(5), 367–377.

George, A., & Mathuranath, P. S. (2007). Community-based naming agreement, familiarity, image agreement and visual complexity ratings among adult Indians. *Annals of Indian Academy of Neurology*, *10*(2), 92.

Goren, A., Montgomery, W., Kahle-Wrobleski, K., Nakamura, T., & Ueda, K. (2016). Impact of caring for persons with Alzheimer's disease or dementia on caregivers' health outcomes: Findings from a community based survey in Japan. *BMC Geriatrics*, *16*(1), 1–12.

Grasso, S. M., Peña, E. D., Kazemi, N., Mirzapour, H., Neupane, R., Bonakdarpour, B., ... & Henry, M. L. (2021). Treatment for anomia in bilingual speakers with progressive aphasia. *Brain Sciences*, *11*(11), 1371.

Henry, M. L., Hubbard, H. I., Grasso, S. M., Dial, H. R., Beeson, P. M., Miller, B. L., & Gorno-Tempini, M. L. (2019). Treatment for word retrieval in semantic and logopenic variants of primary progressive aphasia: Immediate and long-term outcomes. *Journal of Speech, Language, and Hearing Research*, *62*(8), 2723–2749.

Iyer, G. K., Paplikar, A., Alladi, S., Dutt, A., Sharma, M., Mekala, S., ... & ICMR Neurocognitive Tool Box Consortium. (2020). Standardising dementia diagnosis across linguistic and educational diversity: Study design of Indian council of medical research-neurocognitive tool box (ICMR-NCTB). *Journal of the International Neuropsychological Society*, *26*(2), 172–186.

Jathanna, R. P., Latha, K. S., & Bhandary, P. V. (2010). Burden and coping in informal caregivers of persons with dementia: A cross sectional study. *Online Journal of Health Allied Science*, *9*(4), 7.

Jokel, R., Graham, N. L., Rochon, E., & Leonard, C. (2014). Word retrieval therapies in primary progressive aphasia. *Aphasiology*, *28*(8-9), 1038–1068.

Kaul, S., Paplikar, A., Varghese, F., Alladi, S., Sharma, M., Dhaliwal, R. S., ... & Consortium, I. R. N. B. (2022). MoCA in five Indian languages: A brief screening tool to diagnose dementia and MCI in a linguistically diverse setting. *International Journal of Geriatric Psychiatry*, *37*(10).

Kumar CT, S., George, S., & Kallivayalil, R. A. (2019). Towards a dementia-friendly India. *Indian Journal of Psychological Medicine*, *41*(5), 476–481.

Lerman, A., Mais, D., Nissani, Y., & Malcolm, T. (2023). Preserving lexical retrieval skills across languages in a bilingual person with logopenic primary progressive aphasia. *Aphasiology*, *37*(3), 4320–4455.

Livingston, G., Huntley, J., Sommerlad, A., Ames, D., Ballard, C., Banerjee, S., ... & Mukadam, N. (2020). Dementia prevention, intervention, and care: 2020 report of the Lancet Commission. *The Lancet*, *396*(10248), 413–446.

Mathuranath, P. S., Cherian, J. P., Mathew, R., George, A., Alexander, A., & Sarma, S. P. (2007). Mini mental state examination and the Addenbroke's cognitive examination: Effect of education and norms for a multicultural population. *Neurology India*, *55*(2), 106.

Mathuranath, P. S., George, A., Cherian, P. J., Mathew, R., & Sarma, P. S. (2005). Instrumental activities of daily living scale for dementia screening in elderly people. *International Psychogeriatrics*, *17*(3), 461–474.

Mehmedbegovic, D. & Bak, T. H. (2017). Healthy linguistic diet: The value of linguistic diversity and language learning across the lifespan. *Language, Society and Policy*. 10.17863/CAM.9854

Mehrani, I. & Sachdev, P. S. (2022). The role of Memory Clinics in the assessment and management of dementia, now and into the future. *Current Opinion in Psychiatry*, *35*(2), 118–122.

Mekala, S., Paplikar, A., Mioshi, E., Kaul, S., Divyaraj, G., Coughlan, G., ... & Alladi, S. (2020). Dementia diagnosis in seven languages: The Addenbrooke's Cognitive Examination-III in India. *Archives of Clinical Neuropsychology*, *35*(5), 528–538.

Mendis, S. B., Raymont, V., & Tabet, N. (2021). Bilingualism: A global public health strategy for healthy cognitive aging. *Frontiers in Neurology*, *12*, 628368.

Menon, R. N., Varghese, F., Paplikar, A., Mekala, S., Alladi, S., Sharma, M., ... & Vishwanath, Y. (2020). Validation of Indian council of medical research neurocognitive tool box in diagnosis of mild cognitive impairment in India: Lessons from a harmonization process in a linguistically diverse society. *Dementia and Geriatric Cognitive Disorders*, *49*(4), 355–364.

Meyer, A. M., Snider, S. F., Eckmann, C. B., & Friedman, R. B. (2015). Prophylactic treatments for anomia in the logopenic variant of primary progressive aphasia: Cross-language transfer. *Aphasiology*, *29*(9), 1062–1081.

Nielsen, T. R., Vogel, A., Riepe, M. W., de Mendonça, A., Rodriguez, G., Nobili, F., ... & Waldemar, G. (2011). Assessment of dementia in ethnic minority patients in Europe: A European Alzheimer's Disease Consortium survey. *International Psychogeriatrics*, *23*(1), 86–95.

Nulkar, A., Paralikar, V., & Juvekar, S. (2019). Dementia in India–a call for action. *Journal of Global Health Reports*, *3*, e2019078.

Ojha, G. J. & Moharana, S. (2020). Strategies to Improve Communication during ADLs in Dementia: A Short Review. *International Journal of Science and Healthcare Research*, *5*(3), 286–291.

Paplikar, A., Mekala, S., Bak, T. H., Dharamkar, S., Alladi, S., & Kaul, S. (2019). Bilingualism and the severity of poststroke aphasia. *Aphasiology*, *33*(1), 58–72.

Paplikar, A., Vandana, V. P., Mekala, S., Darshini, K. J., Arshad, F., Iyer, G. K., ... & Alladi, S. (2022). Semantic memory impairment in dementia: A cross-cultural adaptation study. *Neurological Sciences*, *43*(1), 265–273.

Paplikar, A., Ballal, D., Varghese, F., Sireesha, J., Dwivedi, R., Rajan, A., ... & Alladi, S. (2020). Assessment of lifestyle experiences across lifespan and cognitive ageing in the Indian context. *Psychology and Developing Societies*, *32*(2), 308–330.

Paplikar, A., Alladi, S., Varghese, F., Mekala, S., Arshad, F., Sharma, M., ... & ICMR-NCTB Consortium. (2021). Bilingualism and its implications for neuropsychological evaluation. *Archives of Clinical Neuropsychology*, *36*(8), 1511–1522.

Paplikar, A., Varghese, F., Alladi, S., Vandana, V. P., Darshini, K. J., Iyer, G. K., ... & ICMR Neuro Cognitive Tool Box Consortium. (2022). Picture-naming test for a linguistically diverse population with cognitive impairment and dementia. *International Journal of Language & Communication Disorders*, *57*(4), 881–894.

Perani, D., Farsad, M., Ballarini, T., Lubian, F., Malpetti, M., Fracchetti, A., ... & Abutalebi, J. (2017). The impact of bilingualism on brain reserve and metabolic connectivity in Alzheimer's dementia. *Proceedings of the National Academy of Sciences, 114*(7), 1690–1695.

Placek, K., Massimo, L., Olm, C., Ternes, K., Firn, K., Van Deerlin, V., ... & McMillan, C. T. (2016). Cognitive reserve in frontotemporal degeneration: Neuroanatomic and neuropsychological evidence. *Neurology, 87*(17), 1813–1819.

Prince, M. J., Comas-Herrera, A., Knapp, M., Guerchet, M. M., & Karagiannidou, M. (2016). *World Alzheimer Report 2016-Improving healthcare for people living with dementia: Coverage, quality and costs now and in the future.*

Ramakrishnan, S., Mekala, S., Mamidipudi, A., Yareeda, S., Mridula, R., Bak, T. H., ... & Kaul, S. (2017). Comparative effects of education and bilingualism on the onset of mild cognitive impairment. *Dementia and Geriatric Cognitive Disorders, 44*(3-4), 222–231.

Rangarajan, S. K., Gorthi, N. V., Selvaraj, S., Akkunje, P. S., Parlikar, R., Sreeraj, V. S., ... & Venkatasubramanian, G. (2022). Feasibility and benefits of intermittent multiple tDCS courses with concomitant language training in semantic dementia: A case report. *Indian Journal of Psychological Medicine*, 02537176211072208.

Ravindranath, V., & Sundarakumar, J. S. (2021). Changing demography and the challenge of dementia in India. *Nature Reviews Neurology, 17*(12), 747–758.

Sathianathan, R., & Kantipudi, S. J. (2018). The dementia epidemic: Impact, prevention, and challenges for India. *Indian Journal of Psychiatry, 60*(2), 165.

Srivastava, G., Tripathi, R. K., Tiwari, S. C., Singh, B., & Tripathi, S. M. (2016). Caregiver burden and quality of life of key caregivers of patients with dementia. *Indian Journal of Psychological Medicine, 38*(2), 133–136.

Swan, K., Hopper, M., Wenke, R., Jackson, C., Till, T., & Conway, E. (2018). Speech-language pathologist interventions for communication in moderate–severe dementia: A systematic review. *American Journal of Speech-Language Pathology, 27*(2), 836–852.

Vega-Mendoza, M., Alladi, S., & Bak, T. H. (2019). Dementia and multilingualism. *The Handbook of the Neuroscience of Multilingualism*, 608–624.

Verma, M., Tripathi, M., Nehra, A., Paplikar, A., Varghese, F., Alladi, S., ... & Vishwanath, Y. (2021). Validation of ICMR Neurocognitive Toolbox for Dementia in the Linguistically Diverse Context of India. *Frontiers in Neurology*, 1828.

Volkmer, A. (2013). *Assessment and Therapy for Language and Cognitive Communication Difficulties in Dementia and Other Progressive Diseases*. J & R Press.

Voits, T., DeLuca, V., & Abutalebi, J. (2022). The nuance of bilingualism as a reserve contributor: Conveying research to the broader neuroscience community. *Frontiers in Psychology, 13.*

Wilson, R. S., Barnes, L. L., & Bennett, D. A. (2013). Assessment of lifetime participation in cognitively stimulating activities. In *Cognitive Reserve* (pp. 173–186). Psychology Press.

Woumans, E. V. Y., Santens, P., Sieben, A., Versijpt, J. A. N., Stevens, M., & Duyck, W. (2015). Bilingualism delays clinical manifestation of Alzheimer's disease. *Bilingualism: Language and Cognition, 18*(3), 568–574.

10

USE OF tDCS in Primary Progressive Aphasia

Behavioral Interventions for Oral Word Naming

Amy Vogel-Eyny and Elizabeth Galletta

Introduction

Noninvasive brain stimulation refers to techniques that modulate the excitability of the brain using transcranial stimulation. Two current brain stimulation methods are transcranial magnetic stimulation (TMS) and transcranial direct current stimulation (tDCS). While these methods are currently drawing interest, people have been attempting to use electricity as a treatment for human ailments for many years, as early as thousands of years BC (Heidland et al., 2013) as seen in drawings of electric fish used to treat pain in stone carvings from Egypt and in Socrates' time, when electric fish were known to be used for the treatment of headaches and arthritis. In relatively recent modern day medicine in the 1940s, applying electricity to the brain was practiced using electroconvulsive therapy (ECT) or "electrical brain stimulation" to treat severe depression (Kellner et al., 2012). Even more recently in 1985, researchers invented the methods used for TMS as we know it today (Barker et al., 1985). This involves application of a coil placed over the scalp that produces a magnetic field and promotes action potential shifts in neurons. With the increased interest and research in TMS in the late 20th century, research evolved to the study and use of electrical stimulation in the form of tDCS as a main method of noninvasive brain stimulation used to help people with acquired neurological conditions in the 21st century. Use of tDCS paired with behavioral treatment is a clinical research focus that has started to be applied innovatively to clinical care in medical settings.

DOI: 10.4324/9781003330318-12

When administering tDCS, there are at least two electrode sponges placed on the scalp, an anode, the positive electrode, and a cathode, the negative electrode. These are connected via a wire to a stimulator that is powered by a battery that provides a low-level direct current that passes through the wire and electrodes and scalp, to the brain. tDCS always involves an anode and a cathode; when the term "anodal" tDCS is used the brain area targeted is under the anode and when the term "cathodal" tDCS is used the brain area targeted is under the cathode. One applies what is referred to as "anodal" tDCS to promote neuronal firing, and "cathodal" tDCS to inhibit neuronal firing. Dosage of tDCS varies, with length of tDCS sessions generally lasting 20 or 30 minutes. In tDCS research studies both active and sham tDCS are administered, with no actual tDCS in the sham condition, but in clinical care, patients only receive active tDCS. Both in research and clinically, tDCS is administered in combination with behavioral treatment. The low-level electricity administered is usually 1-2 mA (Bikson et al., 2016). There is evidence that repetitive tDCS sessions are necessary to produce desired cumulative effects (Bikson et al., 2016; Monte-Silva et al., 2013; Pilloni et al., 2022).

In the aphasia literature, the first paper that reported on the use of tDCS was published in 2008 (Monti et al., 2008). Since then, there have been numerous applications of tDCS paired with behavioral interventions for stroke aphasia, and more recently there has been a focus on the use of tDCS with primary progressive aphasia, as well (Sheppard, 2022). Primary progressive aphasia (PPA) is a disorder that is manifested by gradual, progressive loss of language abilities (Mesulam, 1982, 2001, 2003). There are three criteria that are the core features of PPA: i) the patient presents with errors of word production or comprehension that cannot be attributed to motor or perceptual deficits; ii) language impairment is the most prominent deficit at the initial stages of the illness and the area that most concerns individuals and families; iii) the underlying disease is progressive and gets worse over time (Mesulam, 2013). There are three main variants of PPA: nonfluent/agrammatic, semantic, and logopenic. These are initially classified based on observed language symptoms and then often brain imaging is completed as well to document brain atrophy.

The nonfluent/agrammatic variant of PPA (naPPA; sometimes referred to as nfvPPA) presents as progressive effortful, non-fluent speech with grammatical errors and omissions (Gorno-Tempini et al., 2004; Grossman, 2010; Mesulam, 2001) and includes naming impairment, with greater difficulty in naming actions than objects (Silveri & Ciccarelli, 2007). Comprehension is an initial strength, with the exception of grammatically complex sentences that are difficult to understand (Gorno-Tempini et al., 2011). Imaging evidence of atrophy in the left inferior frontal gyrus, insula, and supplementary motor areas supports the clinical diagnosis of naPPA (Cerami et al., 2017; Gorno-Tempini et al., 2011). People with naPPA can also show variable degrees of dysarthria, phonological disintegration, labored pronunciation, and apraxia of speech (AOS) (Duffy et al., 2021; Mesulam, 2013). The semantic variant of PPA (svPPA) is characterized by fluent speech with difficulties in semantic memory which lead to impaired confrontation naming of objects and single word comprehension. Anterior temporal lobe atrophy is the main imaging feature in these patients (Cerami et al., 2017). The logopenic/phonological variant of PPA (lvPPA) is characterized by slow speech with long word-finding pauses and anomia, poor repetition, and difficulty understanding sentences. In lvPPA, left posterior temporal cortex and left parietal lobule atrophy is seen (Cerami et al., 2017; Henry & Gorno-Tempini, 2010). See also chapter 7, this volume.

Since anomia is a common symptom among all three variants (Cotelli et al., 2020), it is often a treatment focus of PPA. Anomia is common in other neurological and neurodegenerative diseases, as well, and treatment of anomia in PPA is often applied translationally to PPA since there are no widely-used, specific behavioral treatments designed for PPA. The restorative-focused behavioral interventions used with PPA are often borrowed from the resorative-focused anomia treatments clinicians use with patients with nonprogressive aphasia (Robinaugh & Henry, 2022) and include attempts to implement treatments using approaches such as semantic feature analysis (SFA) (Boyle et al., 1995; Hung et al., 2017) and verb network strengthening treatment (VNeST) (Edmonds, 2014; Sheppard, 2022). Along with direct language treatment, counseling and development of a home program is an important part of treatment in PPA. This includes training a family member or caregiver in the area of supported conversation techniques and compensatory strategies to support communicative interactions in the home environment (Robinaugh & Henry, 2022).

While use of compensatory methods is paramount for individuals with progressive disorders including PPA, it is possible that in addition to this, using the standard-of-care, restorative-focused treatments for nonprogressive anomia in conjunction with tDCS may have a beneficial impact on naming treatment for people with PPA. The use of tDCS combined with behavioral treatment for PPA is less well studied than the use of tDCS combined with behavioral treatment for nonprogressive aphasia, yet some researchers are exploring this area. tDCS could potentially enhance language abilities over and above behavioral interventions alone for individuals with PPA. Alternatively, tDCS could potentially slow the progressive decline in language function. The purpose of this review is to examine all studies to date that include behavioral interventions targeting oral word production when paired with the application of tDCS in individuals with PPA.

tDCS and PPA Oral Naming Treatment Studies

Several studies conducted to date have examined the effect of tDCS alongside word production treatment in individuals with PPA (Cotelli et al., 2014, 2016; Gervits et al., 2016; Hosseini et al., 2019; Hung et al., 2017; Roncero et al., 2017; Sheppard et al., 2022). The majority of the research reviewed included participants with nonfluent/agrammatic PPA (6/7 studies; Cotelli et al., 2014, 2016; Gervits et al., 2016; Hosseini et al., 2019; Roncero et al., 2017; Sheppard et al., 2022), followed by the logopenic (5/7 studies; Gervits et al., 2016; Hosseini et al., 2019; Hung et al., 2017; Roncero et al., 2017; Sheppard et al., 2022) and semantic variants (2/7 studies; Hung et al., 2017; Roncero et al., 2017). With respect to tDCS methodological design, 4/7 of the studies included a sham condition as a control (Cotelli et al., 2014; Hosseini et al., 2019; Roncero et al., 2017; Sheppard et al., 2022). A sham-controlled study allows for evaluation of tDCS as an adjuvant to the behavioral intervention. As such, those investigations that did not include a tDCS control cannot determine whether active stimulation and the language intervention acted synergistically. All studies included in this review assessed maintenance of gains in follow-up testing points, with a minimum of 1 month post-testing and a maximum of 6 months post-testing. Consistent with the largely left-hemisphere lateralization of speech and language (Price, 2010), all studies applied active (anodal) tDCS to a neural region in the left hemisphere. See Table 10.1 for study design details.

Semantically-Based Approaches

A few of the studies reviewed have taken a semantic approach to treatment across all three PPA variants (Hung et al., 2017; Sheppard et al., 2022). In these studies, the selection of both the semantic intervention and the PPA population may be motivated by the therapeutic goal. For example, in a study employing SFA (Hung et al., 2017), the researchers trained semantic attributes of targets in individuals with lvPPA and svPPA, reasoning that both variants are characterized by a semantically-based progressive anomia to some extent, with the latter more impaired than the former. Similarly, researchers employing a VNeST protocol included those with naPPA or lvPPA given the presumed necessity of relatively spared semantic knowledge for treatment efficacy (Edmonds, 2018).

TABLE 10.1 Studies combining tDCS and oral word naming intervention in PPA

Study	*Study Design*	*PPA Variant/ Number*	*Mean (SD) Age*	*Sessions*	*Stimulation Parameters*	*Stimulation Location*	*Treatment Approach/ Duration*	*Word Naming Outcomes*
Cotelli et al., 2014	Sham-controlled RCT	naPPA/16	66.9 (8.2)	10	2 mA, 25 mins.	Anode (L-DLPFC), Cathode (CS)	Computerized picture naming/ 25 minutes	Post treatment: • Trained nouns improved in both conditions (Active > Sham). • Untrained nouns improved equally in both conditions.3-month follow-up: • Trained and untrained forms improved equally in both conditions.
Cotelli et al., 2016	Case series	naPPA/18	65.5 (9.5)	10	2 mA, 25 mins.	Anode (L-DLPFC), Cathode (CS)	Computerized picture naming/25 mins.	• Improvement for trained and untrained nouns immediately post-treatment and at 3-month follow-up.
Gervitz et al., 2016	Open label pilot	lvPPA/4; naPPA/2	66.2 (5.7)	10	1.5 mA, 20 mins.	Anode (L-FT) Cathode (L-OP)	Wordless picture book narration/20 mins.	• Improvement in speech production (MLU and speech rate) at post-testing. No difference at 3-month follow-up. • No improvement in semantic processing (BNT, category fluency, PPT).
Hosseini et al., 2019	Sham-controlled, within-subjects crossover	naPPA or lvPPA/6	67 (10.6)	10	1.5 mA, 20 mins.	Anode (L-Prefrontal) Cathode (L-Occipital)	Wordless picture book narration/20 mins.	• Improvement in category fluency for active tDCS alone at post-testing and follow-up.

(Continued)

TABLE 10.1 (Continued)

Study	*Study Design*	*PPA Variant/ Number*	*Mean (SD) Age*	*Sessions*	*Stimulation Parameters*	*Stimulation Location*	*Treatment Approach/ Duration*	*Word Naming Outcomes*
Hung et al., 2017	Case series	lvPPA/1; svPPA/3	68.9 (8.9)	10	1.5 mA, 30 mins.	Anode (L-TP) Cathode (Forehead)	Semantic Feature Training/ 30 mins.	• Trained forms improved at post-testing. • Untrained forms showed no improvement at post-testing • Trained forms > Untrained forms at 6-month follow-up.
Roncero et al., 2017	Sham-controlled, crossover	lvPPA/2; naPPA/6; svPPA/2	67.4 (6.3)	10	2 mA, 30 mins.	Anode (L-TP) Cathode (R-FO)	Computerized picture naming/ ≥ 30 mins.	Post treatment: • Trained forms improved in both conditions (Active > Sham). • Untrained forms improved only in active tDCS. • At 1-month follow-up trained and untrained forms improved for active tDCS.
Sheppard et al., 2022	Sham-controlled crossover	lvPPA/1; naPPA/2	66.3 (9.1)	15	1 mA, 20 mins. 2 mA, 20 mins.	Anode (L-IF) Cathode (CS)	VNeST/ 60 mins.	• No improvement for trained verbs in active tDCS across post-testing and follow-ups (1 month, 2 month). • Untrained verbs improved for 2/3 participants at post-testing and both follow-up points.

Note. PPA = primary progressive aphasia, naPPA = nonfluent/agrammatic variant PPA; lvPPA = logopenic variant PPA; svPPA = semantic variant PPA; L-DLPFC = left dorsolateral prefrontal cortex; CS = contralateral shoulder; L-FT = left fronto-temporal; L-OP = left occipito-parietal; L-TP = left temporoparietal); R-FO = right fronto orbital; MLU = mean length utterance; BNT = Boston Naming Test; PPT = Pyramids and Palm Trees Test; VNeST = Verb Network Strengthening Treatment, RCT = randomized controlled trial.

In their modified SFA study, Hung and colleagues (2017) created a semi-individualized core lexicon of everyday, functional words (common nouns, verbs, and proper nouns) spanning six semantic categories. Targets were represented by digital photographs of participants' personal exemplars (e.g., objects in the home, family and/or friends) and displayed in a communication book. Given this evidence-based and ecologically-valid treatment approach, participants named trained items more accurately than untrained items across testing times, including at 6 months post-treatment. Generalization to untrained items was not observed. In response to this finding, the researchers argue that the rationale for semantic training of functionally relevant and personalized lexical targets is to improve access to a lexical item through contextualized familiarity, which stands against the concept of generalization (i.e., knowledge of my slippers vs. another set). However, it is important to note that the researchers did not include a sham condition. As such, it is difficult to determine the relative contribution of tDCS and the semantic training on the observed naming improvement.

A recent investigation by Sheppard and colleagues (2022) paired tDCS with a modified version of VNeST, representing one of the early applications of the treatment approach in PPA (but see also Lerman et al., 2023). In addition to examining the effect of active tDCS and paired treatment outcomes for trained verbs, the researchers additionally evaluated production of verbs and nouns at the sentence level in three individuals (two with naPPA and one with lvPPA). There was no improvement for trained verbs in either the active tDCS condition or sham (i.e., behavioral treatment alone). However, an examination of participant-level performance showed that individuals with naPPA (n = 2) had a tDCS-mediated benefit for untrained verbs at both post-treatment time points. One of the participants with naPPA also demonstrated a tDCS-related advantage for sentence production (subtests of the Northwestern Assessment of Verbs and Sentences; NAVS). The researchers point out that one possibility as to why a single participant made greater gains (both to untrained verbs and sentence-level production) than the others might be due to the stimulation parameters (receiving 2 mAs rather than 1 mA). This finding is of interest because 1 mA is the lowest intensity delivered across all studies reviewed in the present paper and may represent insufficient neuromodulatory dosing. Of equal importance is that VNeST alone (i.e., sham stimulation) led to maintenance of trained verbs across all testing times for all three participants, including the individual with lvPPA, which provides further support for the efficacy of VNeST in the treatment of PPA.

Computerized Picture Naming Approaches

Another approach taken when pairing tDCS for therapeutic effect alongside behavioral intervention is computerized picture naming. Although computerized single word naming administered without a theoretically motivated cueing hierarchy is not evidence-based or of functional relevance (Galletta & Vogel-Eyny, 2015), two of the three studies reported here included a prompting paradigm. The most common variant included across these reports was participants with naPPA (3/3 studies; Cotelli et al., 2014, 2016; Roncero et al., 2017), with only one study additionally including individuals with lvPPA and svPPA (Roncero et al., 2017). Looking at the tDCS paradigm, 2/3 of the studies were sham-controlled (Cotelli et al., 2014; Roncero et al., 2017), and all studies delivered stimulation at 2 mA intensity with differences only in stimulation duration: 20 mins. vs 25 mins. For all studies, behavioral intervention was paired with stimulation duration and did not exceed the tDCS stimulation window (i.e., the behavioral intervention ended when the tDCS stimulation ceased).

Two studies from the same group employed a similar word naming treatment methodology in their group of participants with naPPA (Cotelli et al., 2014, 2016). The researchers developed a stimulus set composed of common nouns for training and generalization that was individualized given performance on a larger set of nouns (Philadelphia Naming Test; PNT). The treatment approach was previously reported in a prior study by the same research group (Cotelli et al., 2011) and consisted of repetition given a clinician model, articulatory suppression (i.e., to prevent verbal rehearsal), oral naming, reading, and oral naming a second time. Cotelli and colleagues' (2014) sham-controlled investigation found improved naming accuracy for trained and untrained items in both the active and sham groups immediately following treatment and 3-months post; however, the effect was greater in the active tDCS condition. Of functional importance, the researchers also observed gains following active tDCS in a self-reported measure of daily language abilities (Stroke and Aphasia Quality of Life Scale; SAQoL). In their 2016 case series (Cotelli et al., 2016) including a similar population, the authors reported gains for treated and untreated noun targets from baseline to post-treatment time points.

Confrontation naming from picture cues was also examined in all three PPA variants in a sham-controlled tDCS study conducted by Roncero and colleagues (2017). The paired naming activity included computerized picture naming without a cueing hierarchy. Participants cycled through a subset of pictures named incorrectly at the start of the active or sham tDCS conditions. The protocol was not intended to provide therapeutic, evidence-based anomia training. Rather, the picture naming task was used to engage word-naming neural areas of interest. Trained items improved from baseline in both conditions with a greater effect observed for active tDCS relative to sham. Generalization to untrained nouns and maintenance of gains were observed at all post-stimulation testing times, including a 1-month follow-up, in the active tDCS condition. The researchers did not examine performance by PPA subtype, so it is unclear whether the paired intervention was equivalently beneficial for all participants.

Semi-structured Discourse Approach

Only two studies reviewed included narrative discourse as a word-naming intervention for individuals with lvPPA or naPPA (Gervits et al., 2016; Hosseini et al., 2019). Similar to Roncero et al., (2017), the rationale for including an online linguistic task during tDCS is to engage neural regions subserving the domain for remediation (Gill et al., 2015). The authors targeted speech production in discourse given the overall fluency profile of the PPA variants assessed: Individuals with naPPA have speech difficulties characterized by reduced rate and increased effortfulness, and those with lvPPA experience phonologically-mediated word-retrieval impairments. In this open-label pilot, participants narrated wordless picture books during stimulation, with a different book assigned to each of the ten sessions. No further intervention or facilitation was provided. Participants improved in a composite measure of speech production (i.e., Cookie Theft task: Speech rate and MLU) immediately following tDCS; however, gains were not maintained at a 6- or 12-week follow-up.

In a separate sham-controlled investigation by the same group, the researchers combined tDCS with wordless picture book narration and observed a significant benefit in the active tDCS condition relative to sham (Hosseini et al., 2019). More specifically, relative to baseline, participants receiving active tDCS produced more words in the semantic fluency task at 6 and 12 weeks post-stimulation than those in the sham condition. This outcome was observed for individuals with naPPA and for those with lvPPA. They assumed that individuals with naPPA and lvPPA may benefit from wordless picture book narration, given intact verbal semantic processing, over and above those with svPPA. This is consistent with recent findings that those with svPPA produced fewer words in category fluency measures relative to the other variants, evidencing semantic deficits (van den Berg et al., 2022) (see also research indicating no between-group differences for semantic fluency; van den Berg et al., 2017). The researchers also assessed post-treatment performance on a measure of confrontation naming (Boston Naming Test), but there was no effect of tDCS condition (active vs sham). Although there were no significant differences at each testing time point between the two tDCS conditions, the authors note a trend where individuals in the sham condition continued to decline from baseline at each of the three post-stimulation time points while those in the active condition did not. The implication here is that tDCS might serve to stave off cognitive-linguistic decline, which is clinically meaningful for those with a progressive condition due to neurodegenerative processes. Taken together, these findings represent a much-needed addition to the existing literature by targeting speech fluency during tDCS, in comparison to naming at the single-word level.

Conclusion and Future Directions

The purpose of the present review was to highlight the current state of the art in the use of tDCS as an adjuvant to oral word retrieval intervention in PPA, with a particular focus on paired treatment approaches. Given the progressive nature of PPA, the goal of rehabilitation is to stave off further decline of language functioning, which is distinct from post-stroke aphasia treatment where the goal of rehabilitation is to improve language function. Evidence-based interventions are continuing to be developed to address the range of unique and complex language needs of the PPA population (Robinaugh & Henry, 2022). Within the current review, several studies took a restitutive approach to treatment, providing well-founded speech-language therapies such as SFA (Hung et al., 2017) and VNeST (Edmonds, 2018). Furthermore, researchers also turned to prophylactic interventions that target the maintenance of a core lexicon of functionally-relevant words (Hung et al., 2017). These paired treatment approaches to tDCS support the viability of this form of neuromodulation as a therapeutic tool for individuals with PPA. The findings from these early paired investigations are promising as several studies found improvements to both trained and untrained items, with maintenance observed for several weeks beyond intervention. The tDCS-related treatment gains in several studies were significantly greater than behavioral treatment alone. As with any novel area of investigation, there is work to be done. Future studies will need to address the issue of dosage as it relates to neuromodulation (i.e., stimulation site, intensity, and duration), as well as behavioral treatment characteristics (i.e., treatment selection and duration). Additional studies should consider the role of participant-level parameters (i.e., PPA variant, disease duration, and age) in treatment outcomes. Continued development of evidence-based interventions and refinement of tDCS parameters will improve the functional use of this cutting-edge treatment approach to word retrieval for those with PPA.

References

Barker, A. T., Jalinous, R., & Freeston, I. L. (1985). Non-invasive magnetic stimulation of human motor cortex. *Lancet*, *1*(8437), 1106–1107. 10.1016/s0140-6736(85)92413-4

Boyle, M. & Coelho, C. A. (1995). Application of semantic feature analysis as a treatment for aphasic dysnomia. *American Journal of Speech-Language Pathology*, *4*(4), 94–98. 10.1044/1058-0360.0404.94

Bikson, M., Grossman, P., Thomas, C., Zannou, A. L., Jiang, J., Adnan, T., Mourdoukoutas, A. P., Kronberg, G., Truong, D., Boggio, P., Brunoni, A. R., Charvet, L., Fregni, F., Fritsch, B., Gillick, B., Hamilton, R. H., Hampstead, B. M., Jankord, R., Kirton, A., ...& Woods, A. J. (2016). Safety of transcranial Direct Current Stimulation: Evidence based update 2016. *Brain Stimulation*, *9*(5), 641–661. 10.1016/j.brs.2016.06.004

Cerami, C., Dodich, A., Greco, L., Iannaccone, S., Magnani, G., Marcone, A., Pelagallo, E., Santangelo, R., Cappa, S. F., & Perani, D. (2017). The role of single-subject brain metabolic patterns in the early differential diagnosis of Primary Progressive Aphasias and in prediction of progression to dementia. *Journal of Alzheimer's Disease*, *55*(1), 183–197. 10.3233/JAD-160682

Cotelli, M., Fertonani, A., Miozzo, A., Rosini, S., Manenti, R., Padovani, A., Ansaldo, A. I., Cappa, S. F., & Miniussi, C. (2011). Anomia training and brain stimulation in chronic aphasia. *Neuropsychological Rehabilitation*, *21*(5), 717–741. 10.1080/09602011.2011.621275

Cotelli, M., Manenti, R., Brambilla, M., Petesi, M., Rosini, S., Ferrari, C., Zanetti, O., & Miniussi, C. (2014). Anodal tDCS during face-name associations memory training in Alzheimer's patients. *Frontiers in Aging Neuroscience*, *6*, 38. 10.3389/fnagi.2014.00038

Cotelli, M., Manenti, R., Ferrari, C., Gobbi, E., Macis, A., & Cappa, S. F. (2020). Effectiveness of language training and non-invasive brain stimulation on oral and written naming performance in Primary Progressive Aphasia: A meta-analysis and systematic review. *Neuroscience and Biobehavioral Reviews*, *108*, 498–525. 10.1016/j.neubiorev.2019.12.003

Cotelli, M., Manenti, R., Paternicò, D., Cosseddu, M., Brambilla, M., Petesi, M., Premi, E., Gasparotti, R., Zanetti, O., Padovani, A., & Borroni, B. (2016). Grey matter density predicts the improvement of naming abilities after tDCS intervention in agrammatic aariant of Primary Progressive Aphasia. *Brain Topography*, *29*(5), 738–751. 10.1007/s10548-016-0494-2

Duffy, J. R., Utianski, R. L., & Josephs, K. A. (2021). Primary Progressive Apraxia of Speech: From recognition to diagnosis and care. *Aphasiology*, *35*(4), 560–591. 10.1080/02687038.2020.1787732

Edmonds, L. (2018). VNeST. In J. Kreutzer, J. DeLuca, & B. Caplan (Eds.), *Encyclopedia of Clinical Neuropsychology* (pp. 1–5). Springer International Publishing. 10.1007/978-3-319-56782-2_9130-2

Edmonds, L. (2014). Tutorial for Verb Network Strengthening Treatment (VNeST): Detailed description of the treatment protocol with corresponding theoretical rationale. *Perspectives on Neurophysiology and Neurogenic Speech and Language Disorders*, *24*(3), 78. 10.1044/nnsld24.3.78

Galletta, E. E. & Vogel-Eyny, A. (2015). Translational treatment of aphasia combining neuromodulation and behavioral intervention for lexical retrieval: Implications from a single case study. *Frontiers in Human Neuroscience*, *9*, 447. 10.3389/fnhum.2015.00447

Gervits, F., Ash, S., Coslett, H. B., Rascovsky, K., Grossman, M., & Hamilton, R. (2016). Transcranial direct current stimulation for the treatment of primary progressive aphasia: An open-label pilot study. *Brain and Language*, *162*, 35–41. 10.1016/j.bandl.2016.05.007

Gill, J., Shah-Basak, P. P., & Hamilton, R. (2015). It's the thought that counts: Examining the task-dependent effects of transcranial direct current stimulation on executive function. *Brain Stimulation*, *8*(2), 253–259. 10.1016/j.brs.2014.10.018

Gorno-Tempini, M. L., Dronkers, N. F., Rankin, K. P., Ogar, J. M., Phengrasamy, L., Rosen, H. J., Johnson, J. K., Weiner, M. W., & Miller, B. L. (2004). Cognition and anatomy in three variants of primary progressive aphasia. *Annals of Neurology*, *55*(3), 335–346. 10.1002/ana.10825

Gorno-Tempini, M. L., Hillis, A. E., Weintraub, S., Kertesz, A., Mendez, M., Cappa, S. F., Ogar, J. M., Rohrer, J. D., Black, S., Boeve, B. F., Manes, F., Dronkers, N. F., Vandenberghe, R., Rascovsky, K., Patterson, K., Miller, B. L., Knopman, D. S., Hodges, J. R., Mesulam, M. M., & Grossman, M. (2011). Classification of primary progressive aphasia and its variants. *Neurology*, *76*(11), 1006–1014. 10.1212/WNL.0b013e31821103e6

Grossman, M. (2010). Primary progressive aphasia: Clinicopathological correlations. *Nature Reviews. Neurology*, *6*(2), 88–97. 10.1038/nrneurol.2009.216

Heidland, A., Fazeli, G., Klassen, A., Sebekova, K., Hennemann, H., Bahner, U., & Di Iorio, B. (2013). Neuromuscular electrostimulation techniques: Historical aspects and current possibilities in treatment of pain and muscle waisting. *Clinical Nephrology*, *79*(Suppl 1), S12–S23.

Henry, M. L. & Gorno-Tempini, M. L. (2010). The logopenic variant of primary progressive aphasia. *Current Opinion in Neurology*, *23*(6), 633–637. 10.1097/WCO.0b013e32833fb93e

Hosseini, M., McConathey, E. M., Ungrady, M., Grossman, M., Coslett, H. B., & Hamilton, R. H. (2019). Proceedings #10: Transcranial Direct Current Stimulation mediates improvements in verbal fluency for patients with Primary Progressive Aphasia. *Brain Stimulation: Basic, Translational, and Clinical Research in Neuromodulation*, *12*(2), e69–e71. 10.1016/j.brs.2018.12.179

Hung, J., Bauer, A., Grossman, M., Hamilton, R. H., Coslett, H. B., & Reilly, J. (2017). Semantic Feature Training in combination with Transcranial Direct Current Stimulation (tDCS) for progressive anomia. *Frontiers in Human Neuroscience*, *11*, 253. 10.3389/fnhum.2017.00253

Kellner, C. H., Greenberg, R. M., Murrough, J. W., Bryson, E. O., Briggs, M. C., & Pasculli, R. M. (2012). ECT in treatment-resistant depression. *The American Journal of Psychiatry*, *169*(12), 1238–1244. 10.1176/appi.ajp.2012.12050648

Lerman, A., Mais, D., Nissani, Y., & Malcolm, T. (2023). Preserving lexical retrieval skills across languages in a bilingual person with logopenic primary progressive aphasia. *Aphasiology*, *37*(3), 432–455. 10.1080/02687038.2021.2020717

Mesulam, M. (1982). Slowly progressive aphasia without generalized dementia. *Annals of Neurology*, *11*(6), 592–598. 10.1002/ana.410110607

Mesulam, M. (2001). Primary progressive aphasia. *Annals of Neurology*, *49*(4), 425–432.

Mesulam, M. (2003). Primary progressive aphasia—A language-based dementia. *The New England Journal of Medicine*, *349*(16), 1535–1542. 10.1056/NEJMra022435

Mesulam, M. (2013). Primary progressive aphasia: A dementia of the language network. *Dementia and Neuropsychologia*, *7*(1), 2–9. 10.1590/S1980-57642013DN70100002

Monte-Silva, K., Kuo, M.-F., Hessenthaler, S., Fresnoza, S., Liebetanz, D., Paulus, W., & Nitsche, M. A. (2013). Induction of late LTP-like plasticity in the human motor cortex by repeated non-invasive brain stimulation. *Brain Stimulation*, *6*(3), 424–432. 10.1016/j.brs.2012.04.011

Monti, A., Cogiamanian, F., Marceglia, S., Ferrucci, R., Mameli, F., Mrakic-Sposta, S., Vergari, M., Zago, S., & Priori, A. (2008). Improved naming after transcranial direct current stimulation in aphasia. *Journal of Neurology, Neurosurgery, and Psychiatry*, *79*(4), 451–453. 10.1136/jnnp.2007.135277

Pilloni, G., Vogel-Eyny, A., Lustberg, M., Best, P., Malik, M., Walton-Masters, L., George, A., Mirza, I., Zhovtis, L., Datta, A., Bikson, M., Krupp, L., & Charvet, L. (2022). Tolerability and feasibility of at-home remotely supervised transcranial direct current stimulation (RS-tDCS): Single-center evidence from 6,779 sessions. *Brain Stimulation*, *15*(3), 707–716. 10.1016/j.brs.2022.04.014

Price, C. J. (2010). The anatomy of language: A review of 100 fMRI studies published in 2009. *Annals of the New York Academy of Sciences*, *1191*, 62–88. 10.1111/j.1749-6632.2010.05444.x

Robinaugh, G. & Henry, M. L. (2022). Chapter 14—Behavioral interventions for primary progressive aphasia. In A. E. Hillis & J. Fridriksson (Eds.), *Handbook of Clinical Neurology* (Vol. 185, pp. 221–240). Elsevier. 10.1016/B978-0-12-823384-9.00011-6

Roncero, C., Kniefel, H., Service, E., Thiel, A., Probst, S., & Chertkow, H. (2017). Inferior parietal transcranial direct current stimulation with training improves cognition in anomic Alzheimer's disease and frontotemporal dementia. *Alzheimer's and Dementia (New York, N. Y.)*, *3*(2), 247–253. 10.1016/j.trci.2017.03.003

Sheppard, S. M. (2022). Chapter 16—Noninvasive brain stimulation to augment language therapy for primary progressive aphasia. In A. E. Hillis & J. Fridriksson (Eds.), *Handbook of Clinical Neurology* (Vol. 185, pp. 251–260). Elsevier. 10.1016/B978-0-12-823384-9.00018-9

Sheppard, S. M., Goldberg, E. B., Sebastian, R., Walker, A., Meier, E. L., & Hillis, A. E. (2022). Transcranial Direct Current Stimulation aired with Verb Network Strengthening Treatment improves verb naming in Primary Progressive Aphasia: A case series. *American Journal of Speech-Language Pathology*, *31*(4), 1736–1754. 10.1044/2022_AJSLP-21-00272

Silveri, M. C., & Ciccarelli, N. (2007). Naming of grammatical classes in frontotemporal dementias: Linguistic and non linguistic factors contribute to noun-verb dissociation. *Behavioural Neurology*, *18*(4), 197–206. 10.1155/2007/428191 van den Berg, E., Dijkzeul, J. C. M., Poos, J. M., Eikelboom, W. S., van Hemmen, J., Franzen, S., de Jong, F. J., Dopper, E. G. P., Vonk, J. M. J., Papma, J. M., Satoer, D., Jiskoot, L. C., & Seelaar, H. (2022). Differential linguistic features of verbal fluency in behavioral variant frontotemporal dementia and primary progressive aphasia. *Applied Neuropsychology: Adult*, 1–9. 10.1080/23279095.2022.2060748

van den Berg, E., Jiskoot, L. C., Grosveld, M. J. H., van Swieten, J. C., & Papma, J. M. (2017). Qualitative assessment of verbal fluency performance in frontotemporal dementia. *Dementia and Geriatric Cognitive Disorders*, 44(1–2), 35–44. 10.1159/000477538

PART III

Language Processing in Multilingual and Monolingual Adults with Stroke-Induced Aphasia

11

TOWARD AN INTERSECTIONAL NEUROCOGNITIVE APPROACH TO MANAGEMENT OF POST-STROKE APHASIA IN MULTILINGUAL ETHNORACIALLY DIVERSE GERIATRIC POPULATIONS

Jose G. Centeno and Eve Higby

Introduction

The disproportionate burden of the COVID-19 pandemic on underserved and vulnerable populations, such as minoritized ethnoracial groups and individuals with disabilities, including people with aphasia (PWA), has highlighted the urgency to address the health care and social inequities in vulnerable populations in our society (Centeno et al., 2023; Kong, 2021; Shakespeare et al., 2021; Webb Hooper et al., 2020). Intersectionality, a central tenet in Critical Race Theory (Crenshaw, 1989), describes how multiple marginalized social identities intersect to result in unequal social power that translates into oppression or discrimination with detrimental consequences in life quality, access to care, and general well-being (Cho et al., 2013; Crenshaw, 1989; Hankivsky et al., 2017). Intersectionality has been a valuable principle to focus healthcare practitioners and researchers on the multiple factors that coalesce in individuals and social groups to result in discrimination, marginalization, vulnerability to illness, and, in turn, disparities (Bridges et al., 2017; Hankivsky et al., 2017).

Larger caseloads of ethnoracially and linguistically diverse geriatric clients with post-stroke aphasia, a frequent disability after a stroke, are estimated from the increased vulnerability to cardiovascular complications in a rapidly aging diverse population with complex health histories and personal life trajectories (Centeno & Harris, 2021; Feigin et al., 2019). In these growing ethnogeriatric caseloads, intersectionality provides a powerful approach to synergize socially-based principles of aphasia intervention with individual experiential histories and their possible neurological

DOI: 10.4324/9781003330318-14

underpinnings to develop an equity-grounded framework of aphasia rehabilitation. This framework should promote evidence-based services and minimize care inequities among the growing number of multilingual, ethnogeriatric PWA in the U.S. (Centeno et al., 2020; López et al., 2021; LPAA, 2008).

The purpose of this chapter is to propose an aphasia intervention framework that accounts for clients' intersectional life-course profiles, which consist of multiple interconnected factors and experiences, and their interactions with individual patterns of language, cognition, and brain processes throughout their lives. An intersectional neurocognitive approach to aphasia intervention in multilingual speakers in ethnoracially diverse populations incorporates not only their diverse individual life experiences, but also how individual language and cognitive demands from those social experiences shape neurological function and structure (Claussenius-Kalman et al., 2021; DeLuca et al., 2020).

We start with an overview of the ethnogeriatric scenario in the U.S. relevant to aphasia services followed by a summary of multilingualism principles pertinent to aphasia management. We continue with a proposal for intersectional neurocognitive aphasia management of multilingual caseloads and conclude with possible future directions to strengthen socially-responsive neuroscientific aphasia intervention for multilingual speakers. Because multilingual communities include both bilingual and multilingual speakers (i.e., users of two or more than two languages, respectively), we use the term *multilingual* to reflect that language diversity throughout this chapter. Additionally, although the ethnogeriatric illustration in our discussion focuses on the U.S. context, a similar examination of diverse older communities is warranted for aphasia services in other ethnoracially heterogeneous countries.

Ethnogeriatric Scenario in the United States

Consistent with the migration-driven worldwide growth in ethnoracially diverse geriatric populations (e.g., Dwolatzky et al., 2017; Kristiansen et al., 2016), the U.S. population is estimated to continue to become progressively older and more diverse, both linguistically and ethnoracially (Centeno & Harris, 2021; Yeo et al., 2017). By 2060, Black, Indigenous, and People of Color (BIPOC) are predicted to make up about 50% of the U.S. population over 65 years old (Mather et al., 2015). Linguistic and cultural diversity in older communities in the country, consisting of Indigenous groups, settled minorities, and new international migrants, will include individuals with various language backgrounds (i.e., speakers of different dialectal varieties of English, monolingual minority language users, and multilingual speakers) and life circumstances (i.e., varying socioeconomic backgrounds, immigration histories, sociocultural norms, educational experiences, health profiles, etc.) (Centeno et al., 2023; Centeno & Harris, 2021; Cummings & Vaughn, 2017).

Disproportionate vulnerability in older BIPOC groups to conditions such as stroke and other cardiovascular complications has been associated with social and structural determinants of health throughout their life course. While social health determinants refer to the environments in which people live, work, play, and learn, structural health determinants include the economic, judicial, medical, and political policies that impact life and health (Murray, 2021). For geriatric BIPOC groups, complex experiential trajectories that interconnect personal hardships (e.g., low income, language barriers, and minimal insurance coverage), individual health risk factors (e.g., limited physical activity, poor diet, and vulnerable emotional well-being), environmental challenges (e.g., poor water quality, social marginalization, and reduced community safety), and institutional obstacles (e.g., culturally inadequate service, discrimination, and limited specialized care) translate into disparities in health, care, and outcomes (Barr, 2019). Many members of BIPOC communities experience coexisting chronic social and structural challenges throughout their lives that compromise their health and well-being, and ultimately the aging process (Centeno et al., 2023 ; Ferraro et al., 2017). Although multiple health determinants have been implicated in ethnoracial disparities in stroke prevalence and care (Havranek et al., 2015), some factors and their interactions, including race/ethnicity, age, sex, level of education, geographic location, and culturally incongruent care conditions, seem to be critical (Labovitz, 2020; Virani et al., 2021).

Multilingualism Principles in Aphasia Therapy

The heterogeneity in language outcomes in multilingual speakers and the variety of post-stroke aphasia profiles they may exhibit impose specific clinical challenges. Multilingual individuals are a linguistically heterogeneous group whose individual language outcomes reflect their personal language experiences, as shaped by their own life history and personal attributes, as well as the sociopolitical context of language learning (Claussenius-Kalman et al., 2021; López et al., 2021).

Language practices across modalities (i.e., aural comprehension, reading, speaking, and writing) are modulated by each multilingual learner's life trajectory. Experiences that make up a multilingual individual's life history include both formal (i.e., educational and occupational contexts) and informal (i.e., social and leisure contexts) communication environments, as well as personal background (i.e., gender, socioeconomic situation, learning aptitude, immigration history, cultural identity, etc.) and the sociopolitical scenario maintaining linguistic hierarchies (i.e., sociopolitical attitudes and policies toward the ethnic group that speaks the language and toward the language itself) (Bialystok, 2001; López et al., 2021). Furthermore, the broader socio-ecological context of multilingual development, such as interpersonal dynamics, social environments, societal disposition, and historical language-learning trajectory, strongly impacts multilingual individuals' language exposure and use experiences, which ultimately have neurocognitive outcomes (Antolovic et al., 2023; Titone & Tiv, 2023). Despite their effects on neurocognitive processes, these socio-ecological factors in multilingual communication are often minimally or insufficiently acknowledged in research on multilingual people with aphasia (Centeno et al., 2020).

As multilingual learners acquire their languages over time, multiple language-cognition interactions with neurological repercussions occur, which are molded by personal fluctuations in communication contexts, educational and occupational experiences, and acculturation phases (Centeno, 2007). Individual intensity, diversity, and duration of language experiences have neurocognitive consequences for each multilingual speaker (DeLuca et al., 2020). Particularly, evidence for cognitive-control demands in spoken language use by multilingual individuals has shed light on the possible interconnections among language, cognition, and the brain. As multilingual individuals control competition between their languages in their daily monolingual or multilingual communication modes, such monolingual-multilingual communication shifts result in individual neurocognitive adaptations in cognitive control (e.g., attention, monitoring, activation, inhibition) that engage cortical-subcortical networks and enable suitable language choice during monolingual or multilingual communication (Dash & Ansaldo, 2017). The adaptive control hypothesis posits that different types of cognitive control are needed for various types of communication by multilingual speakers, such as intrasentential code-switching (e.g., "I can't run *porque acabo de comer*" [I can't run because I just finished eating]), lexical borrowing (e.g., "She is a great *gobernadora*" [she is a great governor]), or when producing an entire narrative in one language only (Dash & Ansaldo, 2017; Goral & Lerman, 2020; Green & Abutalebi, 2013).

Deficits in cognitive control mechanisms have been implicated in the heterogeneous patterns of post-stroke language recovery in multilingual language users with aphasia (Abutalebi & Green, 2007; Peñaloza & Kiran, 2019). Multilingual persons with post-stroke aphasia may show a similar extent of impairment in both languages relative to pre-morbid language abilities after the brain insult (*parallel recovery pattern*) or different language restitution profiles, in which there is uneven recovery of the two languages (*nonparallel or differential recovery patterns*) (Ansaldo et al., 2008). Brain damage from the stroke can disrupt the cortical-subcortical interactions regulating activation-inhibition control operations, resulting in insufficient activation or excessive inhibition of a language during communication (nonparallel recovery) (Dash & Ansaldo, 2017; Goral & Lerman, 2020; Peñaloza & Kiran, 2019).

Socially-Responsive Neurocognitive Aphasia Management in Multilingual Populations: Intersectionality as a Guiding Principle

Contemporary aphasia intervention principles promote inclusion and life reengagement for PWA through meaningful personal goals and social relationships (Hersch, 2018; LPAA, 2008). Additionally, these principles provide the clinical directions to develop personalized, socially-responsive approaches to serve growing ethnoracially diverse aphasia caseloads. An intersectional life-course approach to aphasia services would create more nuanced, experientially-grounded intervention strategies by synergizing individual profiles, consisting of the sociocultural identities and personal attributes that modulate language attitudes, use, exposure, and proficiency, with the experiential cognitive aptitudes and post-stroke cognitive profile of each multilingual person with aphasia (Claussenius-Kalman et al., 2021; DeLuca et al., 2020). In an intersectional neurocognitive perspective for socially-responsive aphasia intervention, assessment methods explore individual life experiential paths, language practices, and personal identities to collect meaningful diagnostic results that can guide neurocognitive engagement in a socially-attuned individualized remediation plan (Bialystok, 2001; Centeno et al., 2020; López et al., 2021).

Consistent with aphasia services in monolingual-monocultural contexts (Martin et al., 2018; Murray & Coppens, 2022), aphasia management of ethnoracially diverse caseloads relies on the administration of language and cognitive assessment procedures to gather diagnostic results that can inform intervention to facilitate language and communication for social participation (Ansaldo et al., 2008; Centeno et al., 2022; Norvik & Goral, 2021). However, modifications in the standard clinical protocol for aphasia services are necessary when working with multilingual speakers in diverse communities due to the diverse experiences of ethnoracially heterogeneous older populations and limitations in available clinical procedures and research (Beveridge & Bak, 2011; Centeno, 2015; Norvik et al., 2022). These clinical modifications are particularly crucial for the implementation of an intersectional neurocognitive approach to assessment and intervention, as discussed next.

Assessment Considerations

The administration of supplementary intake procedures to gather detailed information about language history (i.e., age, contexts, frequency, and modalities of multilingual use and exposure) and sociocultural affinity (i.e., cultural identity, immigration experiences, and social networks) is needed to estimate the extent of pre-morbid language practice and proficiency and to explore sociocultural affiliation and culturally-shaped attitudes and routines (Norvik & Goral, 2021; Wallace et al., 2010). Although a precise determination of the pre-morbid proficiency may not be possible unless language recordings of the multilingual client are available, using both a multilingualism history questionnaire and self-ratings of proficiency, administered to the client, if possible, as well as the client's family, generate useful insights to estimate pre-morbid levels of language mastery. While a multilingualism history questionnaire typically examines the intensity and frequency of language exposure and use over time (Marian et al., 2007), self-rating scales yield self-assessments of language mastery across multiple modalities (Kiran & Roberts, 2012). Because the site of lesion has consequences for the pattern of language recovery (e.g., parallel/nonparallel; Goral & Lerman, 2020; Lerman et al., 2020), the medical history needs to include this information. Also, administration of acculturation scales, designed to tap into life history, language preference, leisure interests, and social networks (Wallace et al., 2010), would provide important complementary information to standard intake questions (i.e., education, home environment, and health history) and information on post-stroke life quality (i.e., social connections, emotional support, well-being, and sense of self) to develop a comprehensive, historical client profile (Manning et al., 2019; Wilson et al., 2019).

Psychometrically sound assessment of multilingual speakers with aphasia is challenging due to the extensive acquisitional and experiential variability in multilingual adult populations beyond the differences observed between monolingual speakers (Higby et al., 2023; Kiran & Roberts, 2012). In the absence of standardized psychometric aphasia tests for multilingual speakers, aphasia assessment of multilingual individuals requires the use of linguistically and culturally adapted instruments to examine multiple modalities in all of the languages known by the multilingual person pre-stroke, as well as post-morbid cognitive skills, especially in areas relevant to multilingual abilities, such as language switching and translation (Ansaldo et al., 2008; Centeno et al., 2022; Norvik & Goral, 2021). The *Bilingual Aphasia Test* (BAT), a criterion-based assessment instrument available in many different language pairs, is the only aphasia test created to examine post-stroke language recovery in dual language users with aphasia (Paradis, 2022).

For neurocognitive assessment, instruments without high comprehension demands, such as the *Cognitive-Linguistic Quick Test-Plus* (CLQT-Plus; Helm-Estabrooks, 2001) and the *Repeatable Battery for the Assessment of Neuropsychological Status* (RBANS; Randolph, 2012), although developed for monolingual English speakers and also available in Spanish, can be adapted to examine general cognitive skills in multilingual speakers of other languages (Ansaldo et al., 2008; Dash & Ansaldo, 2017). As required in aphasia assessment, given the different life experiences in multilingual adult individuals throughout their lives (e.g., education, language(s), countries of origin, and socioeconomic history) (Lequerica & Panyavin, 2016), cognitive assessment similarly requires linguistic and sociocultural adaptations of available tests.

Therapy Considerations

Regarding intervention, research in multilingual aphasia therapy is scarce. Insights based on monolingual aphasia studies are valuable to describe general variables supporting the therapy process (i.e., prognosis factors, dosage, frequency, and intensity of therapy) (McClung et al., 2010; Plowman et al., 2012; RELEASE Collaborators, 2022). Intervention research in multilingual aphasia, while initially focused on examining the extent and nature of cross-language directionality when one or two languages are chosen for therapy, more recently, stimulated by encouraging neurocognitive control findings, has shifted its emphasis to the study of the therapeutic role of the activation-inhibition control mechanisms in multilingual language use (Goral & Lerman, 2020; Green & Abutalebi, 2008). The cortical-subcortical neurocognitive networks participating in language activation-inhibition operations in multilingual communication seem to be recruited to facilitate therapy-induced language gains, as modulated by multiple important variables (e.g., age of acquisition, language exposure and use, lesion site, focus of therapy). For example, in terms of exposure and use, a communication environment that facilitates the frequent use of a particular language would stimulate the required cortical-subcortical connections to activate that language (Goral & Lerman, 2020). Likewise, based on the contrasting interconnections between language, emotions, and cognition in the languages spoken by bilingual speakers (Marian & Kaushanskaya, 2008), it is possible that positive affective associations with one of the languages spoken by a multilingual person may enhance activation of that language. Thus, language decisions for intervention, grounded on individual acquisitional history and psychosocial language needs, may be useful to engage neurocognitive control mechanisms that enhance therapy-induced language recovery (Ansaldo et al., 2008; Goral & Lerman, 2020; Peñaloza & Kiran, 2019).

To fine-tune intervention in an intersectional neurocognitive direction, the client's experiential profile, especially factors such as estimated pre-morbid language mastery, communication environments, educational history, and acculturation, as well as post-stroke aphasia symptoms, are critical for selecting the stimuli, topics, and formats for socially-responsive, patient-centered therapy contexts that can authentically stimulate cognitive and linguistic abilities. While some research has emphasized treating nonlinguistic neurocognitive control abilities (e.g., working memory, attention, and inhibitory control) (Dash & Kar, 2014; Gray & Kiran, 2016), other studies have focused on linguistic-cognitive stimulation (e.g., code-switching and translation at the word and sentence levels to stimulate attention, memory, and language selection) (Ansaldo & Ghazi Saidi, 2014). Because formal and informal language routines involve different cognitive demands with possible neurocognitive repercussions (Bialystok, 2001; DeLuca et al., 2020; Lopez et al., 2022), therapeutic cognitive stimulation would necessitate alignment with the patient's socioeducational trajectory. Additionally, the interplay of language, cognition, and culture in the elderly population (Harris, 1997), particularly the notion that language is the element to internalize culture (Altarriba, 2003; Marian & Kaushanskaya, 2008), warrants attention. The social-ecological context for aphasia intervention in multilingual environments needs to acknowledge pre-morbid sociolinguistic dynamics and cultural affiliations. Psychological research has highlighted the different emotional associations of vocabulary items to each of the languages of multilingual speakers (Altarriba, 2003) and the more favorable retrieval of autobiographical episodes that are aligned with the language of the experiences (Centeno, 2007; Marian & Kaushanskaya, 2008).

Conclusion and Future Directions

This chapter provided a preliminary framework for the implementation of an intersectional neuroscientific perspective for aphasia intervention that responds to the multidimensional life experiences of the burgeoning ethnogeriatric aphasia populations in post-stroke rehabilitation. By highlighting the possible clinical impact of often overlooked interactions between language, cognition, and brain in multilingualism, this framework aims to strengthen intervention and reduce care disparities in multilingual aphasia caseloads. Research to support aphasia assessment and intervention strategies in multilingual adults, while steadily growing, is still scarce. However, there are promising trends in the emerging theoretical proposals and research strategies.

Theoretical accounts that interconnect the language and communication ecosystem, including its psychosocial aspects, to neurocognitive adaptations throughout the individual life trajectory of each multilingual speaker provide valuable foundations for aphasia intervention strategies (Claussenius-Kalman et al., 2021; DeLuca et al., 2020; López et al., 2021). Similarly, recent multilingualism research in neurotypical individuals with relevance to aphasia services has begun to move away from broad comparisons of multilingual and monolingual speakers and toward the development of models that incorporate individual differences and acknowledge the multidimensionality of multilingual experiences (Bialystok, 2021; Claussenius-Kalman et al., 2021; Higby et al., 2023; López et al., 2021). To incorporate the socio-ecological aspects of language into psycholinguistic or neurolinguistic multilingualism research, data must be collected to capture this information. Language background surveys often focus primarily on the individual experiences of participants (what Titone & Tiv, 2023, refer to as *ego-driven language dynamics*) and not their social contexts. Several more recently developed questionnaires incorporate sociocultural dimensions, including the *Language and Social Background Questionnaire* (LSBQ, Anderson et al., 2018), the *Contextual and Individual Linguistic Diversity Questionnaire* (CILD-Q, Wigdorowitz et al., 2020), and the social network survey (Navarro et al., 2022). Language entropy, a concept recently proposed to capture the social diversity of language use, is a single measure that incorporates language use data from multiple languages across various communicative contexts (Gullifer & Titone, 2020).

Additionally, a number of research methodologies could be employed to generate clinically useful data to enhance intersectional aphasia services in multilingual populations. Specifically, the combined use of complementary data-collection approaches (e.g., mixed quantitative-qualitative methods, longitudinal studies, multifactorial approaches) would be useful to develop multilingual language experience databases and to conduct triangulated intersectional analyses of the multilingual experience based on a variety of data sources (Dash et al., 2022; Higby et al., 2023; López et al., 2021; Marte et al., 2022). Group-specific engagement strategies would help to explore health determinants in individual communities that can inform intervention (Scimeca et al., 2022).

While there is great interest in advancing multilingualism research in the adult population, concerted institutional and individual efforts, bringing together administrators, researchers, faculty, and professional organizations, are still necessary to create the culture and attitudes to maintain the momentum in socially responsive research catalyzed by the COVID pandemic. The research enterprise to advance care in ethnogeriatric communities with communication disabilities requires major self-analysis for the attitudinal changes that will develop and sustain an equity-grounded research agenda (Centeno & Harris, 2021; Ellis et al., 2021). To link individual life-course intersectionality in growing multilingual ethnogeriatric aphasia caseloads to promising neuroscientific evidence warrants the urgent implementation of socially responsive institutional and individual strategies.

References

Abutalebi, J. & Green, D. W. (2007). Bilingual language production: The neurocognition of language representation and control. *Journal of Neurolinguistics*, *20*, 242–275. 10.1016/j.jneuroling.2006.10.003

Altarriba, J. (2003). Does *cariño* equal liking? A theoretical approach to conceptual nonequivalence between languages. *International Journal of Bilingualism*, *3*, 305–322. 10.1177/13670069030070030501

Anderson, J. A. E., Mak, L., Keyvani Chaci, A., & Bialystok, E. (2018). The language and social background questionnaire: Assessing degree of bilingualism in a diverse population. *Behavior Research Methods*, *50*, 250–263. 10.3758/s13428-017-0867-9

Ansaldo, A. I., Marcotte, K., Scherer, L., & Raboyeau, G. (2008). Language therapy and bilingual aphasia: Clinical implications of psycholinguistic and neuroimaging research. *Journal of Neurolinguistics*, *21*, 539–557. 10.1016/j.jneuroling.2008.02.001

Ansaldo, A. I. & Ghazi Saidi, L. (2014). Aphasia therapy in the age of globalization: Cross-linguistic therapy effects in bilingual aphasia. *Behavioural Neurology*, *2014*, 603085. 10.1155/2014/603085

Antolovic, K., Higby, E., & Obler, L. K. (2023). Mechanisms of cognitive aging in multilingualism. In J. Cabrelli, A. Chaouch-Orozco, J. González Alonso, S. M. Pereira Soares, E. Puig-Mayenco, & J. Rothman (Eds.), *The Cambridge Handbook of Third Language Acquisition and Processing* (pp. 606–632). Cambridge University Press.

Barr, D. A. (2019). *Health Disparities in the United States: Social Class, Race, Ethnicity, and the Social Determinants of Health* (3rd ed.). John Hopkins University Press.

Beveridge, M. E. L. & Bak, T. H. (2011). The languages of aphasia: Bias and diversity. *Aphasiology*, *25*, 1451–1468. 10.1080/02687038.2011.624165

Bialystok, E. (2001). *Bilingualism in Development: Language, Literacy, and Cognition*. Cambridge University Press.

Bialystok, E. (2021). Bilingualism as a slice of Swiss cheese. *Frontiers in Psychology*, *12*, 769323. 10.3389/fpsyg.2021.769323

Bridges, K. M., Keel, T., & Obasogie, O. K. (2017). Introduction: Critical race theory and the health sciences. *American Journal of Law and Medicine*, *43*, 179–182. 10.1177/0098858817723657

Centeno, J. G. (2007). Considerations for an ethnopsycholinguistic framework for aphasia intervention. In A. Ardila & E. Ramos (Eds.), *Speech and Language Disorders in Bilinguals* (pp. 213–234). Nova Science.

Centeno, J. G. (2015). Assessing services with communicatively-impaired bilingual adults in culturally and linguistically diverse neurorehabilitation programs. *Journal of Communication Disorders*, *58*, 58–73. 10.1016/j.jcomdis.2015.10.005

Centeno, J. G., Collins, L., Obler, L. K., Wallace, G., Fleming, V. B., & Guendouzi, J. (2023). Focusing our attention on socially-responsive professional education to serve ethnogeriatric populations with neurogenic communication disorders in the United States. *American Journal of Speech-Language Pathology*. 10.1044/2023_AJSLP-22-00325

Centeno, J. G., Ghazi Saidi, L., & Ansaldo, A. I. (2022). Aphasia management in ethnoracially diverse multilingual populations. In I. Papathanasiou & P. Coppens (Eds.), *Aphasia and Related Neurogenic Communication Disorders* (3rd ed., pp. 379–402). Jones and Bartlett Learning.

Centeno, J. G. & Harris, J. L. (2021). Implications of United States service evidence for growing multiethnic adult neurorehabilitation caseloads worldwide. *Canadian Journal of Speech-Language Pathology and Audiology*, *45*(2), 77–97. https://cjslpa.ca/files/2021_CJSLPA_Vol_45/No_2/CJSLPA_Vol_45_No_2_2021_1207.pdf

Centeno, J. G., Kiran, S., & Armstrong, E. (2020). Editorial: Aphasia management in growing multiethnic populations. *Aphasiology*, *34*(11), 1314–1318. 10.1080/02687038.2020.1781420

Cho, S., Crenshaw, K. W., & McCall, L. (2013). Toward a field of intersectionality studies: Theory, applications, and praxis. *Signs: Journal of Women in Culture and Society*, *38*(4), 785–810. 10.1086/669608

Claussenius-Kalman, H., Hernandez, A. E., & Li, P. (2021). Expertise, ecosystem, and emergentism: Dynamic developmental bilingualism. *Brain and Language*, *222*, 105013. 10.1016/j.bandl.2021.105013

Crenshaw, K. W. (1989). Demarginalizing the intersection of race and sex: A black feminist critique of antidiscrimination doctrine, feminist theory and antiracist politics. *University of Chicago Legal Forum*, *138*(1), 8. https://chicagounbound.uchicago.edu/uclf/vol1989/iss1/8/

Cummings-Vaughn, L. (2017). Demographic trends in aging. In L. Cummings-Vaughn & D. M. Cruz-Oliver (Eds.), *Ethnogeriatrics: Healthcare Needs of Diverse Populations* (pp. 35–50). Springer.

Dash, T. & Ansaldo, A. I. (2017). Clinical implications of neurocognitive control deficits in bilingual adults with aphasia. *Perspectives of the ASHA Special Interest Groups, SIG 2*, *2*(3), 117–125. 10.1044/persp2.SIG2.117

Dash, T., Joanette, Y., & Ansaldo, A. I. (2022). Multifactorial approaches to study bilingualism in the aging population: Past, present, and future. *Frontiers in Psychology*, *13*, 917959. 10.3389/fpsyg.2022.917959

Dash, T. & Kar, B. R. (2014). Bilingual language control and general purpose cognitive control among individuals with bilingual aphasia: Evidence based on negative priming and flanker tasks. *Behavioural Neurology*, *2014*, 679706. 10.1155/2014/679706

DeLuca, V., Segaert, K., Mazaheri, A., & Krott, A. (2020). Understanding bilingual brain function and structure changes? U bet! A unified bilingual experience trajectory model. *Journal of Neurolinguistics*, *56*, 100930. 10.1016/j.jneuroling.2020.100930

Dwolatzky, T., Brodsky, J., Azaiza, F., Clarfield, A. M., Jacobs, J. M., & Litwin, H. (2017). Coming of age: Health-care challenges of an ageing population in Israel. *The Lancet*, *389*, 2542–2550. 10.1016/S0140-6736(17)30789-4

Ellis, C., Jacobs, M., & Kendall, D. (2021). The impact of racism, power, prestige, and positionality on communication sciences and disorders research: Time to reconceptualize a pathway to equity. *American Journal of Speech-Language Pathology*, *30*, 2032- 2031. 10.1044/2021_AJSLP-20-00346

Feigin, V. L., Nichols, E., Alam, T., Bannick, M. S., Beghi, E., Blake, N., Culpepper, W. J., Dorsey, E. R., Elbaz, A., Ellenbogen, R. G., Fisher, J. L., Fitzmaurice, C., Giussani, G., Glennie, L., James, S. L., Johnson, C. O. Kassebaum, N. J., Logroscino, G., Marin, B., …& Vos. T. (2019). Global, regional, and national burden of neurological disorders, 1990–2016: A systematic analysis for the Global Burden of Disease Study 2016. *The Lancet Neurology*, *18*, 459–480. 10.1016/S1474-4422(18)30499-X

Ferraro, K. F., Kemp, B. R., & Williams, M. M. (2017). Diverse aging and health inequality by race and ethnicity. *Innovation in Aging*, *1*, 1–11. 10.1093/geroni/igx002

Goral, M. & Lerman, A. (2020). Variables and mechanisms affecting responses to language treatment in multilingual people with aphasia. *Behavioral Sciences*, *10*, 144. 10.3390/bs10090144

Gray, T. & Kiran, S. (2016). The relationship between language control and cognitive control in bilingual aphasia. *Bilingualism: Language and Cognition*, *19*(3), 433–452. 10.1017/S1366728915000061

Green, D. & Abutalebi, J. (2008). Understanding the link between bilingual aphasia and language control. *Journal of Neurolinguistics*, *21*, 558–576. 10.1016/j.jneuroling.2008.01.002

Green, D. W. & Abutalebi, J. (2013). Language control in bilinguals: The adaptive control hypothesis. *Journal of Cognitive Psychology*, *25*(5), 515–530. 10.1080/20445911.2013.796377

Gullifer, J. W. & Titone, D. (2020). Characterizing the social diversity of bilingualism using language entropy. *Bilingualism: Language and Cognition*, *23*(2), 283–294. 10.1017/S1366728919000026

Hankivsky, O., Doyal, L., Einstein, G., Kelly, U., Shim, J., Weber, & Repta, R. (2017). The odd couple: Using biomedical and intersectional approaches to address health inequities. *Global Health Action*, *10*, 1326686. 10.1080/16549716.2017.1326686

Harris, J. L. (1997). Reminiscence: A culturally and developmentally appropriate language intervention for older adults. *American Journal of Speech-Language Pathology*, *6*, 19–25. 10.1044/1058-0360.0603.19

Havranek, E. P., Mujahid, M. S., Barr, D. A., Blair, I. V., Cohen, M. S., Cruz-Flores, S., Davey-Smith, G., Dennison-Himmelfarb, C. R., Lauer, M. S., Lockwood, D. W., Rosal, M., Yancy, C. W., & American Heart Association Council on Quality of Care and Outcomes Research, Council on Epidemiology and Prevention, Council on Cardiovascular and Stroke Nursing, Council on Lifestyle and Cardiometabolic Health, and Stroke Council. (2015). Social determinants of risk and outcomes for cardiovascular disease: A scientific statement from the American Heart Association. *Circulation*, *132*, 873–898. 10.1161/CIR.0000000000000228

Helm-Estabrooks, N. (2001). *Cognitive Linguistic Quick Test-Plus*. The Psychological Corporation.

Hersch, D. (2018). From individual to global: Human rights and aphasia. *International Journal of Speech-Language Pathology, 20*, 39–43. 10.1080/17549507.2018.1397749

Higby, E., Gámez, E., & Holguín Mendoza, C. (2023). Challenging deficit frameworks in research on heritage language bilingualism. *Applied Psycholinguistics*. 10.1017/S0142716423000048

Kiran, S. & Roberts, P. (2012). What do we know about assessing language impairment in bilingual aphasia? In M. Gitterman, M. Goral, & L. K. Obler (Eds.), *Aspects of Multilingual Aphasia* (pp. 35–50). Multilingual Matters.

Kong, A. P. H. (2021). The impact of COVID-19 on speakers with aphasia: What is currently known or missing? *Journal of Speech, Language, and Hearing Research, 64*, 176–180. 10.1044/2020_JSLHR-20-00371

Kristiansen, M., Razum, O., Tezcan-Güntekin, H., & Krasnik, A. (2016). Aging and health among migrants in a European perspective. *Public Health Reviews, 37*, 1–14. 10.1186/s40985-016-0036-1

Labovitz, D. L. (2020). Stroke epidemiology and intersectionality. *Stroke, 52*, 2886–2887. 10.1161/STROKEAHA.120.031848

Lequerica, A. H. & Panyavin, I. (2016). Cultural variables and the process of neuropsychological assessment in the neurorehabilitation setting after brain injury. In J. M. Uomoto (Ed.), *Multicultural Rehabilitation: Clinical Principles for Rehabilitation Professionals* (pp. 49–73). Springer.

Lerman, A., Goral, M., & Obler, L. K. (2020). The complex relationship between pre-stroke and post-stroke language abilities in multilingual individuals with aphasia. *Aphasiology, 34*, 1319–1340. 10.1080/02687038.2019.1673303

Life Participation Approach to Aphasia (LPAA) Project Group. (2008). Life participation approach to aphasia: A statement of values for the future. In R. Chapey (Ed.), *Language Intervention Strategies in Adult Aphasia* (5th ed., pp. 279–289). Lippincott, Williams and Wilkins.

López, B. G., Luque, A., & Piña-Watson, B. (2021). Context, intersectionality, and resilience: Moving toward a more holistic study of bilingualism in cognitive science. *Cultural Diversity and Ethnic Minority Psychology*, 29(1), 24–33. doi.org/10.1037/cdp0000472

Lopez, K., Gravier, M., Vasquez, A., Soto, J., Tollast, A., & Higby, E. (2022). Cross-language generalization in bilingual aphasia: Influence of manner of second language acquisition. *Aphasiology*. 10.1080/02687038.2022.2114289

Manning M., MacFarlane, A., Hickey A., & Franklin S. (2019). Perspectives of people with aphasia post-stroke towards personal recovery and living successfully: A systematic review and thematic synthesis. *PLoS ONE, 14*, e0214200. 10.1371/journal.pone.0214200

Marian, V., Blumenfeld, H. K., & Kaushanskaya, M. (2007). The language experience and proficiency questionnaire (LEAP-Q): Assessing language profiles in bilinguals and multilinguals. *Journal of Speech, Language, and Hearing Research, 50*, 940–967. 10.1044/1092-4388(2007/067)

Marian, V. & Kaushanskaya, M. (2008). Words, feelings, and bilingualism: Cross-linguistic differences in emotionality of autobiographical memories. *The Mental Lexicon*, *3*, 72–90. 10.1075/ml.3.1.06mar

Marte, M. J., Carpenter, E., Falconer, I. B., Scimeca, M., Abdollahi, F., Peñaloza, C., & Kiran, S. (2022). LEX-BADAT: Language EXperience in bilinguals with and without aphasia DATaset. *Frontiers in Psychology*, *13*, 875928. 10.3389/fpsyg.2022.875928

Martin, N., Minkina, I., Kohen, F. P., & Kalinyak-Fliszar, M. (2018). Assessment of linguistic and verbal short-term memory components of language abilities in aphasia. *Journal of Neurolinguistics*, *48*, 199–225. 10.1016/j.jneuroling.2018.02.006

Mather, M., Jacobsen, L. A., & Pollard, K. M. (2015). Aging in the United States. *Population Bulletin*, *70*(2). Population Reference Bureau. https://www.prb.org/

McClung, J. S., Gonzalez Rothi, L. J., & Nadeau, S. E. (2010). Ambient experience in restitutive treatment of aphasia. *Frontiers in Human Neuroscience*, *4*, 183. 10.3389/fnhum.2010.00183

Murray, L. & Coppens, P. (2022). Formal and informal assessment of aphasia. In I. Papathanasiou & P. Coppens (Eds.), *Aphasia and Related Neurogenic Communication Disorders* (3rd ed., pp. 79–108). Jones and Bartlett Learning.

Murray, T. A. (2021). Teaching the social and structural determinants of health: Considerations for faculty. *Journal of Nursing Education*, *60*, 63–64. 10.3928/01484834-20210120-01

Navarro, E., DeLuca, V., & Rossi, E. (2022). It takes a village: Using network science to identify the effect of individual differences in bilingual experience for theory of mind. *Brain Sciences*, *12*, 1–19. 10.3390/brainsci12040487

Norvik, M. I. & Goral, M. (2021). Assessment challenges in acquired aphasia in multilingual individuals. In U. Røyneland & R. Blackwood (Eds.), *Multilingualism Across the Lifespan* (pp. 189–208). Routledge. 10.4324/9781003125815

Norvik, M. I., Lind, M., & Jensen, B. U. (2022). Working with multilingual aphasia: Attitudes and practices among speech and language pathologists in Norway. *International Multilingual Research Journal*. 10.1080/19313152.2021.2015935

Paradis, M. (2022). *The bilingual aphasia test—Online resources*. http://www.mcgill.ca/linguistics/research/bat/

Peñaloza, C. & Kiran, S. (2019). Recovery and rehabilitation patterns in bilingual and multilingual aphasia. In J. W. Schwieter (Ed.), *The Handbook of the Neuroscience of Multilingualism* (pp. 553–571). John Wiley and Sons.

Plowman, E., Hentz, B., & Ellis, C. (2012). Post-stroke aphasia prognosis: A review of patient-related and stroke-related factors. *Journal of Evaluation in Clinical Practice*, *18*, 689–694. 10.1111/j.1365-2753.2011.01650.x

Randolph, C. (2012). *Repeatable Battery for the Assessment of Neuropsychological Status*. The Psychological Corporation.

RELEASE Collaborators. (2022). Dosage, intensity, and frequency of language therapy for aphasia: A systematic review-based, individual participant data network meta-analysis. *Stroke*, *53*, 956–967. 10.1161/strokeaha.121.035216

Scimeca, M., Abdollahi, F., Peñaloza, C., & Kiran, S. (2022). Clinical perspectives and strategies for confronting disparities in social determinants of health for Hispanic bilinguals with aphasia. *Journal of Communication Disorders*, *98*, 106231. 10.1016/j.jcomdis.2022.106231

Shakespeare, T., Ndagire, F., & Seketi, Q. E. (2021). Triple jeopardy: Disabled people and the COVID-19 pandemic. *The Lancet*, *397*, 1331–1333. 10.1016/S0140-6736(21)00625-5

Titone, D. A. & Tiv, M. (2023). Rethinking multilingual experience through a Systems Framework of Bilingualism. *Bilingualism: Language and Cognition*, *26*(1), 1–16. 10.1017/S1366728921001127

Virani, S. S., Alonso, A., Aparicio, H. J., Benjamin, E. J., Bittencourt, M. S., Callaway, C. W., Carson, A. P., Chamberlain, A. M., Cheng, S., Delling, F. N., Elkind, M., Evenson, K. R., Ferguson, J. F., Gupta, D. K., Khan, S. S., Kissela, B. M., Knutson, K. L., Lee, C. D., Lewis, T. T., Liu, J. & …Tsao, C. W. (2021). Heart disease and stroke statistics-2021 update: A report from the American Heart Association. *Circulation*, *143*(8), e254–e743. 10.1161/CIR.0000000000000950

Wallace, P. M., Pomery, E. A., Latimer, A. E., Martinez, J. L., & Salovey, P. (2010). A review of acculturation measures and their utility in studies promoting Latino health. *Hispanic Journal of Behavioral Sciences*, *32*(1), 37–54. 10.1177/0739986309352341

Webb Hooper, M., Nápoles, A. M., & Pérez-Stable, E. J. (2020). COVID-19 and racial/ethnic disparities. *JAMA*, *323*, 2466–2467. 10.1001/jama.2020.8598

Wigdorowitz, M., Pérez, A. I., & Tsimpli, I. M. (2020). A holistic measure of contextual and individual linguistic diversity. *International Journal of Multilingualism*. 10.1080/14790718.2020.1835921

Wilson, Y., White, A., Jefferson, A., & Danis, M. (2019). Intersectionality in clinical practice: The need for a conceptual framework. *The American Journal of Bioethics*, *19*, 8–19. 10.1080/15265161.2018.1557275

Yeo, G., Bell, C. L., Okamoto, L., & Mehta, K. (2017). The future of ethnogeriatrics. In L. Cummings-Vaughn & D. M. Cruz-Oliver (Eds.), *Ethnogeriatrics: Healthcare Needs of Diverse Populations* (pp. 247–259). Springer.

12

FACTORS CONTRIBUTING TO LIFE PARTICIPATION IN PEOPLE WITH APHASIA

Current Knowledge and Future Directions

Lisa Tabor Connor, Sameer Ashaie, and Marjorie Nicholas

Introduction

Within the aphasia rehabilitation community, many intervention programs are modeled on the core values of the Life Participation Approach to Aphasia (e.g., LPAA Project Group, 2008; Nicholas, 2012). A major notion underlying the LPAA is the goal of living well *with* aphasia, rather than focusing primarily on recovering *from* aphasia. The LPAA has five core values that emphasize *participation* in former and new life activities rather than focusing on improving the communicative and cognitive *impairments* associated with aphasia. The values also emphasize that living well with aphasia depends on one's environment and what one brings to the situation as an individual (self-identity, temperament, emotions, etc.). Many of the LPAA key concepts are also represented in commonly used models of functioning and disability such as the World Health Organization (WHO) International Classification of Functioning (ICF) (WHO, 2001), upon which another model called Living with Aphasia–a Framework for Outcome Measurement (A-FROM) was based (Kagan et al., 2008). In both the ICF and A-FROM models, domains representing impairment, participation, environment, and person interact to affect an individual's health and functioning. These frameworks have proven useful to both clinicians and researchers driving intervention models such as our own intensive comprehensive aphasia program (ICAP) (Nicholas et al., 2021). Ultimately, using the LPAA approach, both clinicians and researchers hope to observe that measures of life participation show "improvements" after intervention or during the process of recovery.

DOI: 10.4324/9781003330318-15

First, it is useful to review the A-FROM model developed by Kagan and colleagues (2008) in more detail. As the authors stated, "We aimed to create a user-friendly conceptual framework for outcome measurement in aphasia that included a focus on real-life outcomes of intervention and could be easily accessed by clinicians, researchers, policy makers, funders, and those living with aphasia" (p. 259).

As can be seen in Figure 12.1, domains in the model are represented by four overlapping, intersecting circles. The bottom circle represents impairments associated with aphasia (e.g., severity and details of the language/cognitive disorder); the other three circles represent participation in life situations (top), environmental barriers or supports (left), and personal characteristics including feelings, emotions, and self-identity (right). To evaluate outcomes, the model guides measurement within each domain. In prior years, particularly within the field of speech-language pathology, outcomes would likely have been measured only within the impairment domain. The A-FROM model helps to highlight how narrow an impairment-only focus has been, where only one area out of the four domains was assessed. In the field of occupational therapy, in contrast, a focus on measuring and improving participation in desired life "occupations" has been at the heart of the profession since its inception (e.g., Meyer, 1922).

Using a model like A-FROM helps clinicians understand the overlapping contexts within which interventions take place and can assist them in guiding people with aphasia (PWA) to take an active role in their own adjustments to living with aphasia. It has also been a useful model for researchers who seek to understand the varied factors that might affect participation outcomes, thus pointing toward appropriate targets for intervention programs. In this chapter, we report findings from our research groups related to participation outcomes (participation domain) with respect to how both environmental factors and personal factors predict or interact with participation in desired life activities by PWA post-stroke.

Measuring Participation

Participation in the full array of life activities is the ultimate outcome that PWA hope to achieve after stroke (Worrall et al., 2011). According to the ICF, participation is defined as "involvement in a life situation" (WHO, 2001). More recent research examining how participation is defined by people with a variety of disabilities (Hammel et al., 2008) and by PWA (Dalemans et al., 2010) has revealed that additional essential characteristics include meaningful engagement, choice and control, and feeling of

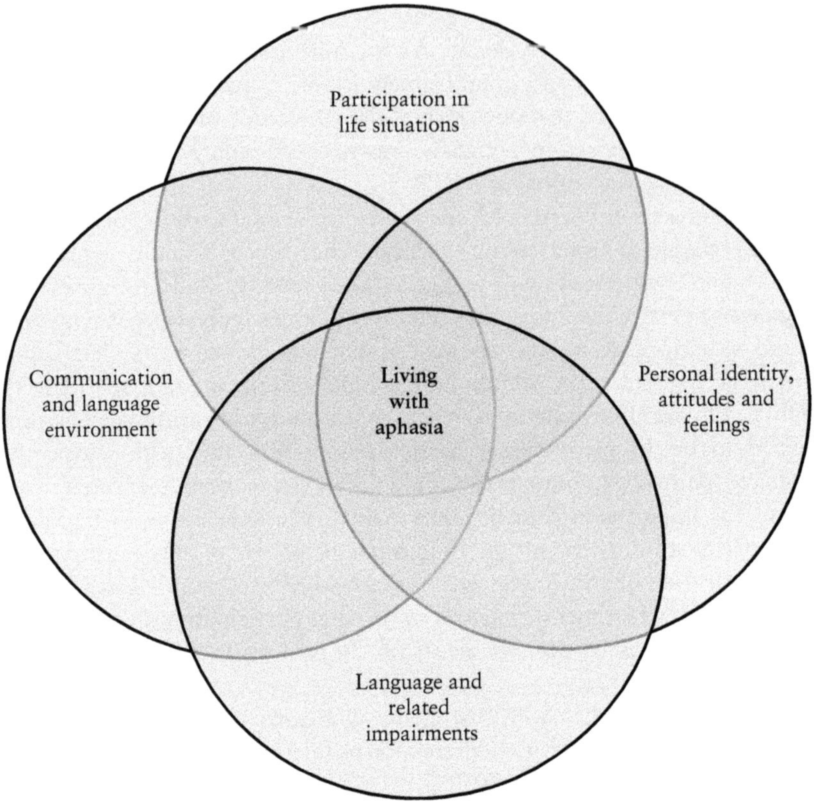

FIGURE 12.1 Living with Aphasia: A Framework for Outcome Measurement (A-FROM). Adapted from Kagan et al., 2008.

belonging. Work in our lab has focused on examining factors that promote or inhibit participation in life activities after stroke in PWA and those without aphasia.

Essential to our efforts has been the explicit inclusion of PWA in our research even though many studies exclude them (e.g., Townend et al., 2007). Crucial to achieving our aims has been the use of aphasia-friendly presentation of written assessments (e.g., Rose et al., 2003), supports for PWA to respond for themselves (e.g., Kagan et al., 2001), adaptations to administration methods when support is needed (Helm-Estabrooks et al., 2007; Tucker et al., 2012), and validating that responses are consistent across measures in similar domains to demonstrate that PWA are capable of "speaking" for themselves (Tucker et al., 2012).

A key participation outcome assessment ideally suited for use in PWA is the Activity Card Sort (ACS: Baum & Edwards, 2008). The ACS is a deck of large-format cards with photographs of activities that people do in their daily lives and a label for those activities. This tool identifies activities that people have given up or do less because of aging or disability. The 89 activities are organized into four domains: Instrumental activities of daily living (e.g., paying bills), low-demand leisure activities (e.g., watching spectator sports), high-demand leisure activities (e.g., biking), and social activities (e.g., getting together with friends and family). People sort cards into piles indicating whether they have ever done or never done the activity, whether they continue to do it at the same level, do it less, or have given it up. For PWA, instructions are adapted so that sorting is done in two steps – one to indicate activities that are ever done and a second to indicate the frequency since stroke.

PWA easily understand the photos to indicate activities and the ACS gives PWA the opportunity to express for themselves activities they find meaningful and would like to do more of, providing treatment targets for clinicians. Additionally, results for each domain are scored in terms of the percentage retained of a person's individual pre-stroke activities. This percent retained score indicates the person's current level of participation vis à vis their prior level of participation, providing a client-centered understanding without assuming activities that a person ought to do. Since the development of the ACS, speech-language pathologists have developed a card sorting assessment, the Life Interest and Values cards (Haley et al., 2010) that show line drawings of activities and also line drawings that express emotional states.

In our study of barriers and facilitators of participation, our sample consists of approximately 130 community-dwelling individuals post stroke, half of whom have aphasia, with mild to moderate stroke severity and mild residual deficits at enrollment at least 6 months later. Although their neurological symptoms were mild, approximately 20% of their pre-stroke activities had been given up or were being done less. They agreed, but not strongly so, that they were able to participate in desired activities as measured by the Reintegration to Normal Living Index (RNL; Wood-Dauphinée et al., 1988). They were able to participate in roles and desired activities most, but not all, of the time as measured by the Stroke Impact Scale Participation/Role Function domain (Duncan et al., 1999). Interestingly, we found no differences in participation outcome in PWA versus people without aphasia post stroke (Foley et al., 2019; Graves et al., 2021; Nicholas et al., 2020), though research indicates that PWA have poorer participation outcomes than their age-matched peers (who have not had a stroke) (Cruice et al., 2006; Davidson et al., 2008; Edwards et al., 2006).

Regarding factors predicting participation outcomes in people post stroke with and without aphasia, we have investigated many potential variables – aphasia status; residual neurological impairment; mental health factors; self-perceived communication; cognitive abilities and physical function; and environmental factors such as social support (Foley et al., 2019; Graves et al., 2021; Ho et al., 2021; Ianni et al., 2022; Lee et al., 2022; Nicholas et al., 2020). Our findings across studies indicate that aphasia status was not a significant predictor of participation, nor was executive ability or residual neurological impairment for the most part. What was important for predicting participation across studies was mental health, social support, and self-perception of capabilities including self-perceived physical function and cognitive ability, though not self-perceived communication ability.

Personal Factors

Depression and Fatigue

Post-stroke depression (PSD) is associated with lower quality of life and increased mortality (Morris et al., 1993; Naess et al., 2012). The prevalence of depression in PWA is particularly concerning given that symptoms of depression may negatively impact rehabilitation outcomes (Lenzi et al., 2008), further increasing social isolation and subverting the road to achieving a better quality of life. PWA have higher rates of depression than those without aphasia with the frequency from 30% to 60% (Ashaie et al., 2019; Kauhanen et al., 2000). For example, Ashaie et al. (2019) found the prevalence of depression and subthreshold depression was 41.64% in 144 people with chronic aphasia. However, other studies (e.g., Kauhanen et al., 2000) have found the prevalence of depression to be around 60% in PWA. This discrepancy in the frequency of depression may be attributed to lack of valid depression measures for PWA (Laures-Gore et al., 2020) and exclusion of PWA from PSD studies. Mitchell et al. (2017) found that only 5 of 108 studies on post-stroke depression reported on depression in PWA. Exclusion of PWA can be attributed to a majority of depression measures being language-based, making their comprehension difficult for PWA.

Depression in PWA has generally been assessed using (a) self-report (including non-verbal) scales and (b) by-proxy measures (e.g., asking caregivers/family members about the patient's symptoms). Van Dijk et al. (2016) reviewed assessments used in PWA including the Aphasic Depression Rating Scale (Benaim et al., 2004), Clinical Global Impression Scale (Busner & Targum, 2007), Signs of Depression Scale (Hammond et al., 2000), Visual Analog Self-Esteem Scale (Brumfitt & Sheeran, 1999), multiple versions of the Stroke Aphasic Depression Questionnaire (SADQ) (Lincoln et al., 2000), and Visual Analog Mood Scale (Kontou et al., 2012; Stern et al., 1997), finding a lack of internal consistency and reliability in the measures, as well as selection bias in studies that used these scales. Therefore, results from studies using the above-mentioned measures should be interpreted with caution. To note, even non-verbal scales of depression may require extensive verbal directions which may make their comprehension difficult for individuals with different aphasia severity levels.

To circumvent these issues, recent work by Ashaie and Cherney (2020) have shown the feasibility of using eye-tracking to assess depression in individuals with aphasia. Ashaie and Cherney (2020) found that eye-tracking can be used to assess how PWA respond to faces representing different mood states which may indicate their own mood state. However, more work with larger samples and different stimuli is needed to validate eye-tracking measures of depression in PWA.

There are few studies that explore treatment options for depression in PWA (Laures-Gore et al., 2020). Depression is often untreated in PWA due to difficulty in partaking in traditional depression "talk" therapies that rely heavily on language. Antidepressants may be effective in treating depression in people with stroke (Villa et al., 2018; Xu et al., 2016), though many studies do not include PWA. Thus, further research is needed on the efficacy of antidepressants in PWA.

Recent studies have also explored the impact of intensive language therapy on depression in PWA. Mohr et al. (2017) investigated the impact of two language treatments (i.e., intensive language-action therapy with a social component and intensive naming therapy) on depression in 18 people with chronic aphasia. Participants received 3.5 hours of therapy daily over 6 consecutive working days. There was a significant decrease in depression symptoms after intensive language therapy with a social component compared to intensive naming therapy. These results suggest that language therapy that has a social component may have benefits beyond linguistic impairment to psychosocial factors in individuals with aphasia.

Another depression treatment option not relying heavily on language is transcranial direct current stimulation (tDCS), a non-invasive form of brain stimulation that may be an efficacious treatment for depression (Brunoni et al., 2016). Patients with depression are assumed to have a hypoactive left dorsolateral prefrontal cortex (DLPFC) so upregulating it with anodal tDCS is presumed to reduce depressive symptoms (Peckham et al., 2010). A recent open-label study in four PWA found that after ten sessions (once a day) of bilateral tDCS to the DLPFC and two additional sessions after 2 and 4 weeks (i.e., 12 total sessions) depression symptoms decreased by more than 40% (Valiengo et al., 2016). This improvement was maintained 4 weeks after the treatment. However, like other depression treatment studies, this tDCS study also had a small sample size and no control group. Thus, further work is needed to explore the impact of tDCS on depression in PWA.

Another factor that impacts quality of life for PWA is post-stroke fatigue (Bullier et al., 2020). Fatigue is highly prevalent after stroke with frequency estimates ranging from 23–85% (e.g., Choi-Kwon & Kim, 2011; Cumming et al., 2016). However, like depression, our understanding of fatigue in PWA is limited due to a majority of fatigue measures being language-based. We recently carried out an extensive systematic review (Riley et al., 2021) that included 161 articles on post-stroke fatigue. Out of 161 studies, only 30% of studies included people with communication disorders, 26% excluded all individuals with communication disorders, and 44% excluded any individual with a severe communication disorder. Moreover, only 10% of studies administered a specific aphasia assessment and 47% did not provide enough information to determine how communication disorders were identified in their study sample, making it difficult to replicate these studies and their findings. Measuring fatigue in PWA is essential since it could also impact their treatment outcomes. For example, it is possible that PWA get fatigued when taking part in treatment sessions, which could impact their treatment adherence or even outcomes. Thus, measuring fatigue before and even during treatment sessions may be important.

Anxiety and Apathy

Although depression and fatigue are recognized factors contributing to poorer outcome and poorer quality of life post-stroke, under-recognized are other mental health factors influencing stroke outcome, participation, and quality of life, namely apathy and anxiety. Lopatkiewicz et al. (2021) found in a sample of 443 individuals with neuropsychiatric evaluations 8 days post stroke that apathetic, but not depressive symptoms, predicted poor 3- and 12-month health outcomes. In a study conducted by Ho et al. (2021) examining contributors to participation in cognitively-demanding activities, participation was significantly influenced by self-reported symptoms of apathy on the Apathy Evaluation Scale (Marin et al., 1991). In an analysis focusing on emotional contributors to participation (Lee et al., 2021), apathy was a significant predictor of participation as measured by both the RNL (Wood-Dauphinée et al., 1988) and the ACS (Baum & Edwards, 2008).

Likewise, anxiety was found to be a predictor of self-perception of performance and participation. In Lee et al. (2021), anxiety as measured as a trait by the State-Trait Anxiety Inventory (Spielberger, 1983) was a significant contributor to variability in RNL score. Anxiety, aphasia status, and residual neurological impairment (NIH Stroke Scale: Brott et al., 1989) were associated with self-perceptions of activities of daily living/instrumental activities of daily living on the Stroke Impact Scale (Juniper & Connor, 2022). Interestingly, in a recent study by our research group, a large number of people post-stroke were found to have anxiety symptoms. For individuals who also had symptoms of depression as measured by the PHQ-9 (Kroenke et al., 2001), anxiety was found to fully mediate the relationship between residual neurological impairment and participation, though not for people without depression (Randolph et al., under review).

The Role of the Environment

In the context of the models introduced in the beginning of this chapter, the ICF and A-FROM, the term environment has been used broadly to refer to everything external to the PWA. This includes the physical world or the built environment, as well as the social/ cultural/economic/community context the person exists in, and the more immediate social/family/home context the person lives in. Aspects of each of these "environments" can serve as either facilitators or barriers to life participation post-stroke.

One feature of the external environments particularly important to communication success in social conversational contexts is awareness of aphasia and skill in facilitating successful communication with a person experiencing language impairment. As part of the LPAA approach, training communication partners has been stressed via what is known as Supported Conversation for Adults with Aphasia or SCA developed by Kagan Kagan, (1998). The foundation of SCA is the idea that communication could be greatly enhanced by educating communication partners such as family members, clinicians, and community volunteers about the characteristics of aphasia and successful strategies to support communication. An environment that included lots of SCA-trained individuals likely would be experienced as more supportive than one where people were ignorant of the types of challenges PWA were likely to encounter. In such a supportive environment, participation in desired life activities may also become more accessible or possible for PWA.

There are many other forms of social support besides SCA that are also likely to serve as facilitators of participation as well. Our results have consistently found that measures of social support are important predictors of engagement in desired life activities post stroke. We have used the Medical Outcomes Study Social Support Scale (MOS SS), a self-report 19-

item survey with items that ask about emotional/information support, tangible support, affectionate support, and positive/social interaction. Social support was an important independent predictor of social participation in one study, where perceived mobility limitations and the built environment were not (Foley et al., 2019). Additionally, positive social interaction correlated with a return to participation in activities from the ACS described as having either high or low cognitive demands, whereas post-stroke aphasia did not impact resumption of participation (Ho et al., 2021). We have found one aspect of post-stroke participation that differs for PWA as compared to those without aphasia. Our research group examined the extent to which the positive association between communication and social participation could be explained by social support (Lee et al., 2022). A mediation analysis indicated that for PWA, but not for people without aphasia, social support fully mediated the relationship between self-perceived communication abilities and social participation. Therefore, although PWA do not participate in pre-stroke activities more or less than those without aphasia, the means by which they participate is different. PWA need social support to engage in social participation. These studies have pointed to the importance of social support experienced by the person with aphasia as a factor leading to better participation in desired life activities, but there are likely numerous other aspects of the environment that are also likely to be important.

Conclusion and Future Directions

This chapter has reviewed current literature and gaps in knowledge regarding factors contributing to participation in daily life activities for PWA as espoused by the LPAA. The focus on living successfully with aphasia, and not simply improving language impairment, broadens our research focus, and ultimately our clinical avenues for intervention, to include psychosocial determinants and environmental supports that may enhance participation and well-being after stroke. Work described in this chapter highlights the need to better understand how PWA resume their pre-stroke activities during the recovery process; the nature of social support crucial to enable participation, including family and community stroke program support; the most appropriate treatment approaches for PWA for mental health issues such as depression, anxiety, and apathy; the role that fatigue may play in limiting participation in treatment and other activities; and how environmental supports such as SCA may enable PWA to experience fewer barriers to social participation. Coupled with psycholinguistic approaches to ameliorate the language impairment experienced by PWA, psychosocial and environmental interventions may help people with aphasia achieve what matters to them most – to be able to participate fully in their daily lives and fulfill their desired roles.

References

Ashaie, S. A., Hurwitz, R., & Cherney, L. R. (2019). Depression and subthreshold depression in stroke-related aphasia. *Archives of Physical Medicine and Rehabilitation*, *100*(7), 1294–1299.

Ashaie, S. A. & Cherney, L. R. (2020). Eye tracking as a tool to identify mood in aphasia: A feasibility study. *Neurorehabilitation and Neural Repair*, *34*(5), 463–471.

Baum, C. M. & Edwards, D. (2008). *Activity Card Sort, 2nd Edition*. Bethesda, MD: American Occupational Therapy Association, Inc.

Benaim, C., Cailly, B., Perennou, D., & Pelissier, J. (2004). Validation of the aphasic depression rating scale. *Stroke*, *35*(7), 1692–1696.

Brott, T., Adams, H. P., Olinger, C. P., Marler, J. R., Barsan, W. G., Biller, J., Spilker, J., Holleran, R., Eberle, R., & Hertzberg, V. (1989). Measurements of acute cerebral infarction: A clinical examination scale. *Stroke*, *20*(7), 864–870. 10.1161/01.str.20.7.864

Brumfitt, S. M. & Sheeran, P. (1999). The development and validation of the Visual Analogue Self-Esteem Scale (VASES). *The British Journal of Clinical Psychology*, *38* (Pt 4), 387–400.

Brunoni, A. R., Moffa, A. H., Fregni, F., Palm, U., Padberg, F., Blumberger, D. M., … & Alonzo, A. (2016). Transcranial direct current stimulation for acute major depressive episodes: Meta-analysis of individual patient data. *The British Journal of Psychiatry*, bjp.bp. 115.164715.

Bullier, B., Cassoudesalle, H., Villain, M., Cogné, M., Mollo, C., De Gabory, I., … & Glize, B. (2020). New factors that affect quality of life in patients with aphasia. *Annals of Physical and Rehabilitation Medicine*, *63*(1), 33–37.

Busner, J. & Targum, S. D. (2007). The clinical global impressions scale: applying a research tool in clinical practice. *Psychiatry (Edgmont)*, *4*(7), 28.

Choi-Kwon, S. & Kim, J. S. (2011). Poststroke fatigue: An emerging, critical issue in stroke medicine. *International Journal of Stroke*, *6*(4), 328–336.

Cruice, M., Worrall, L., & Hickson, L. (2006). Quantifying aphasic people's social lives in the context of non-aphasic peers. *Aphasiology*, *20*(12), 1210–1225. 10.1080/02687030600790136

Cumming, T. B., Packer, M., Kramer, S. F., & English, C. (2016). The prevalence of fatigue after stroke: a systematic review and meta-analysis. *International Journal of Stroke*, *11*(9), 968–977.

Dalemans, R. J. P., de Witte, L., Wade, D., & van den Heuvel, W. (2010). Social participation through the eyes of people with aphasia. *International Journal of Language and Communication Disorders*, *45*(5), 537–550. 10.3109/13682820903223633

Davidson, B., Howe, T., Worrall, L., Hickson, L., & Togher, L. (2008). Social participation for older people with aphasia: The impact of communication disability on friendships. *Topics in Stroke Rehabilitation*, *15*(4), 325–340. 10.1310/tsr1504-325

Duncan, P. W., Wallace, D., Lai, S. M., Johnson, D., Embretson, S., & Laster, L. J. (1999). The stroke impact scale version 2.0. Evaluation of reliability, validity, and sensitivity to change. *Stroke*, *30*(10), 2131–2140.

Edwards, D. F., Hahn, M. G., Baum, C. M., & Dromerick, A. W. (2006). The impact of mild stroke on activity participation and life satisfaction. *Journal of Stroke and Cerebrovascular Diseases*, *15*(4), 151–157.

Foley E. L., Nicholas, M. L., Baum, C. M., & Connor, L. T. (2019). Influence of environmental factors on social participation post-stroke. *Behavioural Neurology*, *73*, 10.1155/2019/2606039.

Graves, R., Connor, L. T., & Nicholas, M. L. (2021). Apathy and residual neurological impairment are associated with community reintegration after mild stroke. *Neuropsychological Rehabilitation.* 10.1080/09602011.2021.2019059.

Hammel, J., Magasi, S., Heinemann, A., Whiteneck, G., Bogner, J., & Rodriguez, E. (2008). What does participation mean? An insider perspective from people with disabilities. *Disability and Rehabilitation*, *30*(19), 1445–1460. 10.1080/09638280701625534

Hammond, M. F., O'Keeffe, S. T., & Barer, D. H. (2000). Development and validation of a brief observer-rated screening scale for depression in elderly medical patients. *Age and Ageing*, *29*(6), 511–515.

Haley, K. L., Womack, J. L., Helm-Estabrooks, N., Caignon, D., & McCulloch, K. L. (2010). *The Life Interest and Values Cards*. University of North Carolina Department of Allied Health Sciences.

Helm-Estabrooks, N., Haley, K. L., & Womack, J. L. (2007). A pictorial, binary-sorting system allowing "self-determination" despite aphasia. *Brain and Language*, 103(1-2), 201–202. 10.1016/j.bandl.2007.07.115

Ho, A., Nicholas, M. L., Dagli, C., & Connor, L. T. (2021). Apathy, cognitive impairment, and social support contribute to participation in cognitively demanding activities poststroke. *Behavioural Neurology*, 1–8. 10.1155/2021/8810632

Ianni, C., Magee, L., Dagli, C., Nicholas, M. L., & Connor, L. T. (2022). Self-reported emotional health and social support but not executive function are associated with participation after stroke. *Topics in Stroke Rehabilitation*, *30*(6), 568–577.

Juniper, A. R. & Connor, L. T. (2022). Self-perceived ADL/IADL function is influenced by stroke severity, aphasia, and anxiety. *Canadian Journal of Occupational Therapy*. 10.1177/00084174221098876.

Kagan, A. (1998). Supported conversation for adults with aphasia: Methods and resources for training conversational partners. *Aphasiology*, *12*, 851–864.

Kagan, A., Black, S. E., Duchan, F. J., Simmons-Mackie, N., & Square, P. (2001). Training volunteers as conversation partners using "Supported Conversation for Adults with Aphasia" (SCA): A controlled trial. *Journal of Speech, Language, and Hearing Research*, *44*, 624–638. 10.1044/1092-4388(2001/051)

Kagan, A., Simmons-Mackie, N., Rowland, A., Huijbregts, M., Shumway, E., McEwen, S., Threats, T., & Sharp, S. (2008). Counting what counts: A framework for capturing real-life outcomes of aphasia intervention. *Aphasiology*, *22*(3), 258–280.

Kauhanen, M. L., Korpelainen, J. T., Hiltunen, P., Määttä, R., Mononen, H., Brusin, E., ... & Myllylä, V. V. (2000). Aphasia, depression, and non-verbal cognitive impairment in ischaemic stroke. *Cerebrovascular Diseases*, *10*(6), 455–461.

Kroenke, K., Spitzer, R. L., & Williams, J. B. W. (2001). The PHQ-9. *Journal of General Internal Medicine*, *16*(9), 606–613. 10.1046/j.1525-1497.2001.016009606.x

Kontou, E., Thomas, S., & Lincoln, N. (2012). Psychometric properties of a revised version of the Visual Analog Mood Scales. *Clinical Rehabilitation*, *26*(12), 1133–1140. doi:10.1177/0269215512442670

Laures-Gore, J. S., Dotson, V. M., & Belagaje, S. (2020). Depression in poststroke aphasia. *American Journal of Speech-Language Pathology*, *29*(4), 1798–1810.

Lee, Y., Fritz, K., Dagli, C., Nicholas, M. L., & Connor, L. T. (2022). Social support fully mediates the association between communication abilities and social participation among persons with post-stroke aphasia. *Aphasiology*, 10.1080/02687038.2022.2063792.

Lee Y., Nicholas, M. L., & Connor, L. T. (2021). Identifying emotional contributors to participation post-stroke. *Topics in Stroke Rehabilitation*, *30*(2), 180–192. doi:10.1080/10749357.2021.2008597.

Lenzi, G. L., Altieri, M., & Maestrini, I. (2008). Post-stroke depression. *Revue Neurologique*, *164*(10), 837–840.

Lincoln, N., Sutcliffe, L., & Unsworth, G. (2000). Validation of the Stroke Aphasic Depression Questionnaire (SADQ) for use with patients in hospital. *Clinical Neuropsychological Assessment*, *1*, 88–96.

Lopatkiewicz, A. M., Pera, J., Slowik, A., & Dziedzic, T. (2021). Early apathetic, but not depressive, symptoms are associated with poor outcome after stroke. *European Journal of Neurology*, *28*(6), 1949–1957. 10.1111/ene.14785

LPAA Project Group. (2008). Life participation approaches to aphasia: A statement of values for the future. In R. Chapey, (Ed.), *Language Intervention Strategies in Aphasia and Related Neurogenic Communication Disorders* (pp. 279–289) 5th ed. Lippincott Williams & Wilkins.

Marin, R. S., Biedrzycki, R. C., & Firinciogullari, S. (1991). Reliability and validity of the Apathy Evaluation Scale. *Psychiatry Research*, *38*(2), 143–162. 10.1016/0165-1781(91)90040-V

Mitchell, A. J., Sheth, B., Gill, J., Yadegarfar, M., Stubbs, B., Yadegarfar, M., & Meader, N. (2017). Prevalence and predictors of post-stroke mood disorders: A meta-analysis and meta-regression of depression, anxiety and adjustment disorder. *General Hospital Psychiatry*, *47*, 48–60.

Mohr, B., Stahl, B., Berthier, M. L., & Pulvermüller, F. (2017). Intensive communicative therapy reduces symptoms of depression in chronic nonfluent aphasia. *Neurorehabilitation and Neural Repair*, *31*(12), 1053–1062.

Morris, P. L., Robinson, R. G., Andrzejewski, P., Samuels, J., & Price, T. R. (1993). Association of depression with 10-year poststroke mortality. *American Journal of Psychiatry*, *150*, 124–124.

Meyer, A. (1922). The philosophy of occupational therapy. *Archives of Occupational Therapy*, *1*(1), 1–10.

Naess, H., Lunde, L., & Brogger, J. (2012). The effects of fatigue, pain, and depression on quality of life in ischemic stroke patients: the Bergen Stroke Study. *Vascular Health and Risk Management*, *8*, 407.

Nicholas, M. (2012). The importance of aphasia community programs in supporting self-determination in people with aphasia. *Perspectives on Neurophysiology and Neurogenic Speech and Language Disorders*, 22(1), 36–43.
Nicholas, M. L., Burch, K., Mitchell, J. R., Fox, A. B., Baum, C. M., & Connor, L. T. (2020). Self-perception of physical function contributes to participation in cognitively- and physically-demanding activities after stroke. *Frontiers in Neurology, 11*. 10.3389/fneur.2020.00474.
Nicholas, M., Pittmann, R., Pennington, S., Hildebrand, M., Connor, L. T., Ambrosi, D., Brady Wagner, L., & Savastano, M. (2021). Outcomes of an interprofessional intensive comprehensive aphasia program's first five years. *Topics in Stroke Rehabilitation*. 29(8), 588–604. 10.1080/10749357.2021.1970452
Peckham, A. D., McHugh, R. K., & Otto, M. W. (2010). A meta-analysis of the magnitude of biased attention in depression. *Depression and Anxiety*, 27(12), 1135–1142. 10.1002/da.20755
Randolph, S. Lee, Y., Nicholas, M. L., & Connor, L. T. (2022). *The mediating effect of anxiety on the association between residual neurological impairment and post-stroke participation among persons with and without post-stroke depression*, [manuscript under review].
Riley, E. A., Hart, E., Preston, J. L., Wu, Y., & Ashaie, S. (2021). Pervasiveness of speech-language disorders and fatigue in stroke: A systematic scoping review. *Journal of Communication Disorders*, 93, 106145.
Rose, T. A., Worrall, L. E., & McKenna, K. (2003). The effectiveness of aphasia-friendly principles for printed health education materials for people with aphasia following stroke. *Aphasiology*, 17, 947–963. 10.1080/02687030344000319
Spielberger, C. D. (1983). *State-trait anxiety inventory for adults*. APA PsychTests.
Stern, R., Arruda, J., Hooper, C., Wolfner, G., & Morey, C. (1997). Visual analogue mood scales to measure internal mood state in neurologically impaired patients: Description and initial validity evidence. *Aphasiology*, *11*(1), 59–71.
Townend, E., Brady, M., & McLaughlan, K. (2007). Exclusion and inclusion criteria for people with aphasia in studies of depression after stroke: A systematic review and future recommendations. *Neuroepidemiology*, 29, 1–17. 10.1159/000108913
Tucker, F. M., Edwards, D. F., Mathews, L. K., Baum, C. M., & Connor, L. T. (2012). Modifying health outcome measures for people with aphasia. *American Journal of Occupational Therapy*, 66, 42–50. 10.5014/ajot.2012.001255
van Dijk, M. J., de Man-van Ginkel, J. M., Hafsteinsdóttir, T. B., & Schuurmans, M. J. (2016). Identifying depression post-stroke in patients with aphasia: A systematic review of the reliability, validity and feasibility of available instruments. *Clinical Rehabilitation*, *30*(8), 795–810.
Valiengo, L., Casati, R., Bolognini, N., Lotufo, P. A., Bensenor, I. M., Goulart, A. C., & Brunoni, A. R. (2016). Transcranial direct current stimulation for the treatment of post-stroke depression in aphasic patients: A case series. *Neurocase*, 22(2), 225–228. doi:10.1080/13554794.2015.1130231
Villa, R. F., Ferrari, F., & Moretti, A. (2018). Post-stroke depression: Mechanisms and pharmacological treatment. *Pharmacology and Therapeutics*, *184*, 131–144.
World Health Organization (2001). *International Classification of Functioning, Disability and Health: ICF*. Geneva: World Health Organization.

Worrall, L., Sherratt, S., Rogers, P., Howe, T., Hersh, D., Ferguson, A., & Davidson, B. (2011). What people with aphasia want: Their goals according to the ICF. *Aphasiology*, *25*(3), 309–322. 10.1080/02687038.2010.508530

Wood-Dauphinée, S., Opzoomer, M., Williams, J. I., Marchand, B., & Spitzer, W. O. (1988). Assessment of global function: The Reintegration to Normal Living Index. *Archives of Physical Medicine and Rehabilitation*, *69*(8), 583–590.

Xu, X. M., Zou, D. Z., Shen, L. Y., Liu, Y., Zhou, X. Y., Pu, J. C., ... & Wei, Y. D. (2016). Efficacy and feasibility of antidepressant treatment in patients with post-stroke depression. *Medicine*, *95*(45), e5349.

13

IMPLEMENTATION OF THE LIFE PARTICIPATION APPROACH TO APHASIA IN AN APHASIA CENTER INTEGRATED WITHIN AN ACADEMIC COMMUNICATION DISORDERS DEPARTMENT

Dafna Olenik and Sara Meilijson

Introduction

The Life Participation Approach to Aphasia (LPAA) offers a paradigmatic shift in the way practitioners view aphasia intervention, focusing on meeting the needs of individuals and their families affected by aphasia. It has been shown that LPAA can generate natural, meaningful enhancement to the quality of life of persons with aphasia (PWA) by transitioning from a medical to a social model of health care and disability (Holland & Elman, 2021). This evolutionary model follows the inclusion of a new framework, the International Classification of Functioning Disability and Health (ICF), published by the World Health Organization (WHO, 2001), along with the publication of the LPAA (LPAA Project Group, 2000).

This paradigmatic shift in aphasia intervention has been implemented since 2007 at the Adler Aphasia Center of the Department of Communication Disorders, Hadassah Academic College (HAC), Jerusalem. Most aphasia centers are based on a service delivery model that provides an interactive community for PWA and their families during the chronic stage (Elman, 2016). The Adler Aphasia Center is physically located and integrated within the Communication Disorders Department, thereby offering significant advantages in establishing the LPAA framework. The LPAA is implemented by educating and creating an active community for PWA. The geographical location of the Adler Aphasia Center dictates the multilingual and multicultural character of its participants, with multicultural

DOI: 10.4324/9781003330318-16

issues influencing all aspects of decision-making. The clinical education program for students at HAC is based upon three main axes: evidence-based learning; reflective practice; and case-based learning (Meilijson & Katzenberger, 2009). The center serves as one of the clinical placements where students perform their clinical practice with PWA and their families. The implementation of the LPAA will be discussed through a presentation of specific vignettes from the activities taking place at the center.

The Implementation of LPAA within Aphasia Centers

According to the traditional medical model, illness and disability are perceived as located within the patient. Consequently, a healthcare provider offers treatment with the desired outcome being a cure for the illness – although persons with aphasia typically do not recover fully, but remain living with communication deficits (Elman, 2016). A social model of healthcare, however, views illness and disability as an interaction among personal, physical, environmental, and societal factors, with the desired outcome being to promote positive functional change even when a cure is not possible. The ICF classification, which integrates medical and social models, requires healthcare professionals to look beyond the impairment and illness and consider domains of body structure and function, activities, and participation, as well as contextual factors (environmental and personal) (Reed et al., 2005).

A transformative document in the area of aphasia intervention entitled "Life Participation Approach to Aphasia - A Statement of Values for the Future" was presented in 2000 by a group of expert aphasiologists (the LPAA Project Group, 2000) (see also chapter 12, this volume). One of the positive developments that followed this statement of values was the formation of aphasia groups in several parts of the world (Canada, USA, New Zealand, and UK), that focused on life participation (Holland & Elman, 2021). Furthermore, Elman and Bernstein-Ellis (1999a) provided evidence for the efficacy of group communication treatment. Participants who took part in group communication treatment demonstrated significant improvements in linguistic and communicative outcomes as well as psychosocial adjustment changes. The LPAA statement and growing evidence of positive outcomes of working in groups led to a proliferation of aphasia centers worldwide (Elman, 2016; Holland & Elman, 2021; Woelders et al. 2018).

Aphasia centers are based on a service delivery model that provides an interactive community for PWA and their families during the chronic stage. Centers offer diverse programs providing tools and support for PWA and their families and a variety of activities based on the life participation approach (Woelders et al., 2018). Activities may include communication groups, partner training programs, support for family members, individual therapy focusing on participation goals, implementation of augmentative and alternative communication (AAC) tools, and more. All these activities share a common underlying belief system regarding the potential for learning to live successfully with aphasia by offering interventions aimed at "Living with Aphasia" (Kagan, 2011).

In order to plan and capture meaningful life participation outcomes, many aphasia centers adopted the Living with Aphasia Framework for Outcome Measurement (A-FROM) (Kagan et al., 2008). The A-FROM captures intervention and outcome domains that are relevant for aphasia centers and is presented in an accessible and explicit format that allows for easy practical application (Kagan, 2011; Simmons-Mackie, 2011). The framework consists of four domains that intersect and create four overlapping constructs that are integrated and influence each other:

1 **Participation** in life situations
2 Language, communication, and related **impairments**
3 Personal **identity**
4 **Environment**

Kagan observes that these overlapping constructs reflect a belief that a person's quality of life is the core and is generated by multiple domains (Kagan et al., 2008) (see Chapter 12, Figure 12.1). The emergence of this approach fulfills the call that Holland and Elman (2021) defined as the "Social Imperative" that requires involvement of the environment, consideration of cultural contexts, as well as supporting participation and well-being (Epstein & Street, 2011).

Correspondingly, a parallel process developed in the experiences of many Speech-Language Pathologists (SLPs). An example follows that illustrates this change of focus for intervention. One of the PWA receiving treatment at a medical rehabilitation center in Israel was Nurit[1], a 60-year-old woman, married with two older children. After having a stroke, she was diagnosed with severe conduction aphasia. The intervention focused on speech production and reading comprehension. Following 8 weeks of intensive treatment, Nurit had significantly improved her ability to convey functional verbal messages during therapy sessions and her SLP was excited about her progress. Her response, however, was "*I disagree with you! When I leave your room, I do not open my mouth because if I speak, everyone will think I am ignorant*". Nurit's perception of her frustration from the therapeutic process made clear the need to make a profound change in the intervention approach. The search for a new and effective treatment approach pointed to the work of Elman and colleagues (Elman & Bernstein-Ellis, 1999a, 1999b). Consequently, the first conversation group was launched at the rehabilitation department, participated in by Nurit and three other women. Following the group intervention, Nurit was able to enhance her communication skills, which in turn allowed her to gradually return to participate in more social activities. Nurit, like other PWA, completed her rehabilitation program at a medical center and returned to her community. Hence, it is imperative to develop rehabilitation centers in the community based on the LPAA model to improve PWAs' participation in society (LPAA, 2000).

The Adler Aphasia Center in Jerusalem is a community rehabilitation center for PWA in the chronic stage and their families. Thanks to the joint support of the Adler foundation and HAC the center functions as a non-profit organization within an academic setting. Students conduct part of their clinical education at the center. Including the social model in the academic and clinical education of SLP students is central to the implementation of LPAA-focused centers.

The main aim of the center is to create a supportive community to improve quality of life for PWA and their families. The center is geared toward developing an efficient and appropriate rehabilitative program tailored specifically for each person. Activities at the center are based on the social model and LPAA for intervention for PWA and focus on the person's strengths, expansion of activities, and involvement in society throughout the life span. The main activities offered at the center include individual treatment focused on LPAA goals, conversation groups, communication art groups, training communication partners, enrichment topic groups, cultural community events, advocacy for aphasia, and an extracurricular education center that educates other healthcare providers.

Education as a Force for Implementing the LPAA

Hoepner (2020) describes the LPAA framework for teaching and learning as including four domains: (1) Experiential learning, (2) Focus on learner development, (3) Emphasis on life experience, and (4) Multipronged learning context. The education program at the Department of Communication Disorders, together with the Center, applies evidence-based practice (EBP), case-based learning, reflective practice, and supervision in order for students to become effective participants in our LPAA-based center. This integrative non-medical model encompasses discipline-specific knowledge and core mental elements (Eggbeer et al., 2007).

Evidence-based practice as a standard is a core component in all clinical education programs (Gillan & Gillan, 2008) and a necessary component of effective and ethical treatment. Reflective practice and supervision involve examining with someone or independently, the thoughts, feelings, actions, and reactions evoked in the course of therapeutic work with clients. It is the context and interpersonal environment that permits self-reflection and professional use of the self after each clinical assignment. Clinicians need to learn the basic mental constructs of reflective practice: a working alliance, developing empathy, understanding the use of self, transference, and counter-transference (Geller & Foley, 2009). Among other methods of supervision, the practice of written reflections included in the program became an important manner of communication between students and supervisors, with students reporting through written reflections. There are three aspects of the reflection that determine their qualitative level: recalling or detailing, attending to feeling, and evaluating experiences that develop parallel to knowledge acquired during courses (Meilijson & Katzenberger, 2009).

Case-based learning is an integrative learning approach that provides practical experience and can lead to lifelong learning. The approach aims to strengthen a student's motivation to inquire and develop critical thinking. It seeks to integrate the contents of students' clinical education and creates an environment which encourages questions (Leahy et al., 2010). As part of this case-based approach, some students accompany a PWA, provide individual treatment, and participate in communication groups. The following is a written reflection which an SLP student presented after an intervention:

> My first challenge as a student clinician at the Adler Center was to do away with the medical model for aphasia intervention. That was the model applied at the rehabilitation department at a medical center which I was assigned previously. The social approach required that I would be focused on initiating communicative interactions and taking responsibility for mutual conversation. Supervision helped me move from the medical to the social model and strengthen the interaction by listening to Hana's mental process and my own as a clinician, that affects the flow of the conversation and the implementation of the goals. Throughout the intervention I became more empathic toward the PWA and her emotional state, and I was able to tune in with her emotionally but without identifying with her, which may have disrupted the therapeutic process.

The above self-reflection shows the huge challenge in development from a beginner clinician to one that feels comfortable implementing LPAA principles. In her reflection, the student described the educational evolution process of theoretical and experiential knowledge in addition to mental constructs that are the basis of reflective practice, such as developing empathy and the use of self.

Reciprocal Benefits of an Aphasia Center in an Academic Setting

A key aspect of the LPAA is its authentic context in the environment (Hoepner, 2020). The location of the center at the college allows for interdepartmental activities as well as the development of extracurricular educational programs. Some students participate in courses offered by the center, others receive a scholarship to work at the center, and others receive instruction in conversation accessibility with the PWA. The administrative and academic personnel at HAC are also integrated in the center's activities, enabling the development of an enriched natural and non-medical relationship for the PWA and their families.

For example, "Aphasia Café" is a round table discussion meeting that is held once a year. Meetings are led by the members (PWA), who invite students and faculty to hear their personal stories and learn about aphasia. This project ensures that new entering students are exposed and directly acquainted with the essence of living with aphasia. These meetings enable the PWA to become self-advocators (Harmon et al., 2019). Their ability to tell their stories becomes one of the ways they develop their new personal identity after the stroke. By talking to others about "who we are and what we have done", PWA were able to maintain and reconfirm a sense of identity. These social interactions can help them establish for themselves and others that regardless of aphasia they still have a past, present, and future (Swart & Horton, 2015). They experience dialogue with unfamiliar people and feel they have a part in influencing the environment of their lives.

The members of the center are encouraged to participate in conferences (for instance, the annual international conference of the MA program in the department) and share their personal experiences as PWA in lectures and panel discussions. Their participation in conferences is an opportunity for them to share their expertise and bring to the table issues that are important to them from their own experience. During one of the conferences, two members of the center, guided by their SLP, described their new identity in their families and in their community. Shadden (2005) suggested that understanding identity may be useful for improving quality of life in PWA. The opportunity to participate in an academic conference heightened their self-esteem and enabled them to reconnect by creating a sense of continuity between who they had been and who they are now (Swart & Horton, 2015). The value of the presentation is depicted well by Ely who presented in the last conference:

> My participation in the academic conference allowed me to express myself and to convey my message. I felt that I was heard and people showed interest in me. I was reinforced by the feedback I received. I felt I returned to the position I was before the stroke – a lecturer in front of a crowd.

Interdepartmental Activities that Focus on Life Participation

To encourage multidisciplinary and cross disciplinary activity between departments, the center upholds active links with other academic departments at the college, such as Inclusive Industrial Design, Photographic Communication, and Optometry. One of the joint projects with the Department of Inclusive Industrial Design was intended to study the effects of the Communication Fan (see Figure 13.1) as an AAC tool designed to support conversation between a family physician and the PWA. The rationale for the development of this tool includes ergonomic and communicative elements. Ergonomically, it was necessary to fix the size and the grip of the fan, which can be used with the left hand, to accommodate those with right hemiparesis. Communicatively, the content of the fan was designed to meet the needs of a consultation with the family physician who knows the PWA and comprises requests that are typical of a medical dialog. The tool comprises special topics such as type of complaints, referrals to specialized physicians and/or treatments, reporting and place of specific pain, and more. This project was designed as a research seminar by students and faculty from both departments.

Another joint interdepartmental project was the Design Research Course that aimed to teach Industrial Design students to generate new insights about how design research could contribute to the rehabilitation processes. All course students participated in a partner training workshop before their meeting with the Adler Aphasia Center's members. The example below describes the outcome of one of these projects.

Eyal, a 45-year-old man, married with seven children, was diagnosed with severe expressive aphasia after a head injury. A group of design students were confronted with the task of finding rehabilitative solutions for Eyal. Following his trauma, Eyal lost interest in his previous occupations, hardly communicated with his children, and spent most of his time in front of the TV. The students met Eyal at his home and found out that before his head injury he had single-handedly renovated his home and had found ingenious solutions for storage. He was proud to show them all his creative work at his home. The home visit was a turning point for the project, as the students realized that Eyal's creativity would be the key for his rehabilitation. Acknowledging his identity as a religious Jew, the

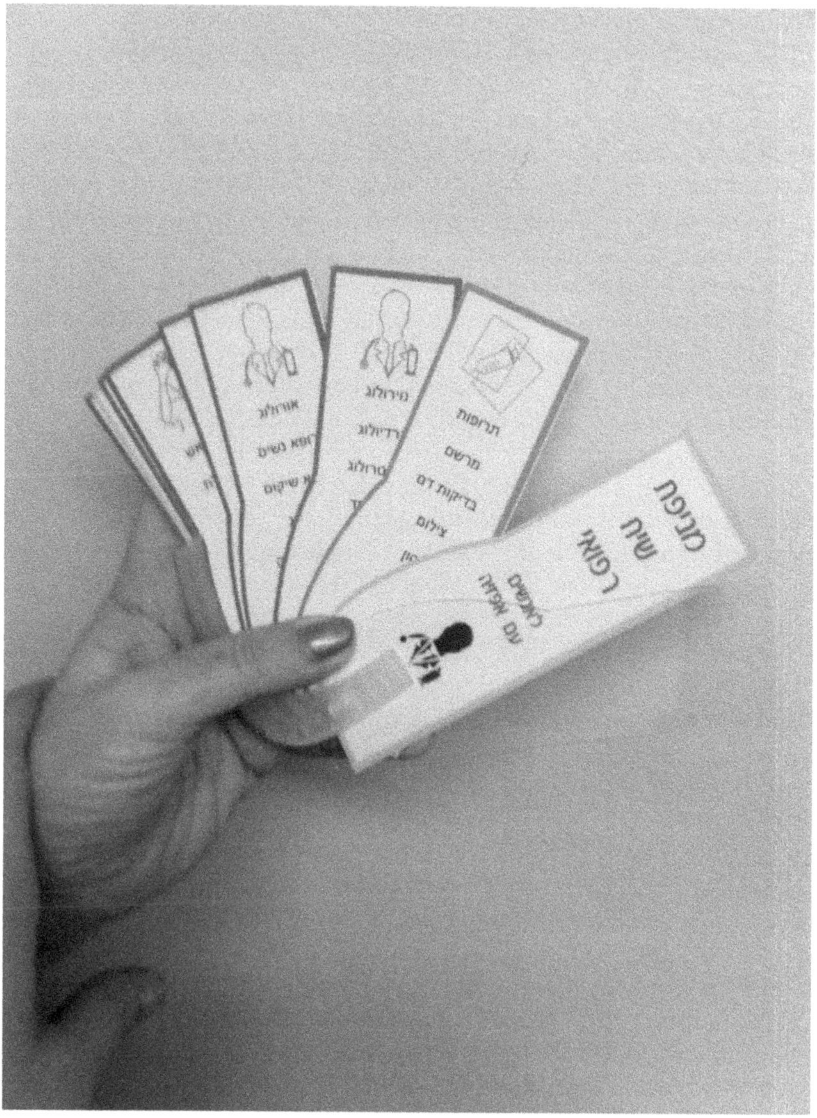

FIGURE 13.1 "Communication Fan"–A medical conversation handheld fan.
Photographer: Haim Kohl.

students created a platform for the design and production of Mezuzahs (a traditional Jewish object that is affixed to the doorpost) at his home. Eyal succeeded in producing Mezuzahs and gave gifts to his family and friends. Later the college administration ordered Mezuzahs to give as presents to the college's guests. Eyal's wife's comment to the students emphasizes the benefits of the project: "*You brought me back my husband, he is motivated and he finds meaning in his creative activity*". Creative-arts-based therapies for stroke survivors has been shown to promote social engagement (Lo et al., 2019), and this is what was observed with Eyal. Shahar and Ventura (2023) described the performance of the design students in the project as skillful and as enabling navigation between the conflicting demands of art and rehabilitation, patient and designer. In addition, they observed that the personal relationship that evolved between the students and their allocated partner proved to be a major factor in the project's success.

A third example is the Photography group, organized in collaboration with the Department of Photographic Communication and aimed to enable PWA to acquire a new mode of self-expression by utilizing their residual abilities. Lo et al. (2019) has described how photography can gradually become a tool for communication, a medium for reintegration and a part of the identity of PWA. An example of this process is described by Mira, the wife of one of the members, that remarked:

> Since he uses his camera, he approaches people on the street, he shows them his "aphasia card" and he asks permission to photograph them. In addition, he takes advantage of his non-verbal communication skills, especially his friendly smile. From this point, the encounter becomes a social event.

Photography allows members to explore their personal identity as PWA. Figures 13.2 and 13.3 describe the feelings of the photographers and their social alienation. The photographs taken by the members are exhibited in an open exhibition to the public. The fact that they are identified as artists and not seen only as persons with aphasia allows them to enhance their personal identity. Moreover, the exhibition provides their family an opportunity to regard them through a different point of view, as creative artists and not as disabled persons, as described by Thompson (2009).

Extracurricular Educational Activities

Extracurricular collaborative practice is an important aspect of education in the community. The center collaborates with the School of Medicine at the Hebrew University in Jerusalem by offering workshops to medical and nursing students about aphasia, partner training, and meetings with the members of the center and their families. Reduced communication opportunities for PWA may result in reduced participation in healthcare decision

FIGURE 13.2 Example of a photograph that expresses the photographer's feelings as a PWA. Haim named the photograph "My Aphasia" describing his social alienation.

Photographer: Haim Kohl.

making and adverse events at hospital (Hemsley et al., 2013). According to the literature, educating health care professionals is one of the reported solutions for those communication barriers (van Rijssen et al., 2022).

The Adler Aphasia Center also offers dedicated seminars for SLPs, focusing on applied aspects of the principles of the life participation approach. SLPs receive tools for implementing the LPAA model, which are adapted to the Hebrew language and to Israeli culture, for example, in Communication Partner Training (CPT). CPT has been shown to be effective in several ways: improving the communication partner's skills in supporting communication with PWA, improving the participation of PWA, and reducing the negative psychosocial consequences for partners and PWA (Simmons-Mackie et al., 2010, 2016). However, it was found that only a small percentage of SLPs apply CPT in their practice (Chang et al., 2018; Simmons-Mackie et al., 2016). Consequently, a study was designed to develop a protocol in Hebrew for working with families of PWA in Israel. The protocol was presented during seminars for SLPs and promoted for further application at other centers. In addition to the seminars, a web

FIGURE 13.3 Example of a photograph that expresses the photographer's feelings as a PWA. Avi named the photograph "My Reflection".

Photographer: Avi Israel.

forum sponsored by the center was opened to reinforce the SLPs' use of CPT and allow them to discuss issues pertaining to the integration of CPT in their clinical work. Moreover, a group of SLPs from the forum collaborated with the Israeli Speech and Language Association to write a position paper with guidelines for the role of SLPs in providing communication partner training for people with acquired communication disorders. The aim of these guidelines is to initiate change at governmental levels.

Multicultural and Multilingual Challenges and Opportunities at the Center

The multilingual character of the members of the center presents another challenge to SLPs in finding the appropriate delivery service that suits language differences. For that purpose, a communication group was started for bilingual members who speak English as their first language and Hebrew as their second language. The group is guided by an SLP whose first language is English. The bilingual members can choose to participate in either the Hebrew or the English-speaking group. Hanan, a bilingual member who arrived in Israel from Canada at age 16, had a stroke at 57 years old and was diagnosed with moderate expressive aphasia. The gap between his first (better-spared English) and second (more-impaired Hebrew) languages was prominent in his speech production. During the first years of his participation at the center, Hanan insisted on participating in Hebrew-speaking groups in spite of having better communicative performance in English. After discussing the issue with Hanan, it was decided that he should participate in the English-speaking group, and that in all other activities he would speak in English although other members and the SLPs would address him in Hebrew. While most persons with aphasia may prefer receiving therapy in their first language, immigrants often find it functionally more efficient to receive therapy in their second language (e.g., Gil & Goral, 2004). Centeno (2008) suggested that in order to understand language choice, it is necessary to consider emotional connections, ethnic identity, and communication contexts associated with each language.

Conclusion and Future Directions

The Life Participation Approach to Aphasia is officially over 20 years old (LPAA Project Group, 2000). Nevertheless, it is important to acknowledge that 50 years ago Marta Taylor Sarno published the "Functional communication approach", thus introducing the paradigm of social participation (Simmons-Mackie, 2021). While, notably, LPAA has not yet become the leading therapeutic approach for clinicians who work with PWA (Fridriksson & Hillis, 2021), establishing the center in the Communication Disorders Department at HAC was a turning point in the implementation of the social approach to intervention in Israel. According to Devanga et al. (2021), academic-based aphasia programs are a vital part of the continuum of care for aphasia. As was shown in this chapter, a strong cooperation between a community aphasia center and an academic program is one setting that can lead to an effective implementation of the LPAA principles. The underlying reciprocal benefits that derive from this integrated approach of service delivery and education can be described in the following domains:

Education

The broad LPAA perspective supported by the A-FROM allows students to develop empathy and gain insights into the lived experience of the person with aphasia. The observation of the experiences of the PWA communicating in different situations enables students, as well as the PWA, to plan goals for intervention in the most efficient way so as to enhance the quality of life of the PWA. LPAA is integrated in the academic curriculum allowing the students to make the connection between theory and practice. Addressing the lived experience of PWA is crucial for LPAA implementation (Harmon et al., 2019). The SLPs and students who participate in the center's activities become LPAA ambassadors in their communities. They advocate for further development of the social approach among health care organizations and administration. Graduates who do not necessarily continue to work with aphasia experience the important influence of the ICF and the LPAA values that are relevant to the lives of all people with communication disorders.

Integration in the Community

Simmons-Mackie (2021) describes the environment of the person with aphasia as a significant theme of the social imperative. The location of an aphasia center in a community opens a variety of opportunities for participation of PWA. The academic setting can become a supportive environment that provides positive experiences and creates a feeling of belonging that enhances wellbeing and social interactions. Armour et al. (2019) claim that one's environment includes the physical and social factors at home and in the community and can take a critical role in promoting communicational opportunities that are enjoyable and healing. We found support for this, in that members' participation in extracurricular activities such as conferences, the "Aphasia Café", and workshops allows them to integrate in their community as self-advocators.

Future Directions

The implementation of the LPAA framework has been developed successfully at the Adler Aphasia Center in Jerusalem in cooperation with the Department of Communication Disorders at HAC and it has had a great impact throughout the country. In the future, we recommend opening more centers in Communication Disorders Departments that have secured mutual cooperation. These new centers will contribute to the enhancement of the skills required for sustained implementation of LPAA and the development of new models of aphasia rehabilitation. We strongly recommend that founders of new centers choose an academic department that values collaboration with the community, as this approach is considered the best fit for a center based on the LPAA, as has been shown in this chapter.

In addition, it is recommended to strengthen financial cooperation between external funding and academic programs. Simmons-Mackie (2021) stated that "funding will be an important consideration as we embark on the next 20 years of LPAA" (p. 219). Participation of PWA and their families in an aphasia center is not supported by the medical insurance programs in Israel. The cooperation of an academic SLP program in addition to external donations may afford the economic base for permanent, long-term care for PWA. The gains of academia from collaborating with the center are substantial, in that it allows students to participate in a unique clinical practice that could not be attained otherwise. As shown, students acquire tools that are central to the development of future SLPs in the implementation of the LPAA model for working with PWA and their families. Finally, the centers may provide a supportive environment for the promotion of advocacy for lifelong intervention for PWA and their families.

Acknowledgments

We wish to thank the founders of the Center – Mike and Elaine Adler and their family, Professor Nava Ben Zvi (former President of HAC), and current HAC President Professor Bertold Fridlender.

Note

1 All names of PWA mentioned in this chapter have been changed to protect their privacy.

References

Armour, M., Brady, S., Sayyad, A., & Krieger, R. (2019). Self-reported quality of life outcomes in aphasia using life participation approach values: 1-year outcomes. *Archives of Rehabilitation Research and Clinical Translation*, *1*(3–4).

Centeno, J. G. (2008). Multidisciplinary evidence to treat bilingual individuals with aphasia. *Perspectives on Communication Disorders and Sciences in Culturally and Linguistically Diverse Populations*, *15*(3), 66–72.

Chang, H. F., Power, E., O'Halloran, R., & Foster, A. (2018). Stroke communication partner training: A national survey of 122 clinicians on current practice patterns and perceived implementation barriers and facilitators. *International Journal of Language and Communication Disorders*, *53*(6), 1094–1109.

Devanga, S. R., Pollens, R. D., & Glista, S. O. (2021). Toward developing outcome measures in university-based aphasia programs: Perspectives from the aphasia communication enhancement program. *Perspectives of the ASHA Special Interest Groups*, *6*(5), 1047–1059.

Eggbeer, L., Mann, L., & Seibel, N. (2007). Reflective supervision – Past, present and future. *Zero to Three*, *5*, 1–9.

Elman, R. (2016). Aphasia centers and the life participation approach to aphasia: A paradigm shift. *Topics in Language Disorders*, *36*, 154–167.

Elman, R. J. & Bernstein-Ellis, E. (1999a). The efficacy of group communication treatment in adults with chronic aphasia. *Journal of Speech, Language, and Hearing Research*, *42*(2), 411–419.

Elman, R. & Bernstein-Ellis, E. (1999b). Psychosocial aspects of group communication treatment: Preliminary findings. *Seminars in Speech and Language*, *20*, 65–71.

Epstein, R. (2011). The values and value of patients-centered care. *Annual of Family Medicine*, *9*, 100–103.

Fridriksson, J. & Hillis, A. E. (2021). Current approaches to the treatment of post-stroke aphasia. *Journal of Stroke*, *23*(2), 183–201.

Geller, E. & Foley, G., (2009). Broadening the "port of entry" for speech-language pathologists: A relational and reflective model for clinical supervision. *American Journal of Speech-Language Pathology*, *18*, 22–41.

Gil, M. & Goral, M. (2004). Nonparallel recovery in bilingual aphasia: Effects of language choice, language proficiency, and treatment. *International Journal of Bilingualism*, *8*(2), 191–219.

Gillan, S. L. & Gillan, R. (2008). Teaching graduate students to make evidence-based intervention decision: Application of a seven-step process within an authentic learning context. *Topics in Language Disorders*, *28*(3), 212–228.

Harmon, T. G., Lin, M. L., Scronce, G., & Jacks, A. (2019). Supporting confidence and participation for PWA through student interaction: A descriptive study on the effects of an interdisciplinary campus program. *Journal of Allied Health*, *48*(4), 107E–112E.

Hemsley, B., Werninck, M., & Worrall, L. (2013). "That really shouldn't have happened": PWA and their spouses narrate adverse events in hospital. *Aphasiology*, *27*(6), 706–722.

Holland, A. L. & Elman, R. J. (Eds.). (2021). *Neurogenic communication disorders and the life participation approach: The social imperative in supporting individuals and families*. Plural Publishing.

Hoepner, J. K. & Sather, T. W. (2020). Teaching and mentoring students in the life participation approach to aphasia service delivery perspective. *Perspectives of the ASHA Special Interest Groups*, *5*(2), 397–413 10.1044/2019_PERSP-19-00159.

Kagan, A., Simmons-Mackie, N., Rowland, A., Huijbregts, M., Shumway, E., McEwen, S., & Sharp, S. (2008). Counting what counts: A framework for capturing real-life outcomes of aphasia intervention. *Aphasiology*, *22*(3), 258–280.

Kagan, A. (2011). A-FROM in action at the Aphasia Institute. *Seminars in Speech and Language*, *32*(3), 216–228.

Leahy, M. M., McTiernan, K., Smith, M. M., Sloane, P., Walsh, I. P., Walshe, M., & Ni Cholmain, C. (2010). Foundation studies in education for therapy practice: Curriculum updating. *Folia Phoniatrica et Logopaedica*, 2, 255–259.

Lo, T. L. T., Lee, J. L. C., & Ho, R. T. H. (2019). Creative arts-based therapies for stroke survivors: A qualitative systematic review. *Frontiers in Psychology*, 1646.

LPAA project group: Chapey, R., Duchan, J. F., Elman, R. J., Garcia, L. J., Kagan, A., Lyon, J. G., & Simmons-Mackie, N. (2000). Life participation approach to aphasia: A statement of values for the future. *The ASHA Leader*, *5*(3), 4–6.

Meilijson, S. & Katzenberger, I. (2009). Reflections on reflections: Learning process in speech language pathology students' clinical education. *Perspectives on Administration and Supervision*, *9*(2), 62–71.

Reed, G. M., Lux, J. B., Bufka, L. F., Trask, C., Peterson, D. B., Stark, S., Threats, T. T., Jacobson, J. W., & Hawley, J. A. (2005). Operationalizing the International Classification of Functioning, Disability and Health in clinical settings. *Rehabilitation Psychology*, *50*(2), 122–131. 10.1037/0090-5550.50.2.122.

Shadden, B. (2005). Aphasia as identity theft: Theory and practice. *Aphasiology*, *19*(3-5), 211–223.

Shahar, D. & Ventura, J. (2023). Bespoke healthcare design. In R. Shusterman & B. Veres (Eds.), *Somaesthetics and Design Culture*. Brill (Netherlands).

Simmons-Mackie, N. (2011). Aphasia centers: A growing trend in North America. *Seminars in Speech and Language*, *32*, 199–202.

Simmons-Mackie, N. (2021). The Life Participation Approach to Aphasia: Looking back and moving forward. In A. L. Holland & R. J. Elman (Eds.). *Neurogenic communication disorders and the life participation approach: The social imperative in supporting individuals and families*. Plural Publishing.

Simmons-Mackie, N., Raymer, A., Armstrong, E., Holland, A., & Cherney, L. R. (2010). Communication partner training in aphasia: A systematic review. *Archives of Physical Medicine and Rehabilitation*, *91*(12), 1814–1837.

Simmons-Mackie, N., Raymer, A., and Cherney, L. R. (2016). Communication partner training in aphasia: An updated systematic review. *Archives of Physical Medicine and Rehabilitation*, *97*(12), 2202–2221.

Swart, J. & Horton, S. (2015). From patients to teachers: The perspectives of trainers with aphasia in a UK Conversation Partner Scheme. *Aphasiology*, *29* (2), 195–213.

Thompson, G. (2009). Artistic sensibility in the studio and gallery model: Revisiting process and product. *Art Therapy*, *26* (4), 159–166.

van Rijssen, M. N., Veldkamp, M., Bryon, E., Remijn, L., Visser-Meily, J. M., Gerrits, E., & van Ewijk, L. (2022). How do healthcare professionals experience communication with people with aphasia and what content should communication partner training entail? *Disability and Rehabilitation*, *44*(14), 3671–3678.

WHO. (2001). International classification of functioning, disability and health. ICF. Geneva, Switzerland.

Woelders, S., van der Borg, W., Schipper, K., & Abma, T. (2018). The meaning of Aphasia Centers from the perspectives of people with aphasia and their relatives: Understanding participation in the Dutch context. *Aphasiology*, *32*(12), 1490–1512.

14

CONVERSATION TREATMENT IN APHASIA IN MONOLINGUAL AND MULTILINGUAL ADULTS

Yael Neumann and Marion C. Leaman

Introduction

Communication in real-life conversation is key to relationships and to establishing social connections (e.g., Maynard & Zimmerman, 1984). It allows one to share what one thinks, feels, and knows. Furthermore, a person's identity and sense of self is woven into their individual communicative style. Consequently, the impact that an acquired language impairment has on people with aphasia (PWA) can be profoundly negative, both personally and socially. This is because changes to language and interactional communication abilities can make PWA appear less competent than they are and as a result may be treated as such. This bears heavily on their sense of self-identity and may lead to a constellation of problems, such as not returning to work and/or hobbies, deteriorating social connections, particularly with one's spouse or significant other, and social isolation. This overall reduction in participating in social and community life can have devastating effects to PWA's self-esteem and quality of life (e.g., Moeller & Carpenter, 2013).

In particular, one very important area of communication impacted by aphasia is that of conversation between couples (Lock et al., 2001). Due to PWA's linguistic impairments, the pattern of interaction between couples, in addition to post-stroke changes in roles and responsibilities, are very different from pre-stroke interactions which can create stress and tension in the relationship. Developing ways of interacting together and adapting to those changes through everyday conversation can help couples rebuild their relationship (e.g., Boles, 2011). Thus, it is not surprising that PWA

DOI: 10.4324/9781003330318-17

and their families place a high value on rehabilitation addressing interactional, conversational level communication that goes far beyond the basic communication needs often prioritized in therapy.

Historical Overview of the Field of Aphasia Rehabilitation

Aware of these unmet needs, aphasia researchers and clinicians began shifting practice over 40 years ago to include real-world communication experiences as a part of the therapeutic process. By the early 1980s, Audrey Holland, the seminal leader focusing on real-world communication, had begun publishing her research on the critical importance of addressing "functional communication" with PWA (Holland, 1982). Previously, researchers and clinicians had focused almost solely on the language impairment caused by aphasia. Therapy was conducted primarily through assessment and treatment of discrete language building blocks such as grammatical structures and lexical retrieval of vocabulary (e.g., Porch, 1967). Therapy programs addressed single word and sentence level production (e.g., Voluntary Control of Involuntary Utterances, Helm & Barresi, 1980; Semantic Feature Analysis, Boyle & Coelho, 1995), with little consideration of discourse production abilities, limitations, or needs in real-life. Conversation was relegated to an activity that happened before and after therapy (Holland, 1998). Minimal therapeutic resources were devoted to supporting PWA in the practical skills of using language within a real-world context to communicate with other people. With so much focus on what PWA could not do linguistically, little attention was given to recognizing, understanding, and promoting what they could do using the broad array of verbal and nonverbal communicative resources used by all people in real-world interactions with others.

During this period, other researchers made critical contributions to a shifting intervention paradigm. For instance, Davis (1980) introduced Promoting Aphasic Communicative Effectiveness, an approach which incorporated the important interactional features of real-world communication by requiring both the clinician and the PWA to communicate novel information in a structured task. Simmons-Mackie and colleagues (1987) and Lyon (1989) reported on the benefits of providing communication and strategy training to conversational partners of PWA. Group therapy had been provided since as early as the 1940s for people with traumatic brain injuries, with extension to PWA (e.g., Turnblom & Myers, 1952). By the 1980s, programs and centers had developed for PWA (e.g., 1979 opening of the Aphasia Institute in Toronto, Canada by Pat Arato) with a focus on authentic group interactions. Thereafter, research showing the impact of group intervention involving naturalistic everyday conversation further emerged (e.g., Wertz et al., 1981). Concurrently, important research was being conducted investigating detailed microlinguistic (e.g., Gleason et al., 1980) and macrolinguistic (e.g., Ulatowska et al., 1981) profiles of discourse production in people with different types of aphasia, which in this early stage focused on monologic language samples.

Models of Conversation Treatments in Aphasia

These lines of innovative research formed a strong foundation for the development of therapy programs centered on conversation using three unique and beneficial delivery models: communication partner training, group therapy, and individual therapy. Of these three delivery models, most of the research involving conversation in aphasia took the form of partner training programs (e.g., Simmons-Mackie et al., 2014). Many programs provide training only to the partner (e.g., Supported Conversation for Aphasia, Kagan, 1998) but several address the conversational needs of the PWA together with the partner (Better Conversations with Aphasia, Beeke et al., 2013; Interaction-focused therapy, Wilkinson, 2010; Couples Therapy, Boles, 2011; Communication Partners, Lyon, 1989).

Our focus in this chapter is on research that involves assessment and intervention of conversation that parallels spontaneous, real-world conversations as closely as possible. We define conversation therapies as those that are primarily focused on interaction, that accept and encourage all communication modalities, and that are situated in an authentic context where there is communicative intent (Doedens & Meteyard, 2022). Further, conversation interventions are those that employ rich communicative environments that are characterized by complexity, voluntary communication, and are specifically relevant to the individual's interests and needs promoting a positive experience in the interaction (Hengst et al., 2019). Consequently, we have not included discussion of therapy programs in which conversation is not the main focus (i.e., when used as a component of a therapy primarily addressing word/sentence-level tasks). Likewise, we do not discuss therapies in which the clinician controls the conversation using a preset agenda e.g., uses a list of questions/topics or asks for a conversation in response to a picture or video clip. These structured conversational contexts represent a subgenre of conversation with features that differ from the unstructured subgenre of conversation used in typical daily interactions (e.g., Drew & Heritage, 1992).

Conversation Therapy Programs Aimed at the Person with Aphasia

Most conversation therapy programs focus on working with the PWA and their primary communication partner; only a few programs exist that focus directly on working one-on-one with the PWA (Simmons-Mackie et al., 2014). In the early part of the past decade, two such therapies were published in the literature; a single case study introducing Natural Conversation for Severe Aphasia (Basso, 2010), and two studies involving the same set of two participants who participated in intervention that alternated between a conversation-focused program and a more common stimulation-focused program in which the clinician directly stimulates language skills (Savage & Donovan, 2017; Savage et al., 2014). Since then, two other interventions targeting authentic conversation with PWA have been introduced. Each of these four conversation-focused treatments is reviewed below.

Facilitating Authentic Conversation (FAC)

FAC is an aphasia intervention that is grounded theoretically on constructivism, a leading theory which posits that adults learn through experiences occurring in natural, everyday contexts (see Damico et al., 2015). This contrasts with the highly structured, clinician-controlled behaviorist approaches and principles of operant conditioning that have been historically predominant in aphasia intervention. FAC provides an outline of five constructivist principles that are critical to the intervention:

1. focus on face-to-face conversation
2. orient toward the interdependence of the interlocutors in the unfolding of the conversation (i.e., what happens in each turn is informed by prior turns)
3. recognize the complexity of conversation as an emergent phenomenon (i.e., not structured or predictable)
4. focus on functional goals, and
5. recognize that conversation is a social activity and is thus a collaborative phenomenon.

The clinician follows the above principles while engaged in spontaneous conversation with the PWA. While so doing, the clinician employs the following therapeutic techniques: a) explicit discussion of the conversational interaction and the behavioral targets of therapy; b) opportunities for the PWA to evaluate their own communication/use of strategies; c) clinician modeling of conversational skills; d) clinician shaping of conversational skills using natural conversational consequences to turns, occasional corrections, and occasional explicit feedback about communicative efforts (i.e., "bracketed critiques").

Three studies (two case studies and one group study) involving 23 individuals with mild to profound aphasia have investigated FAC (Azios et al., 2021; Damico et al., 2015; Tetnowski et al., 2021). Facilitative behaviors taught to the participants included use of writing, drawing, gesturing, intentional circumlocution, and requesting assistance when needed. Behaviors considered inhibitory to the forward movement of conversation, such as when a participant would remain fixated on production of a word that could not be retrieved or abandon the topic when confronted with word retrieval difficulty, were also addressed with the participants as the researchers would describe the behaviors targeted for eradication.

In the two case studies, individual data from three participants showed positive benefits of FAC for generalization of facilitative strategies addressed during intervention to novel conversations (Azios et al., 2021; Damico et al., 2015). One person with profound global aphasia and one with moderate Broca's aphasia each increased use of two out of three facilitative strategies (Azios et al., 2021), and another person with moderate Broca's aphasia did so for both facilitative strategies targeted in intervention (Damico et al., 2015). This participant also reduced both inhibitory behaviors targeted in therapy that were limiting the forward movement of his conversations (i.e., fixation on retrieving specific lexical items and abandoning topic).

In the group study conducted by Tetnowski and colleagues (2021), 19 people with mild to moderate aphasia and one with severe aphasia were included. Therapy entailed a 50-minute group session and a 50-minute individual session on the same day with trained student-clinicians who followed the previously published FAC guidelines. Intervention lasted 3 months, with a total of 40 hours of therapy delivered to each person. Spontaneous conversation was the focus of both group and individual sessions, with a focus on increasing behaviors that facilitate forward movement of the conversation and decrease those that inhibit the desired conversational progressivity. Impact of treatment was analyzed using four measures related to the repair sequences that occurred in pre-/post-treatment conversations. A significant decrease in the rate of communication breakdowns from pre-treatment to post-treatment was reported at the group-level, as well as a decrease in the length of repair sequences, measured in turns. The rate at which PWA initiated self-repairs and completed the repairs did not show a significant change.

Savage and Colleagues' Conversational Therapy

Savage and colleagues (2014, 2017) used a spontaneous conversational context to address goals they described as involving language production, repair, initiation, turn-taking, and topic management with two participants. They identified these intervention target areas via assessment using the Conversation Analysis Profile for People with Aphasia (Whitworth et al., 1997). Conversation therapy was alternated with a stimulation-based therapy, with an assessment phase between the two phases, and was counterbalanced across participants. Each intervention phase consisted of twice weekly, 60-minute sessions for 5 weeks.

Conversation therapy occurred through unstructured conversation on topics of interest to the participants, which had been queried during assessment phase 1, using a questionnaire adapted from the Aphasia Needs Assessment (Garrett & Beukelman, 2006 as cited in Savage et al., 2014). The clinician modulated complexity of the conversation by manipulating turns and using strategies such as modeling, clarifying, and questioning. Following participant turns the clinician manipulated the next turn by using expansions and questions with the intent to improve the organization of the PWA's last turn. Examples of the hierarchical tasks used in the stimulation therapy entailed having the participant point to items, respond to questions and stories, verify sentence integrity, follow instructions, name pictures, provide antonyms and synonyms, complete rhyming exercises, and name items by semantic category.

The authors developed primary outcome measures with a pragmatic focus for the conversational therapy based on the previous work of Pimentel and Algeo (2009). Savage and colleagues (2014) evaluated use of those behaviors that they felt moved the conversation forward, calling them facilitative, and those they felt slowed the conversation down, labeling them non-facilitative. The facilitative measure was an index that incorporated a count of utterance initiations, continuations, and responses. The non-facilitative measure was an index of repairs and revisions. In addition, they employed linguistic measures to evaluate the impact of their conversation therapy, including mean length of utterance in words (MLUwords), type/token ratio (TTR), a raw count of number of different words (NDW), percent of utterance responses, percent of simple utterances, percent of complex utterances, and propositional idea density (Savage & Donovan, 2017). Findings were evaluated by effect size changes from one testing phase to the next and from pre-treatment to post-treatment. Secondary aphasia test battery measures assessing language, functional communication, and quality of life, were administered during each assessment phase.

P1, who received conversation therapy after stimulation therapy, had a significant decrease in facilitative behaviors and a significant increase in non-facilitative behaviors following conversation therapy, in contrast to the study expectations. However, from baseline to post-treatment (i.e., from assessment 1 to assessment 3) findings were reversed, with facilitative behaviors significantly increasing and non-facilitative behaviors significantly decreasing. In terms of linguistic measures, P1 demonstrated negative effects following conversation therapy for MLU, TTR, number of different words, and percent production of simple utterances. However, there was a positive effect for increased number of utterances, increased percent of complex utterances, and propositional density (i.e., number of verbs, adjectives, adverbs, prepositions, and conjunctions divided by total words). No differences in secondary measures were observed, which included test batteries of language, functional communication, and quality of life.

In contrast, P2 demonstrated a significant increase in facilitative behaviors and a significant decrease in non-facilitative behaviors following conversation therapy. There were small treatment effects in the expected directions following the entire intervention (i.e., from assessment 1 to assessment 3). For linguistic measures, P2 demonstrated a significant reduction in the number of words and number of utterances, but significant increases for MLU, TTR, number of different words, percent simple utterances, percent complex utterances, and propositional density. Like P1, no differences in secondary measures were observed.

The authors summarized their findings stating that both participants demonstrated gains for some of the conversation measures following both types of therapy. Greatest gains in conversation were observed for each participant during or following the conversation therapy phase, irrespective of intervention ordering.

Natural Conversation for Severe Aphasia

Basso (2010) developed an intervention for an individual with severe global aphasia based on the workings of typical conversation and guided by Grice's maxims (1975): quality, quantity, relation, and manner. Basso describes the intervention as consisting of a type of conversation one would have with someone who did not have aphasia in which interlocutors have authentic information to share with one another. The clinician first establishes turn-taking behavior, and then focuses on ensuring the PWA comprehends incoming information by using simple language and explicitly stating the speech act to be performed, such as stating "I wish to ask you a question". The clinician further supports comprehension by highlighting new information by producing turns in which the important and new information is fronted, such as "London, do you like it?" rather than asking "Do you like London?". Throughout the intervention the clinician uses all communication modalities.

During the conversation with the PWA, the clinician assumes competence by understanding the person's responses as related to the topic being discussed. The clinician offers interpretations that make relevant connections to information being negotiated. Although some inferences supplied by the clinician may be wrong, the two work together until an agreement is made about the intended meaning. In an effort to aid future retrieval of the word (or words), the clinician then asks the PWA to repeat the correct information more than once.

Basso describes a case study about a participant with global aphasia who engaged in little interaction with others or his environment and participated in few verbal exchanges 18 months following his stroke. He then began attending 2 hours of therapy daily for 9 months. During the first 3 months, the program focused on turn-taking, using structured tasks such as pointing to objects or completing simple tasks. Following this period, he was able to adequately take turns, and the intervention shifted to conversational interactions, as outlined above. The author reported improvement in all tasks except writing following 6 months, with additional gains in all language modalities and newfound engagement with others following the full 9 months of daily intervention.

Expanding Communication and Language Opportunities Generated in Conversation (ECoLoGiC-Tx)

Leaman and Edmonds (under review) reported preliminary data for ECoLoGiC-Tx, an intervention aimed at improving conversational language and communication that incorporates principles from Conversation Analysis (Schegloff, 2007), neuroplasticity (Kleim & Jones, 2008), experiential learning (Kolb & Kolb, 2017), effortful learning (Schuchard & Middleton, 2018), and complexity theory (Kiran & Thompson, 2003). The treatment has two primary components which are alternated throughout the session according to need: Therapeutic Conversation and Therapeutic Repair. During Therapeutic Conversation, the clinician uses behaviors typical of everyday social interaction, following the Social Conversation Collection Protocol (Leaman & Edmonds, 2021) developed from Conversation Analysis (Schegloff, 2007), Systemic Functional Linguistics (Eggins & Slade, 2004; Halliday & Matthiessen, 2014) and related interactional literature (Norrick, 2000; Ochs & Capps, 2002). For instance, the clinician makes comments, tells stories, shows engagement with back-channeling behaviors (i.e., saying "mhm"), and uses (and accepts) multiple communication modalities, all while pausing at appropriate junctures to provide increased time for the PWA to contribute to the conversation. Simultaneously, the clinician also avoids typical clinical behaviors such as phonemic and semantic cueing, question/answer cycles typical of an interview, and telling the PWA how to communicate because these behaviors are atypical of everyday interactions.

During Therapeutic Repair, the clinician or the PWA identifies the communication needing repair work by remarking on it and by providing a concrete referent to it such as writing, drawing, or pointing to an item in the environment relevant to the breakdown (e.g., the clinician might point to the person's baseball cap if the breakdown occurred around something to do with the cap or the logo on it). The clinician then proceeds with a flexible 7-step least-to-most hierarchy of support allowing the PWA time to complete their own communicative problem-solving to provide more information. For instance, in Step 1 the clinician first says something like "I'm not sure that I understand how your Yankees cap is related to your son and Florida" (if these concepts have been communicated). When the PWA responds (via any modality), the clinician provides them with the interpretation and time to make a judgment about the effectiveness of the communication based on what the clinician has understood.

If the clinician has understood correctly, the clinician provides feedback, and the dyad discusses what was helpful and/or what was not helpful during the communication breakdown and repair. The conversational partners then return to the Therapeutic Conversation. However, if the PWA decides that the clinician's understanding was incorrect, the PWA might add more clarifying information spontaneously. If the PWA does not do so, the clinician takes a turn by returning to the least-to-most hierarchy, now asking for a bit more specific information, again accepting all modalities of communication. The repair cycle continues until the PWA indicates repair has been successful, and the partners can return to the Therapeutic Conversation.

ECoLoGiC-Tx is in its earliest stages of development, with preliminary results collected for four participants: one with moderate Broca's aphasia (P1); one with severe Broca's aphasia (P2); one with moderate Conduction aphasia (P3); one with severe Conduction aphasia (P4). Intervention was delivered for 60 minutes twice weekly for 10 weeks with a licensed Speech Language Pathologist. Post-therapy, each participant demonstrated a change on the Aphasia Quotient of the Western Aphasia Battery–Revised (Kertesz, 2006), surpassing the meaningful improvement criterion set by Hula and colleagues (2010) (occurring at maintenance for P4, rather than immediately post-treatment). Likewise, improved scores of functional communication as per the Communication Activities of Daily Living– 3 (Holland et al., 2018) exceeded the standard error of measurement (4 points; Holland et al., 2018) for all participants (occurring at maintenance for P3). Generalization of language production was assessed in standard monologue samples and unstructured conversation samples with the SLP using the Social Conversation Collection Protocol. Measures included: (1) Communicative Success (verbal/nonverbal communication); (2) % Correct Information Unit (vocabulary informativeness); (3) Complete Utterance (a two component measure including integrity of the Subject-Verb-Object sentence frame and Relevancy of the words produced in the sentence frame); (4) Global Coherence Scale (extent of coherence); and (5) Grammaticality (presence of grammatical errors not evaluated by the Subject-Verb-Object measure, e.g., plurality, verb tense).

Participants 2, 3, and 4 demonstrated meaningful change for 90% of the measures in both types of discourse (i.e., 38/42), defined as at least a small effect size (Cohen, 1988) or change exceeding the minimal data change criteria (Leaman & Edmonds, 2021). However, Participant 1 demonstrated changes on fewer measures than the other participants, with meaningful change only for the Complete Utterance (and its two subcomponents) in conversation, and for Communicative Success, Subject-Verb-Object, Complete Utterance, and Global Coherence in monologue. At the 6-week follow-up, gains were maintained across participants for 87% of the discourse measures. Overall, ECoLoGiC-Tx shows promising pilot results for improved language production on formal tests, and generalization to untrained discourse.

Implications for Conversation Treatment with Bilingual/Multilingual Speakers

As reviewed above, there is a growing, yet nominal, body of literature on conversation therapy for PWA. However, to date, studies have concentrated on monolingual speakers. Thus, there is a need for research on conversation-level aphasia therapy for bilingual/multilingual speakers as well as for speakers of languages other than English whose conversation rules might be expected to be similar/different. In this section, we explore some general principles in intervention with bilingual PWA that can be extended to bilingual conversation treatment. We also present findings from research on conversational discourse and narrative production in bilingual PWA, which, though not intervention, can still be informative for the field of bilingual aphasia therapy.

In creating an optimized and personalized intervention for bilingual PWA, clinicians should include aspects of bilingual aphasia that are different from monolingual aphasia, such as, sociocultural history, output abilities, translation abilities, acquisitional and communicative experiences, and cognitive factors (e.g., Cuetos & Centeno, 2009; Lorenzen & Murray, 2008). Also, variables that differ across bilingual speakers with aphasia must be considered, such as premorbid language proficiency, use of the two languages, psychocognitive factors like motivation and affect in language processing, and post-morbid language abilities, e.g., morphosyntax, lexical access, reading, writing (e.g., Brozgold & Centeno, 2007; Neumann et al., 2022; Paradis, 2004).

Furthermore, an even more ecologically valid method would be to adopt a therapeutic approach that mirrors the daily discourse pattern of the bilingual PWA, namely, therapy that focuses on stimulating both languages. This dual-language strategy would use translation and codeswitching to maximally stimulate premorbid cognitive-linguistic mechanisms, spared cross-linguistic L1-L2 connections, and the bilingual language system as a whole (e.g., Ansaldo et al., 2010).

Evidence from the conversational discourse of four Spanish-English PWA and four healthy counterparts revealed that PWA codeswitch more as compared to their healthy counterparts (Muñoz et al, 1999). They do so to facilitate fluency or to manage instances of expressive difficulties by using the less-impaired language (see Goral et al., 2019). Similarly, Neumann et al. (2017) conducted a case study of a Yiddish-English bilingual PWA and found that codeswitching in the PWA's narratives was used to enhance fluency and compensate for ungrammaticality in each language. Moreover, Neumann et al. also reported differential motivations for the use of codeswitching across the two languages. In L1 codeswitching was motivated by efforts to improve lexical access difficulties, whereas in L2 codeswitching was employed for both lexical access and cross-linguistic lexicalization differences. Taking these important factors of bilingual aphasia intervention into account can help guide an approach to enhancing conversation therapy for bilingual speakers with aphasia.

Conclusion and Future Directions

PWA and their families report that they want intervention that has an impact on their everyday, real-world communication which will allow them to actively participate in a variety of conversational situations. This state of affairs has resulted in an evolving face of aphasia rehabilitation, moving from heavily constrained, modular, and impairment-focused treatments to more interactional, holistic, and life participation-based approaches. It has resulted in a growing interest in conversational interventions focusing on the PWA; however, the research is still scant. Thus far, the studies that have been conducted are of relatively weak study designs (e.g., case descriptions, small group designs) that often failed to control for confounding variables. Additionally, they have singularly focused on monolingual speakers. Therefore, further empirical exploration of the issues pertaining to understanding and managing real-life conversation is needed in both monolingual and bilingual PWA. Furthermore, research is needed to critically evaluate treatment protocols for authenticity and complexity critical to spontaneous real-world conversation. It is not yet clear to what extent treatment of different conversation variables influences communication success. Consequently, this requires further investigation.

References

Ansaldo, A. I., Saidi, L. G., & Ruiz, A. (2010). Model-driven intervention in bilingual aphasia: Evidence from a case of pathological language mixing. *Aphasiology*, *24*(2), 309–324.

Azios, J. H., Archer, B., & Lee, J. B. (2021). Detecting behavioral change in conversation: Procedures and preliminary data. *Aphasiology*, *35*(7), 961–983.

Basso, A. (2010). 'Natural' conversation: A treatment for severe aphasia. *Aphasiology*, *24*, 466–479.

Beeke, S., Sirman, N., Beckley, F., Maxim, J., Edwards, S., Swinburn, K., & Best, W. (2013). Better Conversations with Aphasia: An e-learning resource. Available at: https://extend.ucl.ac.uk/

Boles, L. (2011). A review of aphasia couples therapy. *Asia Pacific Journal of Speech, Language and Hearing*, *14*(3), 159–163.

Boyle, M. & Coelho, C. A. (1995). Application of semantic feature analysis as a treatment for aphasic dysnomia. *American Journal of Speech-Language Pathology*, *4*(4), 94–98.

Brozgold, A. Z. & Centeno, J. G. (2007). Sociocultural, societal, and psychological aspects of bilingualism: Variables, interactions, and therapeutic implications in speech-language pathology. In *Communication Disorders in Spanish Speakers* (pp. 67–81). Multilingual Matters.

Cohen, J. (1988). *Statistical Power Analysis for the Behavioral Sciences* (2nd ed.). Lawrence-Erlbaum Associates.

Cuetos, F. & Centeno, J. G. (2009). Applying cognitive neuropsychological principles to the rehabilitation of Spanish readers with acquired dyslexia. *Seminars in Speech and Language*, *30*, 187–197.

Damico, J., Tetnowski, J., Lynch, K., Harwell, J., Weill, C., Heels, J., & Simmons-Mackie, N. (2015). Facilitating Authentic Conversation: An intervention employing principles of constructivism and conversation analysis. *Aphasiology*, *29*(3), 400–421.

Davis, G. A. (1980). A critical look at PACE therapy. In R. Brookshire (Ed.), *Proceedings of the Clinical Aphasiology Conference*. BRK Publishers.

Doedens, W. J. & Meteyard, L. (2022). What is functional communication? A theoretical framework for real-world communication applied to aphasia rehabilitation. *Neuropsychology Review*. *32*, 937–973 10.1007/s11065-021-09531-2.

Drew, P. & Heritage, J. (1992). *Talk At Work: Interaction in Institutional Settings*. Cambridge University.

Eggins, S., & Slade, D. (2004). *Analysing Casual Conversation*. Equinox Publishing Ltd.

Garrett & Beukleman. (2006). Aphasia needs assessment. Retrieved May 29, 2013, from http://aac.unl.edu/screen/aphasianeeds.pdf

Gleason, J. B., Goodglass, H., Obler, L., Green, E., Hyde, M. R., & Weintraub, S. (1980). Narrative strategies of aphasic and normal-speaking subjects. *Journal of Speech, Language, and Hearing Research*, *23*(2), 370–382.

Goral, M., Norvik, M., & Jensen, B. U. (2019). Variation in language mixing in multilingual aphasia. *Clinical Linguistics and Phonetics*, *33*(10-11), 915–929.

Grice, H. P. (1975). Logic and conversation. In P. Cole & G. Morgan (Eds.), *Speech Acts: Syntax and Semantics* (Vol 3, pp.113–128). Academic Press.

Halliday, M. A. K. & Matthiessen, C. M. I. (2014). *An Introduction to Functional Grammar*. Routledge.

Helm, N. A. & Barresi, B. (1980). Voluntary control of involuntary utterances: A treatment approach for severe aphasia. In *Clinical Aphasiology: Proceedings of the Conference 1980* (pp. 308–315). BRK Publishers.

Hengst, J. A., Duff, M. C., & Jones, T. A. (2019). Enriching communicative environments: Leveraging advances in neuroplasticity for improving outcomes in neurogenic communication disorders. *American Journal of Speech-Language Pathology*, *28*, 216–229.

Holland, A. L. (1982). Observing functional communication of aphasic adults. *Journal of Speech and Hearing Disorders*, *47*(1), 50–56.

Holland, A. L. (1998). Why can't clinicians talk to aphasic adults? Comments on supported conversation for adults with aphasia: Methods and resources for training conversational partners. *Aphasiology*, *12*(9), 844–847.

Holland, A. L., Fromm, D., & Wozniak, L. (2018). *Communication Activities of Daily Living – Third Edition*. Pro-Ed.

Hula, W., Donovan, N. J., Kendall, D. L., & Gonzalez-Rothi, L. J. (2010). Item response theory analysis of the Western Aphasia Battery. *Aphasiology*, *24*(11), 1326–1341.

Kagan, A. (1998). Supported conversation for adults with aphasia: Methods and resources for training conversation partners. *Aphasiology*, *12*(9), 816–830.

Kertesz, K. (2006). *Western Aphasia Battery-Revised*. Psychological Corporation.

Kiran, S. & Thompson, C. K. (2003). The role of semantic complexity in treatment of naming deficits: Training semantic categories in fluent aphasia by controlling exemplar typicality. *Journal of Speech, Language, and Hearing Research*, *46*, 608–622.

Kleim, J. A. & Jones, T. A. (2008). Principles of experience-dependent neural plasticity: Implications for rehabilitation after brain damage. *Journal of Speech Language Hearing Research*, *51*, S225–S239.

Kolb, A. Y. & Kolb, D. A. (2017). Experiential learning theory as a guide for experiential educators in higher education. *Experiential Learning and Teaching in Higher Education*, *1*(1), 7–44.

Leaman, M. C. & Edmonds, L. A. (2021). Assessing language in unstructured conversation in people with aphasia: Methods, psychometric integrity, normative data, and comparison to a structured narrative task. *Journal of Speech, Language, and Hearing Research*, *64*, 4344–4365.

Leaman, M. C. & Edmonds, L. A. (under review). *Pilot results for ECoLoGiC-Tx: A new conversation-level intervention improving language in people with moderate to severe aphasia.*

Lock, S., Wilkinson, R., Bryan, K., Maxim, J., Edmundson, A., Bruce, C., & Moir, D. (2001). Supporting partners of people with aphasia in relationships and conversation (SPPARC). *International Journal of Language and Communication Disorders*, *36*(sup1), 25–30.

Lorenzen, B. & Murray, L. L. (2008). Bilingual aphasia: A theoretical and clinical review. *American Journal of Speech-Language Pathology*, *17*, 299–317.

Lyon, J. G. (1989). Communicative partners: Their value in reestablishing communication with aphasic adults. *Clinical Aphasiology*, *18*, 11–17.

Maynard D. & Zimmerman, D. (1984). Topical talk, ritual and the social organization of relationships. *Journal of Social Psychology*, *47*, 301–316.

Moeller, D. & Carpenter, C. (2013). Factors affecting quality of life for people who have experienced a stroke. *International Journal of Therapy and Rehabilitation*, *20*(4), 207–216.

Muñoz, M. L., Marquardt, T. P., & Copeland, G. (1999). A comparison of the codeswitching patterns of aphasic and neurologically normal bilingual speakers of English and Spanish. *Brain and Language*, *66*(2), 249–274.

Neumann, Y., Walters, J., & Altman, C. (2017). Codeswitching and discourse markers in the narratives of a bilingual speaker with aphasia. *Aphasiology*, *31*, 221–240.

Neumann, Y., Chang, A., Echavarria, W., & Webman Shafran, R. (2022, June). *A case study of a bilingual person with non-fluent aphasia and a neurogenic stutter: The relationship between dysfluency and emotion*. Poster presentation at International Aphasia Rehabilitation Conference, Philadelphia, PA.

Norrick, N. R. (2000). *Conversational Narrative: Storytelling in Everyday Talk*. John Benjamins Publishing Company.

Ochs, E. & Capps, L. (2002). *Living Narrative: Creating Lives in Everyday Storytelling*. Harvard University Press.

Paradis, M. (2004). *A Neurolinguistic Theory of Bilingualism* (Vol. 18). John Benjamins Publishing.

Pimentel, J. & Algeo, D. (2009). Effects of environmental props on communication in aphasia group therapy. *Perspectives on Gerontology*, *14*(1), 12–18.

Porch, B. E. (1967). *Porch Index of Communicative Ability: Theory and Development* (Vol. 1). Consulting Psychologists Press.

Savage, M. C., Donovan, N. J., & Hoffman, P. R. (2014). Preliminary results from conversation therapy in two cases of aphasia. *Aphasiology*, *28*(5), 616–636.

Savage, M. C. & Donovan, N. J. (2017). Comparing linguistic complexity and efficiency in conversations from stimulation and conversation therapy in aphasia. *International Journal of Language and Communication Disorders*, *52*(1), 21–29.

Schegloff, E. A. (2007). *Sequence Organization in Interaction: A Primer in Conversation Analysis I* (Vol. 1). Cambridge university press.

Schuchard, J. & Middleton, E. L. (2018). The roles of retrieval practice versus errorless learning in strengthening lexical access in aphasia. *Journal of Speech, Language, and Hearing Research*, *61*(7), 1700–1717.

Simmons-Mackie, N., Kearns, K., & Potechin, G. (1987). Treatment of aphasia through family member training. In R. Brookshire (ed.), *Clinical Aphasiology Conference Proceedings* (Minneapolis, MN), pp. 106–113.

Simmons-Mackie, N., Savage, M. C., & Worrall, L. (2014). Conversation therapy for aphasia: A qualitative review of the literature. *International Journal of Language Communication Disorders*, *49*(5), 511–526.

Tetnowski, J. T., Tetnowski, J. A., & Damico, J. S. (2021). Patterns of conversation trouble source and repair as indices of improved conversation in aphasia: A multiple-case study using conversation analysis. *American Journal of Speech-Language Pathology*, *30*(1S), 326–343.

Turnblom, M. & Myers, J. S. (1952). A group discussion program with the families of aphasic patients. *Journal of Speech and Hearing Disorders*, *17*(4), 393–396.

Ulatowska, H. K., North, A. J., & Macaluso-Haynes, S. (1981). Production of narrative and procedural discourse in aphasia. *Brain and Language*, *13*, 345–371.

Wertz, R. T., Collins, M. J., Weiss, D., Kurtzke, J. F., Friden, T., Brookshire, R. H., ... & Resurreccion, E. (1981). Veterans Administration cooperative study on aphasia: A comparison of individual and group treatment. *Journal of Speech, Language, and Hearing Research*, *24*(4), 580–594.

Whitworth, A., Perkins, L., & Lesser, R. (1997). *Conversation Analysis Profile for People with Aphasia (CAPPA)*. Whurr.

Wilkinson, R. (2010). Interaction-focused intervention: A conversation analytic approach to aphasia therapy. *Journal of Interactional Research in Communication Disorders*, *1*(1), 45–68.

15

DISENTANGLING BILINGUALISM AND APHASIA USING NARRATIVE ANALYSIS

Aviva Lerman, Joel Walters, Merav Raveh-Malka, Mali Gil, and Carmit Altman

Introduction

From the publication of Albert and Obler's (1978) ground-breaking book *The Bilingual Brain* it took almost 20 years for the field of bilingualism and aphasia to take off. Much of the research on aphasia in bilingual people has taken its lead from monolingual studies in aphasiology, investigating brain organization, attempting to refine classification of deficits, and developing assessment techniques and therapeutic approaches, but the majority has focused on a single linguistic phenomenon or a single aphasia diagnosis/syndrome (e.g., agrammatism, anomia) in case study designs (Del Maschio & Abutalebi, 2019; Gitterman, 2005). Bilingualism and aphasia can present with the same linguistic manifestations in areas such as morphology, syntax, word retrieval, and fluency, particularly when one language is only acquired to a moderate level of proficiency (e.g., Albert & Obler, 1978; Altman et al., 2012; Fiestas & Peña, 2004; Lerman et al., 2022). Thus, it is important to disentangle the two, and consider the independent contributions of each to post-morbid language abilities. Narrative analysis has been shown to be a useful platform to do this (Goral et al., 2012; Lerman et al., 2022; Paplikar et al., 2014), since a broad scope of linguistic parameters can be examined, including macrostructure and microstructure features, as well as fluency indicators. We begin by briefly reviewing the current literature on narrative production in bilingual populations and in people with aphasia (PWA).

DOI: 10.4324/9781003330318-18

Narrative Analysis

There has been growing interest in narrative and discourse analysis across the lifespan, with researchers developing comprehensive approaches to analysis that have also advanced the field of aphasia, informing assessment and intervention (e.g., Altman et al., 2012; Coelho et al., 2023; Dipper et al., 2021; Marini et al., 2011; Stark et al., 2021, 2022). These approaches are grounded in linguistics and discourse analysis (Labov, 1997, 2013; Labov & Waletzky, 1967; Longacre, 1996) as well as clinical assessment (Westby, 2005). They are similar in that they all contain both structural and functional elements, involve both macrostructure (discourse level) and microstructure (clause/word level) components, examine fluency and lexical choice, and cover different narrative genres (e.g., personal, fictional) (Olness, 2006; Stark, 2019).

For example, Dipper, et al. (2021) reviewed ten theoretical models of discourse processing and proposed a comprehensive framework which involves four main components (pragmatic, macrostructure planning, propositional and linguistic) covering a wide range of skills and constructs aimed at guiding intervention research and clinical practice. Marini et al. (2011) proposed a multi-level model involving productivity, lexical and grammatical processing, narrative organization, and informativeness. Similarly, Altman et al. (2012) developed an integrative model of discourse structure, sentence structure, fluency, and lexical choice. In our study, we analyzed many variables that were included in Altman et al.'s (2012) integrated narrative analysis (INA), thus this is the framework we outline below.

Narratives offer a number of advantages over more structured approaches to assessment. First, narratives generate rich, authentic language, in many ways similar to natural speech. Second, elicited narratives allow assessment of multiple linguistic domains in a single task, including lexis, grammar, discourse, and fluency. Finally, narratives ground language in the social world, where linguistic performance is enveloped in pragmatic abilities.

Macrostructure

Narrative macrostructure involves an episode and its components. Originally proposed as a universal structural framework for story knowledge, Stein and Glenn (1979) described the following components: *Setting, Initiating event, Internal response, Goal, Attempt, Consequence,* and *Ending*. Longacre's (1996) functional approach to discourse analysis simplified these components, and included *Setting* and *Background* as one component, *Storyline* as a second component, and added to the analysis a functional element, *Irrealis*, the reconstruction of the story's world via possible alternatives to a sequence of events, (Longacre 1989, 1996; Olness, 2006). Furthermore, *Evaluation*, the beliefs about characters' motives, intentions, and feelings, has also been shown to be another important component in macrostructure (Armstrong & Ulatowska, 2007; Labov, 2013).

Narrative macrostructure has been investigated with a variety of data elicitation techniques, e.g., story generation and retelling of personal and fictional narratives with and without picture stimuli, in both impaired and non-impaired populations (e.g., Altman et al., 2012, 2022). These studies have shown that in healthy adults, macrostructure is similar across languages in both bilingual adults, regardless of proficiency or age of acquisition (e.g., Antonijevic et al., 2022) and monolingual adults (e.g., Gagarina et al., 2019). In PWA, macrostructure features are largely intact (Altman et al., 2012; but see Schneider et al., 2006 for exceptions).

Microstructure

Microstructure elements are centered at the level of sentences and clauses and cover a wide range of linguistic features, including general measures of utterance length and lexis (e.g., mean length of utterance, lexical variation, and richness, percentage of content words), aspects of morphosyntax (e.g., agreement, tense), syntax (e.g., subordination) and cohesion (e.g., temporal and tense reference, connectives), among others. Together these features comprise lexicon, grammaticality, and sentence complexity. In healthy bilingual adults, microstructure has been observed to be dependent on language proficiency in a second language (e.g., Krasnoshchekova & Kashleva, 2019). In PWA, microstructure features such as mean length of utterance and thematic units (pre-determined units produced in a picture description task, for example) can be useful as a measure of severity and change over time (Brisebois et al., 2022; Stark & Fukuyama, 2021). Furthermore, in PWA verb use is often less diverse than that of neurologically healthy speakers (Bastiaanse, et al., 2006; Edwards & Bastiaanse 1998; Faroqi-Shah & Waked 2010; Lerman et al., 2018).

Fluency

Fluency in narrative production has been investigated with a wide variety of constructs, including speech rate, errors, and dysfluencies. Speech rate is measured as words or syllables per time unit (Andreetta, et al., 2012; Wilson et al., 2010). Dysfluency includes filled and unfilled pauses, false starts, repetitions, and prolongations (Lundgren et al., 2010; Wilson et al., 2010). In bilingual adults, both proficiency in and exposure to a second language affect fluency measures in that language (Chakraborty et al., 2017). Aphasia-related fluency phenomena include the measures described above, plus semantic and phonemic paraphasias, neologisms, circumlocutions, and comments on word retrieval in monolingual PWA (Hickin et al., 2007) as well as language mixing in bilingual PWA (Neumann et al., 2016).

The Present Study

Our aim was to examine a wide range of narrative features in an attempt to identify the features which best distinguish bilingualism effects from aphasia effects on language production. Narrative data from people with conductive aphasia (PWA-C) and people with anomic aphasia (PWA-A) as well as from healthy adults were transcribed and coded for several macrostructure, microstructure, and fluency features (described in detail below) in order to address the following research question and predictions:

> Which narrative features best distinguish the narratives of monolingual speakers of Hebrew from the narratives of speakers of Hebrew as a second language (L2) in people with and without aphasia?

Considerable research has reported similar performance on narrative macrostructure for monolingual and bilingual people using diverse narrative frameworks and stimuli (e.g., Altman et al., 2012, but see Schneider et al., 2006 for exceptions). In contrast, microstructure features generally differ across languages and populations due to the language specific nature of lexis and morphosyntax (Gagarina et al., 2014). For example, grammaticality is grounded in the microstructure of narrative production, and might be expected to distinguish between the narratives of bilingual and monolingual healthy adults, particularly if the bilingual adults are not highly proficient in L2 (although grammatical errors would still be expected to be above atypical levels; Krasnoshchekova & Kashleva, 2019). Similarly, dysfluency measures in bilingual adults should be higher than in monolingual adults, particularly in bilingual adults with low proficiency and exposure of L2 (Chakraborty et al., 2017).

Much less research has examined the narratives of PWA and still less has investigated the narratives of bilingual PWA (but see: Altman et al., 2012; Armstrong, 2000; Marini et al., 2011). It is predicted that the narratives of PWA, both monolingual and bilingual, will not differ from those of healthy participants in terms of macrostructure, but will likely show deficits in terms of microstructure features such as total number of tokens (TNT) and verb use. Additionally, grammaticality, and to some extent fluency, which are both grounded in the microstructure of narrative production, are expected to distinguish the narratives of bilingual and monolingual PWA (e.g., Brisebois et al., 2022; Hickin et al., 2007; Neumann et al., 2016). Thus, all PWA are expected to produce more ungrammatical utterances than healthy adults. Regarding fluency, PWA-A are expected to be more fluent as compared to PWA-C except for when they search for words and therefore produce filled or silent pauses, while PWA-C may use more fluency markers due to phonemic retrieval difficulties.

Method

Participants

Narratives were elicited from 48 healthy adults (23 monolingual Hebrew speakers and 25 bilingual speakers, with a variety of native languages and Hebrew as a later-acquired language). Narratives were also elicited from eight PWA (four monolingual and four L2 Hebrew). See Table 15.1 for information on age, gender, level of education, years of residence in Israel, etiology, and aphasia severity of the participants. No data were collected for this study in the native languages of the bilingual participants. Four PWA (PC1-PC4) were diagnosed with conduction aphasia and four (PA5-PA8) were diagnosed with anomic aphasia.

Materials and Procedures

PWA were evaluated for aphasia type and severity using the Israeli Lowenstein Aphasia Test (ILAT, Schechter, 1965). For elicitation of narratives, "The Thief Story" (Byrne, 1967) was used. It consists of four black and white line drawings of a thief stealing a woman's purse, when an old man trips the thief with his cane and returns the purse to the woman, and the thief is arrested. The narratives were collected by speech-language pathologists (SLPs) from the Communication Disorders Department in Loewenstein Rehabilitation Hospital, Israel.

Participants were instructed as follows: "Here is a story in pictures. Please tell me as much as possible about the story, tell me about every detail you think is relevant to the story". SLPs who elicited the narratives minimized involvement by confining themselves to use only continuation regulators such as "okay, uh-huh" and general questions such as "what else can you tell me?".

Narratives were recorded and transcribed in conventional Hebrew orthography by SLP graduate students. Transcripts were converted to Latin orthography following CHILDES conventions (MacWhinney, 2000) before being analyzed (see below for details).

TABLE 15.1 Background data for monolingual and bilingual healthy adults and people with aphasia

	Healthy Adults		*People with Aphasia*							
			Conduction aphasia				*Anomic aphasia*			
	Monolingual N=23	*Bilingual* N=25	*Monolingual*		*Bilingual*		*Monolingual*		*Bilingual*	
			PC1	*PC2*	*PC3*	*PC4*	*PA5*	*PA6*	*PA7*	*PA8*
Age (years)	20–85	17–86	27	49	47	51	17	49	21	52
Etiology	n/a	n/a	TBI	TBI	CVA	CVA	CVA	TBI	TBI	CVA
Aphasia severity	n/a	n/a	Mod	Mild/Mod	Mod	Mod	Mild	Mild	Mild/Mod	Mild
Gender	11 M 12 F	9 M 16 F	M	F	F	F	M	M	M	M
Education (years)	10–20	10–20	12	15	12	10	10	11	10	12
Bilinguals' L1	n/a	Varied	n/a	n/a	Arabic	French	n/a	n/a	Arabic	Russian
Years since Immigration	n/a	10–30	n/a	n/a	20+	32	n/a	n/a	0	38
Country of origin (if not born in Israel)		Varied			Libya	Morocco				USSR

Note. n/a = not applicable; Mod = Moderate; TBI = traumatic brain injury; CVA = cerebrovascular accident.

Data Analysis

Narrative analysis was based on the INA model for macrostructure and microstructure features (Altman et al., 2012). The narratives were divided into Analysis of Speech Units (AS-units), where each AS-Unit is an utterance consisting of an independent clause or a sub-clause (Foster, et al., 2000). Each AS-Unit (hereafter we use "sentences" for clarity) was then classified for its number of clauses.

For macrostructure analysis, grounded in Longacre (1996) and Labov (2013) and applied to language impairment (Altman et al., 2012), the following categories were coded: mean number of clauses representing the Setting (time/place, introduction of protagonists), Storyline (description of events), Irrealis (reconstruction of the story's world), and Evaluation (attitudes and beliefs about characters and events).

For microstructure analysis, we coded for Lexis (productivity and lexical variety), Complexity, and Grammaticality. Sentence complexity was coded on a 5-point scale (Altman et al., 2012): 1 point for an incomplete sentence, 2 points for a complete simple sentence, 3 points for an attempt to produce a complex sentence, 4 points for a complex coordinated sentence, and 5 points for a complex sentence with a subordinate clause. Clauses were identified as grammatical or ungrammatical. Fluency was classified following Altman et al. (2012) by measuring: silent pauses, filled pauses, repetitions, false starts, self-corrections, and rephrasing.

Coding reliability was assessed by two of the authors and found to be high, with disagreements resolved by a third author. Descriptive statistics (frequencies, means, and standard deviations) are presented.

Results

Macrostructure

All four macrostructure categories (Setting, Storyline, Irrealis, Evaluation), showed general similarity between the narratives of healthy adults and those of PWA as well as between the narratives of monolingual and bilingual participants (see Table 15.2). Among the exceptions to this overall trend were:

1 Three of the four bilingual PWA (PC3, PC4, PA8) produced fewer Setting clauses than monolingual PWA (whose Setting clauses ranged from 19%–35%). The Setting clauses for the three bilingual PWA showed lower percentages (0%–6%) than the average of both the bilingual and monolingual healthy adult groups (17%–18%).

TABLE 15.2 Macrostructure features in the narratives of healthy adults and PWA

	Healthy Adults		*People with Aphasia (PWA)*							
			Conduction aphasia				*Anomic aphasia*			
	Monolingual N=23	*Bilingual* N=25	*Monolingual*		*Bilingual*		*Monolingual*		*Bilingual*	
	Mean (Range)	*Mean (Range)*	*PC1*	*PC2*	*PC3*	*PC4*	*PA5*	*PA6*	*PA7*	*PA8*
% Setting clauses	18 (0–36)	17 (0–41)	26	19	6	6	19	35	29	0
% Storyline clauses	79 (61–100)	80 (54–100)	68	71	89	82	80	59	58	100
% Irrealis clauses	5 (0–6)	5 (0–12)	0	0	0	0	0	3	0	0
% Evaluation clauses	8 (0–14)	2 (0–14)	7	10	6	6	0	3	13	0

2 Two PWA-A, one monolingual (PA6) and one bilingual (PA7) used fewer Storyline clauses (59% and 58%, respectively) in their narratives than the other PWA, whose Storyline clauses were above 68% (indeed, one PWA produced only Storyline clauses). PA6's percentage of Storyline clauses was lower than the healthy monolingual range, while PA7's percentage was within the healthy bilingual range.

Two additional notable findings were the following:

1 Irrealis statements were relatively rare among all participants. Among PWA, only PA6 produced even a single Irrealis clause.
2 Evaluation clauses were also rare, ranging from 0%–14% in the narratives of healthy adults. Those with conduction aphasia had similar percentages. Two of the four PWA-A (PA5, PA8) had no Evaluation clauses (but this was observed for some healthy adults too).

Microstructure

Lexis: Tokens and Verb Diversity

Three monolingual PWA (PC1, PC2, and PA6) produced narratives longer than the range produced by healthy monolingual adults, as measured by TNT (see Table 15.3). One bilingual PWA (PA7) produced a narrative marginally longer than the range produced by healthy bilingual adults. Verb diversity, a measure of lexical variation, indicated differences between the narratives of healthy adults and PWA. Two monolingual PWA (PC2 and PA6) and one bilingual PWA (PC3) had lower than or were at the lower end of the range produced by healthy monolingual or bilingual adults respectively.

Length and Sentence Level Complexity

Narrative length, as measured by the number of sentences, was similar for all monolingual and bilingual healthy adults, ranging from 5–12 sentences, averaging 8–9 (see Table 15.3). Monolingual PWA-C and PWA-A conformed to this pattern. Two of the four bilingual PWA produced longer narratives than the healthy bilingual adults (PC3 and PA7: 14 sentences each). Complexity averaged 3.5 out of 5 for healthy participants' narratives and was within range for PWA except for one bilingual PWA-A whose narrative was less complex (PA8 – 1.89).

Grammaticality

Grammaticality clearly distinguished the narratives of PWA from those of healthy adults. The data show very few ungrammatical clauses in the

TABLE 15.3 Narrative length (TNTs and sentences), verb diversity, and complexity in the narratives of monolingual and bilingual healthy adults (N=48) and monolingual and bilingual people with conduction and anomic aphasia (N=8)

	Healthy Adults		*People with Aphasia (PWA)*							
			Conduction				*Anomic*			
	Monolingual N=23	*Bilingual* N=25	*Monolingual*		*Bilingual*		*Monolingual*		*Bilingual*	
	Mean (Range)	*Mean (Range)*	*PC1*	*PC2*	*PC3*	*PC4*	*PA5*	*PA6*	*PA7*	*PA8*
TNT	91.39 (44–165)	105.88 (57–176)	195	170	171	90	106	174	177	80
Different verbs (%)	90.43 (69.6–100)	81.49 (55–100)	72.4	65.23	54.54	85.0	53.84	69.4	61.29	90
Number of sentences	8.17 (5–12)	8.78 (5–12)	10	8	14	10	12	9	14	9
Complexity (1–5)	3.47 (2–4.44)	3.53 (2.58–4.2)	4	4.38	3.79	3	3	4.44	3.43	1.89

Note. TNT = total number of tokens.

narratives of healthy monolingual adults (6%) and two to six times as many ungrammatical clauses in the narratives of monolingual PWA (10%–32%). For healthy bilingual adults, the data show about twice as many ungrammatical clauses as for healthy monolingual adults (11% on average). The highest percentages of ungrammaticality were found in the narratives of bilingual PWA, where three of the four bilingual PWA produced narratives with 38%–47% ungrammatical clauses. The fourth (PA8) was an exception to this pattern, with only 13% ungrammatical clauses. Figure 15.1 displays the findings for Grammaticality.

Fluency

The narratives of six out of eight PWA had more total dysfluencies than the narratives of healthy adults (see Table 15.4), with a large degree of individual variation. Two of the PWA stood out in this respect. At the upper end of the fluency range, one monolingual PWA-C (PC2) had many dysfluencies, 45 of which were silent pauses almost half of the total for all eight PWA for silent pauses). Most of the rest of her dysfluencies were evenly divided between repetitions (23) and false starts (23). At the lower end of the fluency range, one bilingual PWA-A (PA7) had an average

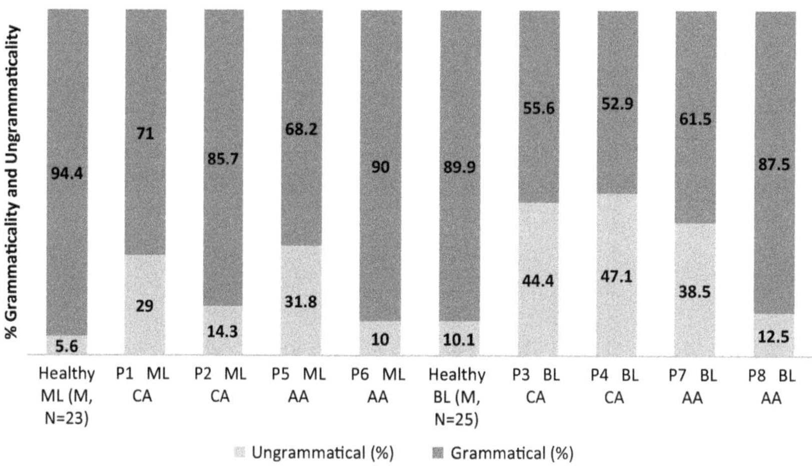

Notes: ML=Monolingual, BL=Bilingual, CA=Conduction Aphasia, AA=Anomic Aphasia, M =Mean

FIGURE 15.1 Percentage of grammatical and ungrammatical clauses in the narratives of monolingual and bilingual healthy adults (N=48) and monolingual and bilingual people with conduction and anomic aphasia (N=8).

TABLE 15.4 Mean fluency markers per sentence in the narratives of monolingual and bilingual healthy adults and PWA (N=8)

	Healthy Adults		*Conduction*				*Anomic*			
	Monolingual N=23	*Bilingual* N=25	*Monolingual*		*Bilingual*		*Monolingual*		*Bilingual*	
Fluency marker	*Mean (range)*	*Mean (range)*	*PC1*	*PC2*	*PC3*	*PC4*	*PA5*	*PA6*	*PA7*	*PA8*
Silent pauses	0.24 (0–1.57)	0.19 (0–0.75)	0.7	5.62	0.14	1.8	0.42	1.56	0.07	1.33
Filled pauses	0.1 (0–0.33)	0.09 (0–0.71)	0	0.13	0.29	0.2	0	0.3	0	0.11
Repetitions	0.02 (0–0.22)	0.07 (0–0.42)	0.3	2.88	0.57	0.5	0.08	0.44	0	0.22
False starts	0.03 (0–0.2)	0.01 (0–0.1)	1.1	2.88	0.71	0.7	0.08	0	0.07	0.22
Self-corrections	0.04 (0–0.2)	0.05 (0–0.375)	0.4	0.38	0.29	0.1	0.08	0.33	0.14	0
Rephrasing	0.03 (0–0.2)	0.06 (0–0.25)	0.1	0.38	0.14	0	0.08	0.22	0.07	0.33
Total dysfluencies	0.76 (0.49–1.17)	0.7 (0.49–1.18)	2.5	12.2	2.14	3.3	0.66	2.85	0.38	2.21

Note. Mean and range – calculated as frequency out of total number of sentences.

of only 0.38 dysfluency markers per sentence in total, close to the mean for the healthy adults (0.49-1.18 per narrative).

Discussion

We investigated the features that best distinguish narratives of monolingual speakers of Hebrew from narratives of L2 speakers of Hebrew in people with and without aphasia. To address the research question, we discuss distinguishing features of PWA compared to healthy adults, incorporating the potential contribution of bilingualism to the results.

First, we found that PWA can potentially be distinguished from healthy adults by grammaticality, verb diversity, and fluency, but not by macrostructure categories, narrative length, or sentence complexity, although there was variability across PWA. The most salient feature distinguishing PWA from healthy participants' narratives was grammaticality, where PWA had overall higher rates of ungrammatical sentences than healthy adults. Moreover, for bilingual people with conduction aphasia, grammaticality was impaired at a higher rate than people with anomic aphasia, with almost half of their utterances being ungrammatical. The higher rate of ungrammaticality in the narratives of bilingual PWA, as compared to both healthy bilingual adults and healthy monolingual adults, supports current literature (e.g., Altman et al., 2012; Neumann et al., 2016), and may be the best way to disentangle the relative contribution of aphasia from bilingualism in language impairment. However, in order to clarify the dissociation between grammaticality and the other measures and to show how individual analysis can assist in distinguishing monolingual PWA from bilingual PWA, we took a closer look at the PWA at the extremes in terms of grammaticality, i.e., those with high levels of ungrammaticality (PC1, PC3) and relatively low levels (PA8).

The importance of analysis of individual data can be illustrated as follows: PC1 and PC3 both presented with conduction aphasia. Their narratives stood out for the high levels of ungrammaticality (29% and 44% of the clauses, respectively). Yet, when examining the complexity of PC1's and PC3's narratives, we find repeated attempts at producing complex sentences, which may explain their high level of ungrammaticality. Similarly, a closer look at PA8's narrative shows that he had the lowest level of ungrammaticality of any of the eight PWA, on par with the narratives of healthy bilingual adults. His narrative was the shortest, only 90 words, with all his utterances concentrated in the Storyline. He also had the lowest complexity score (1.89) of all seven PWA. In summary, he produced a very short, syntactically simple, grammatical narrative, characteristic of unimpaired bilingual speech, and only his level of unfilled pauses was anomic-like. Thus, each participant with aphasia has their own way of getting a message across, one at the price of using only simple sentences and speaking to the point and another attempting to be more complex with a cost in ungrammaticality.

Another example of the importance of individual analysis can be seen from the dysfluency measures. The individual differences point to the possibility that dysfluencies are not always indicative of impairment. Rather, silent pauses and repetitions may be useful to a speaker for planning and formulation in narrative production. Clinically, for example, people with anomic aphasia often do not produce semantic paraphasias; rather, they search for a word or give a definition (paraphrase), and that may explain the relatively high rate of silent pauses in two PWA-A. Furthermore, false starts in conduction aphasia are considered markers of impairment in both monolingual and bilingual PWA; conduction aphasia patients may use false starts due to phonemic retrieval difficulties (e.g., ga ... zaha ... zan ... zagan ... zaken [target: *zaken* "old man"]). While the four PWA-C all produced more false starts than the healthy adults, notably, the two bilingual PWA-C had fewer false starts than the two monolingual PWA-C, but more filled pauses, indicating that other underlying mechanisms may be influencing phonemic retrieval processes in a later acquired language.

Only by examining a large range of features can we identify the source of language difficulty and any strategies adopted for compensation. This study provides some initial directions as to which features of language production might indicate that bilingualism is an addition burden on top of someone's aphasia. However, concluding that bilingualism represents a double challenge for PWA would be too simple.

Conclusion and Future Directions

This study examined a broad range of macrostructure, microstructure, and fluency features in a narrative framework. The most consistent differences which emerged in this study were between the narratives of healthy adults and those of PWA rather than between monolingual and bilingual speakers, particularly for grammaticality and partially for verb diversity and fluency. However, we observed that there is a complex relationship between bilingualism and grammaticality, verb diversity, and fluency, together with other measures such as sentence complexity and word retrieval. Our results showed the importance of examining a wide range of linguistic indicators and the effectiveness of narratives in eliciting these features. Future work should examine data from both the first and second language and include analyses of factors common in bilingualism (e.g., codeswitching) and in aphasia (e.g., paraphasias) in addition to the factors described in this study. Furthermore, more specific analyses of grammaticality may be useful in distinguishing the effect of bilingualism on narratives of PWA.

References

Albert, M. L. & Obler, L. K. (1978). *The Bilingual Brain: Neuropsychological and Neurolinguistic Aspects of Bilingualism*. Academic Press.

Altman, C., Goral, M., & Levy, E. (2012). Integrated narrative analysis in multilingual aphasia: The relationship among narrative structure, grammaticality and fluency. *Aphasiology*, *26* (8), 1029–1052.

Altman, C., Avraham, I., Meirovich, S. S., & Lifshitz, H. (2022). How do students with intellectual disabilities tell stories? An investigation of narrative macrostructure and microstructure. *Journal of Applied Research in Intellectual Disabilities*, *35*(5), 1119–1130.

Andreetta, S., Cantagallo, A., & Marini, A. (2012). Narrative discourse in anomic aphasia. *Neuropsychologia*, *50*, 1787–1793.

Antonijevic, S., Colleran, S., Kerr, C., & Mhíocháin, T. N. (2022). Online assessment of narrative macrostructure in adult Irish-English multilinguals. *Frontiers in Psychology*, *13*.

Armstrong, E. M. (2000). Aphasic discourse: The story so far. *Aphasiology*, *14*(9), 875–892.

Armstrong, E. & Ulatowska, H. (2007). Making stories: Evaluative language and the aphasia experience. *Aphasiology*, *21*(6-8), 763–774.

Bastiaanse R., Hurkmans, J., & Links, P. (2006). The training of verb production in Broca's aphasia: A multiple-baseline across-behaviours study. *Psychology Press*, *20*, 298–311.

Brisebois, A., Brambati, S. M., Boucher, J., Rochon, E., Leonard, C., Désilets-Barnabé, M., ... & Marcotte, K. (2022). A longitudinal study of narrative discourse in post-stroke aphasia. *Aphasiology*, 1–26.

Byrne, D. (1967). *Progressive Picture Compositions*. Longman.

Chakraborty, R., Morales, N., Fritsch, K., & Gonzales, M. D. (2017). Second language proficiency and maze: Marathi-English bilinguals. *Clinical Archives of Communication Disorders*, *2*(2), 103–115.

Coelho, C. A., Cherney, L. R., & Shadden, B. B. (2023). *Discourse Analysis in Adults with and without Communication Disorders*. Plural Publishing.

Del Maschio, N. & Abutalebi, J. (2019). Language organization in the bilingual and multilingual brain. In J. Schweiter (ed.), *The Handbook of the Neuroscience of Multilingualism* (197–213). John Wiley & Sons Ltd.

Dipper, L., Marshall, J., Boyle, M., Hersh, D., Botting, N., & Cruice, M. (2021). Creating a theoretical framework to underpin discourse assessment and intervention in aphasia. *Brain Sciences 11*, 183–201.

Edwards, S. & Bastiaanse, R. (1998). Diversity in the lexical and syntactic ability of fluent aphasic speakers. *Aphasiology*, *12*, 99–117.

Faroqi-Shah, Y. & Waked, A. (2010). Cross-linguistic priming in multilingual aphasia. *Cognitive Neuropsychology*, *27*, 181–203.

Fiestas, C.E. & Peña, E.D. (2004). Narrative discourse in bilingual children: Language and task effects. *Language, Speech and Hearing Services in Schools*, *35*(2), 155–168.

Foster, P., Tonkyn, A., & Wigglesworth, G. (2000). Measuring spoken language: A unit for all reasons. *Applied Linguistics*, *21*(3), 354–375.

Gagarina, N., Bohnacker, U., & Lindgren, J. (2019). Macrostructural organization of adults' oral narrative texts. *ZAS Papers in Linguistics*, *62*, 190–208.

Gagarina, N., Klop, D., Kunnari, S., Tantele, K., Välimaa, T., Balčiūnienė, I., Bohnacker, U. & Walters, J. (2014). Assessment of narrative abilities in bilingual children. In S. Armon-Lotem, J. de Jong & N. Meir (Eds.), *Methods for Assessing Multilingual Children: Disentangling Bilingualism from Language Impairment*. Multilingual Matters.

Gitterman, M.R. (2005). Aphasia in multilingual populations. In Martin J. Ball (Ed.), *Clinical Sociolinguistics*. Blackwell.

Goral, M., Rosas, J., Conner, P. S., Maul, K. K., & Obler, L. K. (2012). Effects of language proficiency and language of the environment on aphasia therapy in a multilingual. *Journal of Neurolinguistics*, *25*(6), 538–551.

Hickin, J., Herbert, R., Best, W., Howard, D., & Osborne, F. (2007). Efficacy of treatment: Effects on word retrieval and conversation. In S. Byng, K. Swinburn, & C. Pound (Eds.), *Aphasia Therapy File* (Vol. II), (69–82). Psychology Press.

Krasnoshchekova, S. & Kashleva, K. (2019). Narrative competence of adult L2 Russian learners. *Journal of Psycholinguistic Research*, *48*(3), 617–641.

Labov, W. (1997). Some further steps in narrative analysis. *Journal of Narrative and Life History*, *7*, 395–415.

Labov, W. (2013). *The Language of Life and Death: The Transformation of Experience in Oral Narrative*. Cambridge University Press.

Labov, W. & Waletzky, J. (1967). Narrative analysis. Essays on the verbal and visual arts. *Proceedings of the 1966 Spring Meeting of the American Ethnological Society*. University of Washington Press.

Lerman, A., Goral, M., & Obler, L. K. (2022). Rehabilitating an attrited language in a bilingual person with aphasia. *Clinical Linguistics and Phonetics*, 1–19.

Lerman, A., Pazuelo, L., Kizner, L., Borodkin, K., & Goral, M. (2018). Language mixing patterns in a bilingual individual with non-fluent aphasia. *Aphasiology*, *33*(9), 1137–1153.

Longacre, R.E. (1989). Two hypotheses regarding text generation and text analysis. *Discourse Processes*, *12*, 413–460.

Longacre, R.E. (1996). *The Grammar of Discourse: Topics in Language and Linguistics*. Plenum.

Lundgren, K., Helm-Estabrooks, N., & Klein, R. (2010). Stuttering following acquired brain damage: A review of the literature. *Journal of Neurolinguistics*, *23*(5), 447–454.

MacWhinney, B. (2000). *The CHILDES Project: Tools for Analyzing Talk*. Erlbaum.

Marini, A., Andreetta, S., Del Tin, S., & Carlomagno, S. (2011). A multi-level approach to the analysis of narrative language in aphasia. *Aphasiology*, *25*(11), 1372–1392.

Neumann, Y., Walters, J., & Altman, C. (2016). Codeswitching and discourse markers in the narratives of a bilingual speaker with aphasia. *Aphasiology*, *31*(2), 221–240.

Olness, G.S. (2006). Genre, verb, and coherence in picture elicited discourse of adults with aphasia. *Aphasiology*, *20*(2/3/4), 175–187.

Paplikar, A., Goral, M., Gitterman, M. and Obler, L. K. (2014). Language-mixing, discourse length and discourse quality in bilingual aphasia. *Frontiers in Psychology. Conference Abstract: Academy of Aphasia – 52nd Annual Meeting*. doi: 10.3389/conf.fpsyg.2014.64.00053

Schechter, I. (1965). *Israeli Lowenstein Aphasia Test* (ILAT-Hebrew version), Loewenstein Hospital Rehabilitation Center, Raanana, Israel.

Schneider, P., Hayward, D., & Dubé, R.V. (2006). Storytelling from pictures using the Edmonton narrative norms instrument. *Journal of Speech Language Pathology and Audiology*, *30*(4), 224–238.

Stark, B. C. (2019). A comparison of three discourse elicitation methods in aphasia and age-matched adults: Implications for language assessment and outcome. *American Journal of Speech-Language Pathology*, *28*(3), 1067–1083.

Stark, B. C., Dutta, M., Murray, L. L., Bryant, L., Fromm, D., MacWhinney, B., ... & Sharma, S. (2021). Standardizing assessment of spoken discourse in aphasia: A working group with deliverables. *American Journal of Speech-Language Pathology*, *30*, 491–502.

Stark, B. C., Bryant, L., Themistocleous, C., den Ouden, D. B., & Roberts, A. C. (2022). Best practice guidelines for reporting spoken discourse in aphasia and neurogenic communication disorders. *Aphasiology*, 1–24.

Stark, B. C. & Fukuyama, J. (2021). Leveraging big data to understand the interaction of task and language during monologic spoken discourse in speakers with and without aphasia. *Language, Cognition and Neuroscience*, *36*(5), 562–585.

Stein, N. L. & Glenn, C. G. (1979). An analysis of story comprehension in elementary school children. In R. Freedle (Ed.), *New directions in discourse processing*. Ablex.

Westby, C.E. (2005). Assessing and remediating text comprehension problems. In H. W. Catts & A. G. Kamhi (Eds.), *Language and Reading Disabilities* (2nd ed., pp. 157–232). Pearson Education.

Wilson S. M., Henry M. L., Besbris, M., Ogar, J. M., Dronkers, N. F., Jarrold, W ... & Gorno-Tempini, M. L. (2010). Connected speech production in three variants of primary progressive aphasia. *Brain*, *133*, 2069–2088.

16

TRACKING EYE MOVEMENTS

Language Processing in Bilingualism and Aphasia

E. Susan Duncan and Peggy S. Conner

Introduction

The increased precision and affordability of eye-tracking technology over the past 2 decades have offered new opportunities for researchers in the fields of bilingualism and aphasia to investigate what the eyes reveal about the language system(s). For studies of bilingualism, research questions typically involve how the two languages interact during linguistic processing. Target factors that influence language activation, selection, and interference are used to elucidate the organization of the underlying dual-language network. In aphasia research, a principal focus is how acquired deficits following brain damage have altered the integrity of the language system. The nature of these deficits in word retrieval, grammaticality, and other aspects of language in people with aphasia has been examined through the analysis of eye movements during processing of carefully selected stimuli and tasks. In this chapter, we explore the application of eye tracking to expand knowledge of linguistic processing in these two populations and suggest avenues for further research.

Eye-Tracking Measures

Eye tracking is a noninvasive, inexpensive, and versatile technology that provides an opportunity to measure the field of active vision in real time. Infrared light from the eye tracker is reflected on the fovea, the point of greatest visual acuity, to measure the eye's fixations, or brief stationary moments, and saccades, the rapid jumps to the next point of (visual) regard. Though we may perceive smooth and continuous motion as we are

DOI: 10.4324/9781003330318-19

engrossed for 3 minutes in a page of text, our eyes, moving three to five times per second, will complete 540–900 fixations with intervening saccades (Fischer & Weber, 1993). Our lack of awareness of these frequent, abrupt shifts of the image on our retina is due to the masking effect of saccadic suppression, whereby visual information at the point of fixation overrides the prior saccade (Burr et al., 1994). As we scan a page, a visual display, or our surroundings, our ocular responses provide a way to measure gaze patterns and visual attention.

Eye-tracking metrics are numerous and vary dependent upon the nature of the research questions and methodology. Fixation analyses are the most common in eye-tracking studies of language. For example, fixation count, or the number of fixations that occur in a region of interest, may reflect an area's salience or an observer's difficulty in processing information. Fixation duration, whether for a single fixation or averaged across multiple gaze intervals, may indicate an area of interest, processing speed, or other ongoing cognitive activity (Brunyé et al., 2019). Saccade dynamics also vary with task. In general, there is a close tie between speed (velocity) and distance traveled (amplitude), with longer saccades being proportionally faster. Saccades tend to become shorter when task demands increase, which may be due to the required inspection of more distractors or reduced perceptual span in the presence of an overall greater cognitive load (Pomplun et al., 2001). In studies on reading, longer sentences lead to longer saccades, likely due to skipping of words that become predictable as sentence length constrains context (Cop et al., 2015). Other measures of pupil diameter and blink rate/amplitude can serve as valuable proxies for arousal, motivation, and processing difficulty, but are less frequently used in studies of language processing. (See Mahanama et al., 2022 for a review.)

The quality of eye-tracking data, including temporal and spatial precision, is dependent upon the equipment, measurement technique, selected model, and environmental conditions of the experiment (e.g., set-up, lighting, head restriction). (See Holmqvist et al., 2022 for guidelines.) Currently, eye trackers offer high temporal resolution with sampling frequencies of up to 2,000 Hz, which provides ample sensitivity for active measurements during language tasks (Chabal & Marian, 2015a). The most frequent applications of eye tracking in language research are the visual world paradigm for spoken language and text-based eye tracking for reading. In this chapter, we focus on the use of visual world paradigms in studies of bilingualism and in aphasia.

Tanenhaus and colleagues (1995) first coined the phrase "visual world paradigm" based on pioneering work by Cooper (1974) to describe a display of objects, pictures, or words as referents for auditory language stimuli (see Figure 16.1). Eye movements are recorded and time-locked to

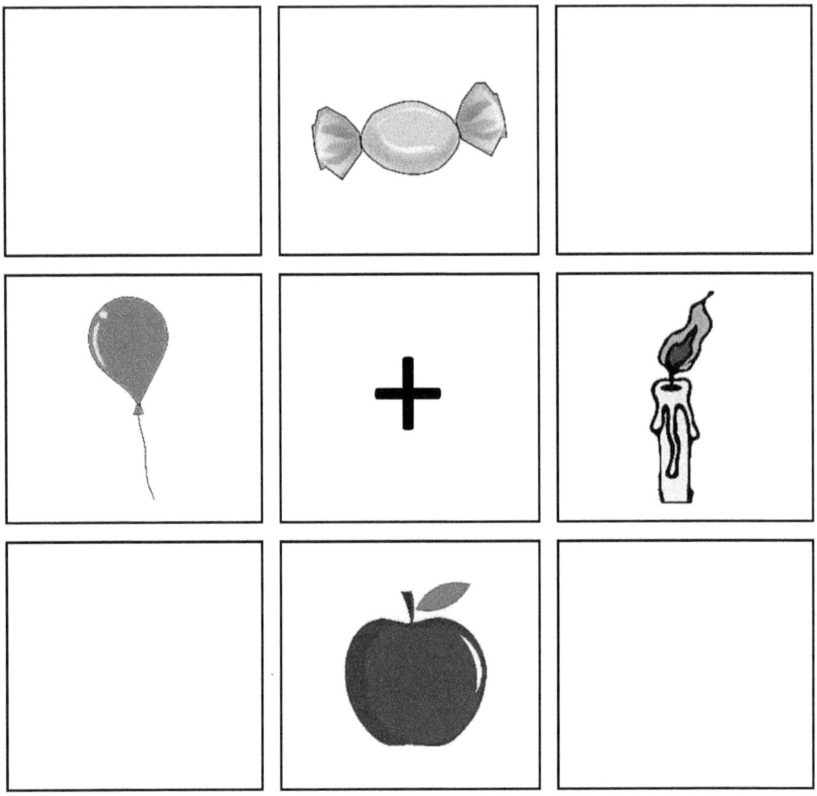

FIGURE 16.1 Visual World Paradigm.

spoken words or sentences, providing a real-time measure as participants perform a task. In an example they provided, when presented with several objects, an instruction to "Pick up the candy" in the presence of a *fork* would yield a more rapid response than in the presence of a *candle* that shares the initial phonemes with the target. Eye movements to the competitor and target object precede the behavioral response and permit measurement of ongoing word recognition as it unfolds. With the proper stimulus constraints and experimental conditions, research questions regarding morphology, syntax, and pragmatic aspects of language are readily addressed by this paradigm (Chabal & Marian, 2015a).

Eye Tracking in Bilingualism Research

Recent advances using eye tracking have uniquely contributed to the substantial evidence for parallel language activation in bilingual individuals. That is, bilingual individuals possess an integrated linguistic system, and both languages are active even within a monolingual context. This non-selective language activation has been demonstrated using eye-tracking research at all stages of linguistic processing from sublexical (Freeman & Marian, 2022; Ju & Luce, 2004; Marian et al., 2008) to sentence and discourse effects (Balling, 2013; Cop et al., 2017; Schwartz & Tarin, 2021). These effects may be modulated by many factors including language proficiency (e.g., Berghoff et al., 2021, Blumenfeld & Marian, 2007; Mishra & Singh, 2016), age of acquisition (e.g., Berghoff et al., 2021, Canseco-Gonzalez et al., 2010), language mode (e.g., Marian & Spivey, 2003a, 2003b), and language status (e.g., Weber & Cutler, 2004). We present examples of research that used the visual world paradigm and discuss their contributions to our understanding of bilingualism.

Eye tracking in bilingual individuals during a spoken word recognition task indexes the parallel co-activation of both languages. At the word level, recognition proceeds sequentially as auditory input unfolds and is subject to competition from lexical items in either language that share initial phonemes (Allopenna et al., 1998). Cross-linguistic competition was demonstrated by Spivey and Marian (1999) in an influential study of bilingual participants whose eye movements were monitored during verbal instructions to move objects in either Russian or English sessions. For example, during a Russian session, when instructed to move the "loshka" (spoon), participants' glances to phonological distractors in the non-target language (e.g., lock) significantly exceeded those to filler items (e.g., unrelated phonologically or semantically in either language). Competition was greater from English, the second language (L2), to Russian, the first language (L1), than vice versa. The investigators posit that participant awareness of the bilingual nature of the experiment may have influenced the relative activation of their two languages. In a subsequent study using rigorous controls to present a solely monolingual context, these investigators reproduced between-language competition, yet with greater competition in the opposite direction (L1 to L2), suggesting context affects the relative strength of language activation. Simultaneous between- and within-language competition was also documented. For example, the target object "plug" was shown alongside a within-language distractor "plum" and between-language distractor "plat'e" (dress), accompanied by a fourth filler object unrelated to the stimuli in either language (Marian & Spivey, 2003b). Both the within- and between-language distractor items received proportionately greater looks than fillers. Although further investigation is needed to understand how additional factors – such as language background, context, and inherent properties of the stimuli – may influence results, this work clearly indicates that bilingual individuals experience competition from similar-sounding words within their lexicon(s), regardless of whether these words exist in the language they are manifestly using.

Interestingly, evidence for parallel language processing suggests an integrated language system even across different language modalities. Shook and Marian (2012) investigated language coactivation in bimodal bilingual participants (American Sign Language [ASL] - English) using target-competitor pairs sharing three of four phonological parameters in ASL (i.e., handshape, palm orientation, location in space, motion). For example, when participants were instructed in English to find the "cheese," they looked more frequently and longer at "paper," which shares all ASL parameters except sign motion. Thus, spoken word recognition showed cross-linguistic influence by feature-specific sign characteristics unrelated to auditory-visual input. The authors posited that, even without auditory overlap, semantic information activates the relevant phonology in both languages, which then activates the lexical level, or that activation ensues via direct excitatory lexical connections.

This dual language activation occurs even in the absence of linguistic input. Chabal and Marian (2015b) showed Spanish-English bilingual participants a picture of an object and then asked them to locate it in a four-item search display. Distractor pictures included items in English or Spanish that shared initial phonemes with the target, such as a "clock" (reloj) presented with the English competitor, "cloud," or Spanish competitor, "regalo" (gift). Competitors in either language garnered proportionately more and longer fixations than filler objects, even though the words were never heard or spoken. (For a second group of monolingual English speakers this phenomenon was limited to the English competitors.) As the authors note, these results suggest phonological features of objects in both languages are automatically activated in bilingual speakers, and linguistic background influences processing of visual information.

These studies in bilingualism have contributed to evidence for the strong, unconscious role that language plays as we operate in the world. Even when one specific language, or indeed any language at all, is not present in the immediate environment, these deeply ingrained arbitrary symbols are inexorably activated and, if task-irrelevant, must be inhibited. Though omnipresent, these subtle, fleeting influences would be imperceptible in the absence of a sensitive tool such as eye tracking. This remarkable finding – of the consistent influence of all languages at one's disposal across a multitude of tasks – naturally leads to the question of how this system is altered following the disruption of language, as in aphasia.

Eye Tracking in Aphasia Research

In aphasia, brain regions and networks that support language are damaged, resulting in a variety of functional deficits that may affect speaking, listening, reading, writing, and related abilities to varying degrees. While aphasia can be caused by neurodegenerative processes (i.e., primary progressive aphasia), we focus here on the more common presentations that follow aphasia's chief etiology, stroke. Eye tracking is an invaluable tool in individuals with aphasia, for whom behavioral responses can be highly inconsistent. Similarly, people with aphasia show greater within- and between-subject performance variability than healthy individuals on eye-tracking tasks, especially as difficulty increases (e.g., Dickey et al., 2007). However, patient data also show stronger test-retest reliability than control participants, establishing good sensitivity for measuring changes over time and in response to treatment (Mack et al., 2016). In this section, we review research on specific linguistic deficits, differences from healthy individuals and among aphasia subtypes, and post-therapy changes in eye-tracking metrics in monolingual speakers with aphasia.

Agrammatism refers to the relative inaccessibility of grammatical forms for some speakers with aphasia. Agrammatic production may be largely telegraphic, lacking function words (e.g., articles, auxiliaries) and bound morphemes (e.g., plural -s, past tense -ed) to complement content words (e.g., nouns, verbs). Agrammatic comprehension can reflect the same underlying deficits, yielding difficulties with more complex forms, such as noncanonical phrases. For example, in English, the underlying structure for a sentence is S-V-O (subject-verb-object), and despite a relatively rigid word order, passive forms such as "The dog was chased by a cat" exchange subject and object placement. Listeners with agrammatism may incorrectly interpret which of the two potential actors, or agents, is performing the action.

Much eye-tracking research in aphasia has centered on the numerous linguistic challenges characteristic of agrammatic aphasia. The time-locked nature of eye movements provides a moment-to-moment measure of attentional focus and elucidates latent decision-making processes. When healthy individuals hear spoken sentences, prompt recognition of disambiguating grammatical markers leads to immediate fixation on the intended target. Unsurprisingly, many studies of aphasia indicate that longer delays in fixation accompany increases in grammatical complexity (Choy & Thompson, 2010; Schumacher et al., 2015), despite final gaze responses that may be at ceiling (e.g., Bos et al., 2014). This delay may result in no detectable fixation preference when simultaneously viewing images portraying either an accurate or competing meaning while hearing a complex sentence, even when it is ultimately understood (Schumacher et al., 2015). These studies demonstrate that, although behavioral performance may be indistinguishable from control participants, the decoding processes facilitating these behaviors do not emerge on the same schedule. Eye tracking can also provide insight into processes underlying behavioral errors in aphasia. When stimuli are not correctly decoded, responses are significantly more likely to be followed by increased gaze to competitors (Choy & Thompson, 2010; Dickey & Thompson, 2009). This finding suggests that the lack of fixation preference during delayed processing may also be due to decreased inhibition of alternate interpretations, even when the individual is ultimately able to appropriately integrate the relevant information and arrive at the correct response.

Anterior lesions affecting the left frontal lobe typically cause nonfluent forms of aphasia that are characterized by sparse, halting, agrammatic verbal output with relatively spared comprehension. In contrast, posterior lesions in the left temporo-parietal lobe may result in fluent forms of aphasia with preservation of rhythmic speech features, fluent output, and (variably correct) grammatical markers but lacking content and with impaired auditory comprehension. These distinct behavioral profiles have traditionally been labeled Broca's and Wernicke's aphasias, respectively; however, these absolute classifications are not without controversy. All speakers with aphasia demonstrate challenges of lexical access (i.e., anomia). Anomia is associated with inadequate activation of retrieval targets or overactivation of closely related words that function as competitors, typically words with similar semantic or phonological characteristics that activate overlapping neural substrates and must consequently be inhibited for correct selection.

Eye-tracking studies have permitted comparative investigation into comprehension difficulties associated with aphasia subsequent to different lesion locations by analyzing competitive processes when a target word is presented with words similar in meaning or sound (Mirman & Graziano, 2012; Mirman et al., 2011; Yee et al., 2008). For example, people with fluent aphasia from posterior lesions divert more visual attention than control participants to competing words with the same phonological onset; whereas people with nonfluent aphasia subsequent to anterior lesions attend *less* than control participants to competitors with the same onset but are more distracted than either group by rhyming words (i.e., same offset). Semantically, people with anterior lesions experience long-lasting competition from taxonomic foils that share a category (e.g., dog vs. cat), while those with posterior lesions are *less* distracted by thematic foils, which share an association (e.g., dog vs. leash). Greater exploration of eye-tracking responses will further our understanding of the nature of specific deficits and can help develop new treatment techniques to re-establish fundamental phonological skills and semantic associations.

In daily life, unimpaired listeners effectively apply phonological, semantic, and syntactic processes online (i.e., rapidly unfolding in real-time) while using context to predict upcoming words and ascertain meaning. People with aphasia, however, may be less able to process and integrate verbal input as it becomes available. Nozari et al. (2016) found that when only one of four images could appropriately complete a sentence by using semantically-restrictive verbs (i.e., drive → car) or phonologically-restrictive determiners (i.e., an → eagle), individuals with posterior lesions oriented quicker and fixated more on permissible targets than those with anterior lesions. However, when ambiguous nouns with multiple meanings were contextually disambiguated in the last sentence of three-sentence stories, people with fluent aphasia demonstrated consistently poorer performance and lesser fixation on the target compared to the competing (incorrect) image (Laurinavichyute et al., 2014). Combined, these findings suggest that anterior regions play a key role in forming predictions (see also Mack et al., 2013), with posterior regions more critical for inhibiting competing activation.

In addition to providing insight into linguistic phenomena, eye tracking can probe navigation of social environments. People with aphasia attend less to speakers' faces and more to their gesturing hands than do healthy individuals, and this is more pronounced in severe aphasia or apraxia (Eggenberger et al., 2016; Preisig et al., 2018). When faces show affect, however, whether happy or sad, they yield more rapid fixations from people with aphasia than control participants (Ashaie & Cherney, 2020). Yet those with aphasia also spend more time looking at a photograph's background, with less attention to salient features – such as a person looking at the camera or an object being used in the foreground – when compared to control participants (Thiessen et al., 2014). This work suggests utility of eye tracking for discerning extralinguistic attentional and pragmatic differences that may impair functional communication in aphasia and might be directly targeted in therapy.

Few studies have examined changes in eye-tracking metrics following behavioral intervention for aphasia. Past work demonstrates that healthy speakers of most languages show an agent-first processing bias (i.e., expect the first noun in a sentence to be performing an action), while people with aphasia do not apply this heuristic (in addition to being slower to fixate and poorer in performance; e.g., Meyer et al., 2012). Following a therapy that trained active and passive sentence forms, people with agrammatic aphasia demonstrated more accurate responses and a higher proportion of target fixations after hearing passive sentences, similar to their patterns for simpler active sentences (Mack & Thompson, 2017). Additional treatment studies have indicated that improved post-therapy production is accompanied by adaptation of eye movements to be more consistent with those of control participants, supporting improved encoding of active and passive sentence roles as well as early structural planning (Barbieri et al., 2019; Mack et al., 2017). This corresponds with work showing stronger nonverbal semantic abilities are associated with fixation patterns more similar to healthy individuals (van Scherpenberg et al., 2021). Of great practical importance, no changes were found in untreated control groups of people with aphasia, reinforcing that eye tracking may be a sensitive tool for detecting treatment-related changes in this population.

The principal value of eye-tracking studies in aphasia is that they not only identify the existence of impairments but offer possible explanations for why these exist. From a theoretical standpoint, this knowledge will help complete a picture of how the language system works and the types of implicit computations the brain is performing. From a clinical perspective, such information offers new avenues for developing rehabilitative approaches and monitoring change in the underlying skills that will support progress toward therapy goals. Both these ambitions, whether targeting elucidated language fundamentals or effective treatment applications, could be further enhanced with appreciation of how disruptions manifest when aphasia occurs in a system that commands two or more languages.

Eye Tracking in Bilingual Aphasia

There are only three investigations known to have used eye tracking with bilingual participants with aphasia. These studies targeted various aspects of sentence comprehension in a visual world paradigm. Given the paucity of eye-tracking data derived from bilingual speakers with aphasia, and the possibility for each domain to inform investigation of the other via such combined inquiry, we describe these studies in some detail below.

In the first, Kuzmina and colleagues (2018) presented a brief abstract reporting results from the syntactic comprehension subtest of the Bilingual Aphasia Test (Paradis, 1987), which includes canonical S-V-O sentences as well as more difficult constructions including negative, passive, and cleft forms. Two multilingual participants with aphasia completed the subtest in Norwegian (their third and fourth language, respectively) in two formats. Both performed more poorly when asked to select the correct image from a field of four via gaze than on a traditional pointing task, although the discrepancy between formats was only statistically significant for one participant. Despite limitations of the study, which included sample size, varying time constraints for the two formats, and assessment in a single language, these findings support a role for eye tracking that complements, rather than duplicates, other performance measures. Poorer performance for eye tracking than overt responses suggests that measures of gaze provide additional information on attention and unconscious processing. It would be of great interest to see this study replicated and expanded by (1) testing one or more additional languages using both response formats, and (2) conducting an eye-tracking analysis that considered not only binary response accuracy, but the time-varying nature of attention to target and competitor images.

The second study shared more characteristics with the eye-tracking investigations into bilingualism and aphasia discussed in the sections above. Arantzeta and colleagues (2019) contrasted performance of participants with aphasia who were either monolingual (Spanish; n=7) or bilingual (Spanish-Basque; n=7), in addition to 14 control participants matched in age, education, and language status. Participants were presented a target image, which depicted an action featuring the correct agent and recipient ("theme"), alongside a competitor in which semantic roles were reversed. The precise structure of the sentence stimuli varied depending on the language but used either a canonical form (agent first) or a noncanonical form (theme first). As expected, participants with aphasia performed more slowly and less accurately than control participants, regardless of language or bilingualism. In Spanish, both monolingual and bilingual speakers with aphasia performed more slowly and less accurately with noncanonical than canonical sentences, while control participants performed similarly for both sentence types. Both bilingual groups performed more poorly overall in Basque, which relies on case markers to convey the appropriate meaning, than in Spanish, which relies on prepositions. For healthy bilingual individuals, poorer performance in Basque was present for noncanonical forms only, yet those with aphasia demonstrated multiple cross-linguistic patterns that varied by participant.

Thus, eye-tracking data revealed differences due to bilingualism (but not aphasia) in attention to competitor stimuli for correct vs. incorrect trials, which may reflect the heterogeneous impairments present in the aphasia group. Given the differing cross-linguistic patterns found for performance accuracy in bilingual speakers with aphasia, unique deficit profiles potentially negated each other and obscured between-group differences in gaze fixation. While not reported in this study, it would be interesting to know how eye-tracking data may have correlated with individual performance patterns, particularly due to relative proficiency differences between languages in the bilingual speakers with aphasia. Considering the lack of statistical power with only seven participants per group, it is unsurprising that additional significant contrasts were not uncovered.

In the third study, Ribu and colleagues (2022) used eye tracking to examine predictive processing in highly proficient Norwegian-English bilingual participants, including four individuals with aphasia. Preferential looking patterns were analyzed while listening to sentences in each language that used either neutral or constraining verbs (e.g., Anna sees/eats Mary's pizza). Among those with aphasia, performance was varied and unrelated to presentation language or aphasia severity. One young participant predicted upcoming nouns in L1 and L2 (like younger control participants), two older participants showed preferential looking at verb offset in L1 and L2 (like older control participants), and a third older participant showed no preferential or predictive patterns. Data collection is reportedly ongoing, which may provide further insight into factors associated with language processing in bilingual individuals with aphasia.

These studies highlight the potential role of eye tracking in elucidating linguistic processing in bilingual people with aphasia. Larger studies that include multiple control groups, carefully curated stimuli, an established theoretical linguistic framework, and the use of eye tracking as a complement to behavioral data have the potential to provide insight into commonalities, differences, and interactions between dual-language systems and post-stroke language deficits.

Conclusion and Future Directions

Eye tracking has, to date, provided several interesting and instructive findings in the field of language science. However, it remains underused and has not yet provided the full complement to behavioral and neuroimaging studies that such a tool could promise. Free from the constraints and demands of volitional motor responses and decision-making, eye movements provide the opportunity to observe automatic cognitive and language processes in a near-unfiltered form. For studies of bilingualism and aphasia in particular, this methodology provides a means of interrogating the biological organization of one of our most complex and uniquely human abilities.

We anticipate an expanding body of work will exploit the sensitivity of eye tracking to more comprehensively explore subtle cross-linguistic deficit patterns that might be missed with solely behavioral testing in bilingual aphasia. The many areas that remain unexplored or understudied – multilingualism, naturalistic paradigms, and diagnostic/therapeutic indexing – offer ripe ground for advancing our knowledge of the language system and benefiting individual performance.

References

Allopenna, P. D., Magnuson, J. S., & Tanenhaus, M. K. (1998). Tracking the time course of spoken word recognition using eye movements: Evidence for continuous mapping models. *Journal of Memory and Language*, *38*(4), 419–439.

Arantzeta, M., Howard, D., Webster, J., Laka, I., Martinez-Zabaleta, M., & Bastiaanse, R. (2019). Bilingual aphasia: Assessing cross-linguistic asymmetries and bilingual advantage in sentence comprehension deficits. *Cortex*, *119*, 195–214.

Ashaie, S. A. & Cherney, L. R. (2020). Eye tracking as a tool to identify mood in aphasia: A feasibility study. *Neurorehabilitation and Neural Repair*, *34*(5), 463–471.

Balling, L. W. (2013). Reading authentic texts: What counts as cognate? *Bilingualism: Language and Cognition*, *16*(3), 637–653.

Barbieri, E., Mack, J., Chiappetta, B., Europa, E., & Thompson, C. K. (2019). Recovery of offline and online sentence processing in aphasia: Language and domain-general network neuroplasticity. *Cortex*, *120*, 394–418.

Berghoff, R., McLoughlin, J., & Bylund, E. (2021). L1 activation during L2 processing is modulated by both age of acquisition and proficiency. *Journal of Neurolinguistics*, *58*, 100979.

Blumenfeld, H. K. & Marian, V. (2007). Constraints on parallel activation in bilingual spoken language processing: Examining proficiency and lexical status using eye-tracking. *Language and Cognitive Processes*, *22*(5), 633–660.

Bos, L. S., Hanne, S., Wartenburger, I., & Bastiaanse, R. (2014). Losing track of time? Processing of time reference inflection in agrammatic and healthy speakers of German. *Neuropsychologia*, *65*, 180–190.

Brunyé, T. T., Drew, T., Weaver, D. L., & Elmore, J. G. (2019). A review of eye tracking for understanding and improving diagnostic interpretation. *Cognitive Research: Principles and Implications*, *4*(1), 1–16.

Burr, D. C., Morrone, M. C., & Ross, J. (1994). Selective suppression of the magnocellular visual pathway during saccadic eye movements. *Nature*, *371*(6497), 511–513.

Canseco-Gonzalez, E., Brehm, L., Brick, C. A., Brown-Schmidt, S., Fischer, K., & Wagner, K. (2010). Carpet or Cárcel: The effect of age of acquisition and language mode on bilingual lexical access. *Language and Cognitive Processes*, *25*(5), 669–705.

Chabal, S. & Marian, V. (2015a). In the mind's eye: Eye-tracking and multi-modal integration during bilingual spoken-language processing. In *Attention and Vision in Language Processing* (pp. 147–164). Springer.

Chabal, S. & Marian, V. (2015b). Speakers of different languages process the visual world differently. *Journal of Experimental Psychology: General*, *144*(3), 539.

Choy, J. J. & Thompson, C. K. (2010). Binding in agrammatic aphasia: Processing to comprehension. *Aphasiology*, *24*(5), 551–579.

Cooper, R. M. (1974). The control of eye fixation by the meaning of spoken language: A new methodology for the real-time investigation of speech perception, memory, and language processing. *Cognitive Psychology*, *6*, 84–107.

Cop, U., Dirix, N., Van Assche, E., Drieghe, D., & Duyck, W. (2017). Reading a book in one or two languages? An eye movement study of cognate facilitation in L1 and L2 reading. *Bilingualism: Language and Cognition*, *20*(4), 747–769.

Cop, U., Drieghe, D., & Duyck, W. (2015). Eye movement patterns in natural reading: A comparison of monolingual and bilingual reading of a novel. *PloS One*, *10*(8), e0134008.

Dickey, M. W., Choy, J. J., & Thompson, C. K. (2007). Real-time comprehension of wh-movement in aphasia: Evidence from eyetracking while listening. *Brain and Language*, *100*(1), 1–22.

Dickey, M. W. & Thompson, C. K. (2009). Automatic processing of wh-and NP-movement in agrammatic aphasia: Evidence from eyetracking. *Journal of Neurolinguistics*, *22*(6), 563–583.

Eggenberger, N., Preisig, B. C., Schumacher, R., Hopfner, S., Vanbellingen, T., Nyffeler, T., ... & Müri, R. M. (2016). Comprehension of co-speech gestures in aphasic patients: an eye movement study. *PloS One*, *11*(1), e0146583.

Fischer, B. & Weber, H. (1993). Express saccades and visual attention. *Behavioral and Brain Sciences*, *16*(3), 553–567.

Freeman, M. R. & Marian, V. (2022). Visual word recognition in bilinguals: Eye-tracking evidence that L2 proficiency impacts access of L1 phonotactics. *Studies in Second Language Acquisition*, *44*(3), 759–787.

Holmqvist, K., Örbom, S. L., Hooge, I. T., Niehorster, D. C., Alexander, R. G., Andersson, R., ... & Hessels, R. S. (2022). Eye tracking: Empirical foundations for a minimal reporting guideline. *Behavior Research Methods*, 1–53. 10.1017/S136672892100016X

Ju, M. & Luce, P. A. (2004). Falling on sensitive ears: Constraints on bilingual lexical activation. *Psychological Science*, *15*, 314–318.

Kuzmina, E., Knoph, M. N., Goral, M., & Simonsen, H. G. (2018). Auditory comprehension in bilingual aphasia: What can eye-tracking data tell us? *Aphasiology*, *32*(sup1), 117–118.

Laurinavichyute, A. K., Ulicheva, A., Ivanova, M. V., Kuptsova, S. V., & Dragoy, O. (2014). Processing lexical ambiguity in sentential context: Eye-tracking data from brain-damaged and non-brain-damaged individuals. *Neuropsychologia*, *64*, 360–373.

Mack, J. E., Ji, W., & Thompson, C. K. (2013). Effects of verb meaning on lexical integration in agrammatic aphasia: Evidence from eyetracking. *Journal of Neurolinguistics*, *26*(6), 619–636.

Mack, J. E., Nerantzini, M., & Thompson, C. K. (2017). Recovery of sentence production processes following language treatment in aphasia: Evidence from eyetracking. *Frontiers in Human Neuroscience*, *11*, 101.

Mack, J. E. & Thompson, C. K. (2017). Recovery of online sentence processing in aphasia: Eye movement changes resulting from treatment of underlying forms. *Journal of Speech, Language, and Hearing Research*, *60*(5), 1299–1315.

Mack, J. E., Wei, A. Z. S., Gutierrez, S., & Thompson, C. K. (2016). Tracking sentence comprehension: Test-retest reliability in people with aphasia and unimpaired adults. *Journal of Neurolinguistics*, *40*, 98–111.

Mahanama, B., Jayawardana, Y., Rengarajan, S., Jayawardena, G., Chukoskie, L., Snider, J., & Jayarathna, S. (2022). Eye movement and pupil measures: A review. *Frontiers in Computer Science*, *3*, 733531.

Marian, V., Blumenfeld, H. K., & Boukrina, O. V. (2008). Sensitivity to phonological similarity within and across languages. *Journal of Psycholinguistic Research*, *37*(3), 141–170.

Marian, V. & Spivey, M. (2003a). Bilingual and monolingual processing of competing lexical items. *Applied Psycholinguistics*, *24*(2), 173–193.

Marian, V. & Spivey, M. (2003b). Competing activation in bilingual language processing: Within-and between-language competition. *Bilingualism: Language and Cognition*, *6*(2), 97–115.

Meyer, A. M., Mack, J. E., & Thompson, C. K. (2012). Tracking passive sentence comprehension in agrammatic aphasia. *Journal of Neurolinguistics*, *25*(1), 31–43.

Mirman, D. & Graziano, K. M. (2012). Damage to temporo-parietal cortex decreases incidental activation of thematic relations during spoken word comprehension. *Neuropsychologia*, *50*(8), 1990–1997.

Mirman, D., Yee, E., Blumstein, S. E., & Magnuson, J. S. (2011). Theories of spoken word recognition deficits in aphasia: Evidence from eye-tracking and computational modeling. *Brain and Language*, *117*(2), 53–68.

Mishra, R. K. & Singh, N. (2016). The influence of second language proficiency on bilingual parallel language activation in Hindi–English bilinguals. *Journal of Cognitive Psychology*, *28*(4), 396–411.

Nozari, N., Mirman, D., & Thompson-Schill, S. L. (2016). The ventrolateral prefrontal cortex facilitates processing of sentential context to locate referents. *Brain and Language*, *157*, 1–13.

Paradis, M. (1987). *Bilingual Aphasia Test*. Hillsdale, NJ, USA.

Pomplun, M., Reingold, E. M., & Shen, J. (2001). Investigating the visual span in comparative search: The effects of task difficulty and divided attention. *Cognition*, *81*(2), B57–B67.

Preisig, B. C., Eggenberger, N., Cazzoli, D., Nyffeler, T., Gutbrod, K., Annoni, J. M., ... & Müri, R. M. (2018). Multimodal communication in aphasia: Perception and production of co-speech gestures during face-to-face conversation. *Frontiers in Human Neuroscience*, *12*, 200.

Ribu, I., Goral, M., Theimann, A., Iacorossi, M., Lehtonen, M., Norvik, M., ... , & Murstad, J. (2022, August). Eye tracking measures of prediction in L1 and L2 in bilingual people with and without aphasia. [Conference presentation] 4th International Symposium on Bilingual and L2 Processing in Adults and Children. 10.13140/RG.2.2.18501.32484.

Schumacher, R., Cazzoli, D., Eggenberger, N., Preisig, B., Nef, T., Nyffeler, T., ... & Müri, R. M. (2015). Cue recognition and integration–eye tracking evidence of processing differences in sentence comprehension in aphasia. *PloS One*, *10*(11), e0142853.

Schwartz, A. I. & Tarin, K. S. (2021). The impact of a discourse context on bilingual cross-language lexical activation. *Bilingualism: Language and Cognition*, *24*(5), 879–890.

Shook, A. & Marian, V. (2012). Bimodal bilinguals co-activate both languages during spoken comprehension. *Cognition*, *124*(3), 314–324.

Spivey, M. J. & Marian, V. (1999). Cross talk between native and second languages: Partial activation of an irrelevant lexicon. *Psychological Science*, *10*(3), 281–284.

Tanenhaus, M. K., Spivey-Knowlton, M. J., Eberhard, K. M., & Sedivy, J. C. (1995). Integration of visual and linguistic information in spoken language comprehension. *Science*, *268*(5217), 1632–1634.

Thiessen, A., Beukelman, D., Ullman, C., & Longenecker, M. (2014). Measurement of the visual attention patterns of people with aphasia: A preliminary investigation of two types of human engagement in photographic images. *Augmentative and Alternative Communication*, *30*(2), 120–129.

van Scherpenberg, C., Abdel Rahman, R., Regenbrecht, F., & Obrig, H. (2021). Semantic interference through multiple distractors in picture naming in people with aphasia. *Journal of Cognitive Neuroscience*, *33*(8), 1612–1633.

Weber A. & Cutler A. (2004). Lexical competition in non-native spoken-word recognition. *Journal of Memory and Language*, *50*, 1–25.

Yee, E., Blumstein, S. E., & Sedivy, J. C. (2008). Lexical-semantic activation in Broca's and Wernicke's aphasia: Evidence from eye movements. *Journal of Cognitive Neuroscience*, *20*(4), 592–612.

17

CONCLUSION

Swathi Kiran, Aviva Lerman, and Mira Goral

This book covers a range of topics on language processing in monolingual and multilingual adults with a specific focus on the field of neurolinguistics. Every chapter in this book has relevance to work that Loraine Obler conducted over the past 50 years. Several salient themes emerge from this book, each directly influenced by Loraine's previous work and interests. One distinctive flair of Loraine's work is the integration of targeting the impairment with the holistic perspective of the individual and their successful participation in their individual lives. This impetus is captured in several chapters in the book. A second focus of Loraine's work has been the interface between behavioral studies and technological and/or medical advances. Finally, and most importantly, Loraine's work has been instrumental in helping us understand how bilingualism is not an outlier, rather, the norm in most parts of the world.

Consistent with the structure of the book, this conclusion chapter is organized into three sections. In each section, we highlight Loraine's pioneering work that laid the foundation for our understanding of the topic, followed by chapters in this book that present the current state of the art. In some cases, the chapters highlight the advancements in our understanding of the field, and in several cases, highlight how Loraine's early work laid the foundation for subsequent work.

In Part I, the chapters review language processing in monolingual and multilingual adults. In 1978, Albert and Obler published a seminal book focusing on aphasia in multilingual individuals, in which they identified patterns of impairments and the variables that contribute to them, and raised key questions pertaining to patterns and theories of bilingual

DOI: 10.4324/9781003330318-20

language processing and impairment (Albert & Obler, 1978). A follow up paper by Goral et al. (2002) reviewed the state of the art in our understanding of the neurolinguistic aspects of bilingualism, especially in the context of bilingual and polyglot aphasia. Over the years, Loraine and her students' work influenced the integration of multilingualism into the fabric of how we talk about language processing. The chapters in Part I focus on how different contexts and cultures necessitate research in translanguaging, the dynamic interaction between proficiency and attrition, and the obvious observation that in most societies in the world, monolingualism is the exception, not the rule. Chapters in this section also address the interrelations between linguistic and non-linguistic cognition, another topic that has gained much interest in recent years.

Another area of research that Loraine had a tremendous influence on is our understanding of the aging brain and its relevance to language decline. Part II addresses research on these topics. In a 1985 paper published in the journal *Cortex* (Nicholas et al., 1985), Obler and colleagues evaluated over 100 healthy individuals on their naming skills and found that for older adults, naming difficulty was related to the difficulty of specific lexical retrieval of items (i.e., related to their psycholinguistic characteristics). A follow up study by Au et al. (1995) showed a clear decline in naming abilities in older adults, captured over a 7-year time span. This seminal finding that naming abilities decline as a function of normal aging set the stage for discriminating between normal aging and naming deficits due to pathological decline. Around the same time, in 1983 Loraine authored a chapter where she described the different types of dementia, including distinguishing the cognitive-linguistic manifestations of dementia from those of stroke (Obler, 1983). A most astute observation was that memory and attention interact with language processes, and in dementia the locus of atrophy is more diffuse than stroke, hence the pathophysiology of dementia is more complicated than stroke-induced aphasia. To this end, several chapters in this book tackle current aspects of the aging brain, including current diagnosis and treatment options for people with dementia. Additional chapters also address the nature of dementia in bilingual individuals, especially how a first language (L1) and a second language (L2) can be differentially impaired. Understanding the interplay between languages in bilingual people naturally extends to the extensive evidence around cognitive- and social-consequences of being bilingual with dementia. One of the most exciting research directions of late is the potential to slow/stall the decline of language function in individuals with dementia and neurodegenerative language decline through noninvasive brain stimulation methods. It is only fitting that a book honoring Loraine Obler includes chapters highlighting forward-thinking research methods with profound implications for the aging brain.

Loraine's research interests also span the psycholinguistic and psychosocial aspects of language processing in aging, aphasia, and dementia, topics discussed in detail throughout the book and especially in Part III. One of Loraine's prescient observations was that looking at single-word naming provides a limited window into understanding the failures that underlie language impairments in neurological dysfunction. To this end, an early study of Loraine's attempted to distinguish between patients with aphasia and patients with dementia on the basis of their speech measures on a discourse task (Nicholas et al., 1985). A separate study, also using narrative speech, found important differences between patients diagnosed with either Broca's or Wernicke's aphasia and made the insightful observation that the proportion of nouns to verbs was high in patients with Broca's aphasia but low in patients with Wernicke's aphasia (Gleason et al., 1980). This distinction between informative yet telegraphic speech in Broca's aphasia and fluent but empty speech in Wernicke's aphasia has withstood the test of time in aphasia research, even though the way that aphasia is categorized and/or described today has changed. Several chapters in Part III address current innovations in assessment and intervention of connected speech (narratives, conversations) for people with aphasia as they are a more comprehensive approach to understanding and treating communication deficits in aphasia.

Loraine was also interested in understanding the psychosocial aspects of aphasia and how they may influence clinical care. For instance, Connor et al. (2001) examined the effect of socioeconomic status on aphasia severity and recovery, and found that lower educational and occupational groups had more severe aphasia early in their recovery process even though the rate of recovery was the same over time. It is thus natural that the book includes chapters that focus on the holistic perspective of management of multilingual geriatric populations in the U.S. and the inclusion of the Life Participation Approach in Aphasia (LPAA) rehabilitation management. Within this framework, several new strands of research have emerged, including the development of conversation therapy approaches for people with aphasia, the analyses of narrative discourse in bilingual individuals, and how they can inform the richness of language processing and new methodological approaches that can augment our understanding of language processing, especially in bilingual adults. Again, the chapters in this section set the stage for an exciting new phase of research in our ability to understand how language processing occurs in bilingual individuals, not just at the single word level, but at the conversational level and how we can begin to think about interventional management for bilingual individuals when they have aphasia.

In summary, the field of neurolinguistics has evolved since its inception and is continually changing. The chapters of this book, influenced by the contribution of Loraine's distinguished body of work, point to a number of exciting new directions in the field. Even though the world is becoming more connected and globalized – and the field of neurolinguistics with it – the field is, at the same time, moving in the direction of individualization, identity, and toward the study of marginalized languages. There is a consensus among many researchers that future research in neurolinguistics needs to be less focused on Anglo-centric studies and be more inclusive of marginalized and heritage languages and cultures, in order to enrich our current knowledge of how language is processed and used. In this respect, diversity of the populations and languages studied, including cross-linguistic investigations and studies of multilingual people, will play a crucial role in better understanding the topics at hand and how they affect the biodiversity of our world.

The future of neurolinguistics also points toward the individual, and their identity, as a focus point for more ecologically valid language assessments and intervention protocols, such as those that are discourse- and conversation-based. Although such approaches are frequently more challenging for researchers and clinicians to execute, compared to assessment and intervention based around single words and sentences, they provide a clearer picture of how cognitive, linguistic, and communication skills are interdependent and dynamic across the lifespan in both healthy aging and clinical populations, particularly those with post-stroke aphasia and with dementia. Combining these more ecologically valid behavioral approaches together with tapping into the continually developing advances in technology and medicine, can broaden our understanding of language processing in the brain. This interdisciplinary and individualized approach has the potential to improve neural and behavioral functioning in people with varying abilities and challenges.

References

Albert, M. L. & Obler, L. K. (1978). *The Bilingual Brain: Neuropsychological and Neurolinguistic Aspects of Bilingualism*. Elsevier Science.

Au, R., Joung, P., Nicholas, M., Obler, L. K., Kass, R., & Albert, M. L. (1995). Naming ability across the adult life span. *Aging, Neuropsychology, and Cognition*, 2(4), 300–311. 10.1080/13825589508256605

Connor, L. T., Obler, L. K., Tocco, M., Fitzpatrick, P. M., & Albert, M. L. (2001). Effect of socioeconomic status on aphasia severity and recovery. *Brain and Language*, *78*(2), 254–257. 10.1006/brln.2001.2459

Gleason, J. B., Goodglass, H., Obler, L. K., Green, E., Hyde, M. R., & Weintraub, S. (1980). Narrative strategies of aphasic and normal-speaking subjects. *Journal of Speech, Language, and Hearing Research*, *23*(2), 370–382.

Goral, M., Levy, E. S., & Obler, L. K. (2002). Neurolinguistic aspects of bilingualism. *International Journal of Bilingualism*, *6*(4), 411–440. 10.1177/13670069020060040301

Nicholas, M., Obler, L., Albert, M., & Goodglass, H. (1985). Lexical retrieval in healthy aging. *Cortex*, *21*(4), 595–606. 10.1016/S0010-9452(58)80007-6

Nicholas, M., Obler, L. K., Albert, M. L., & Helm-Estabrooks, N. (1985). Empty speech in Alzheimer's disease and fluent aphasia. *Journal of Speech, Language, and Hearing Research*, *28*(3), 405–410. 10.1044/jshr.2803.405

Obler, L. K. (1983). Language and brain dysnfunction in dementia. In S. J. Segalowitz (Ed.), *Language Functions and Brain Organization* (pp. 267–282). Academic Press. 10.1016/B978-0-12-635640-3.50020-5

INDEX

For Product Safety Concerns and Information please contact our EU representative GPSR@taylorandfrancis.com
Taylor & Francis Verlag GmbH, Kaufingerstraße 24, 80331 München, Germany

www.ingramcontent.com/pod-product-compliance
Ingram Content Group UK Ltd.
Pitfield, Milton Keynes, MK11 3LW, UK
UKHW022351190926
475702UK00015B/2228
* 9 7 8 1 0 3 2 3 6 0 9 6 6 *